EARLY MODERN HISTORY
[1800–1940]

PATRON

Dato' Seri Dr Mahathir Mohamad

SPONSORS

The Encyclopedia of Malaysia was made possible thanks to the generous and enlightened support of the following organizations:

DRB-HICOM GROUP

MAHKOTA TECHNOLOGIES SDN BHD

MALAYAN UNITED INDUSTRIES BERHAD

MALAYSIA NATIONAL INSURANCE BERHAD

MINISTRY OF EDUCATION MALAYSIA

PERNAS INTERNATIONAL HOLDINGS BERHAD

PETRONAS BERHAD

RENONG BERHAD

STAR PUBLICATIONS (MALAYSIA) BERHAD

SUNGEIWAY GROUP

TENAGA NASIONAL BERHAD

UNITED OVERSEAS BANK GROUP

YAYASAN ALBUKHARY

YTL CORPORATION BERHAD

Note for Readers

The dates in this book are followed by the letters CE or BCE, which mean 'Common Era' and 'Before Common Era', respectively. These terms are synonymous with AD Anno Domini *(in the year of our Lord) and BC, which means 'Before Christ'.*

Published by Archipelago Press *an imprint of* Editions Didier Millet Pte Ltd
121, Telok Ayer Street, #03–01, Singapore 068590
Tel: 65-324 9260 Fax: 65-324 9261 E-mail: edm@edmbooks.com.sg

Kuala Lumpur Office:
25, Jalan Pudu Lama, 50200 Kuala Lumpur, Malaysia
Tel: 03-2031 3805 Fax: 03-2031 6298 E-mail: edmbooks@edmbooks.com.my
Websites: www.edmbooks.com
www.encyclopedia.com.my

First published 2001
Reprinted 2003, 2006

Colour separation by Overseas Colourscan Sdn Bhd (236702-T)
Printed by Tien Wah Press (Pte) Limited
ISBN 981-3018-47-X

ACKNOWLEDGMENT

The Encyclopedia of Malaysia was first conceived by Editions Didier Millet and Datin Paduka Marina Mahathir. The Editorial Advisory Board, made up of distinguished figures drawn from academic and public life, was constituted in March 1994. The project was publicly announced in October that year, and eight months later the first sponsors were in place. By 1996, the structure of the content was agreed; later that year the appointment of Volume Editors and the commissioning of authors were substantially complete, and materials for the work were beginning to flow in. By early 2001, seven volumes were completed for publication, and the remaining eight volumes fully commissioned and well under way.

The Publishers are grateful to the following for their contribution during the preparation of the first seven volumes:
Dato' Seri Anwar Ibrahim,
who acted as Chairman of the Editorial Advisory Board;
and the following members of the Board:
Tan Sri Dato' Dr Ahmad Mustaffa Babjee
Prof. Dato' Dr Asmah Haji Omar
Puan Azah Aziz
Dr Peter M. Kedit
Dato' Dr T. Marimuthu
Tan Sri Dato' Dr Noordin Sopiee
Tan Sri Datuk Augustine S. H. Ong
Ms Patricia Regis
the late Tan Sri Zain Azraai
Datuk Datin Paduka Zakiah Hanum bt Abdul Hamid

SERIES EDITORIAL TEAM

PUBLISHER
Didier Millet

GENERAL MANAGER
Charles Orwin

PROJECT COORDINATOR
Marina Mahathir

EDITORIAL DIRECTOR
Timothy Auger

PROJECT MANAGER
Noor Azlina Yunus

EDITORIAL CONSULTANT
Peter Schoppert

EDITORS
Dianne Buerger
Alice Chee
Chuah Guat Eng
Elaine Ee
Irene Khng
Jacinth Lee-Chan
Nolly Lim
Kay Lyons
Premilla Mohanlall
Wendy (Khadijah) Moore
Alysoun Owen
Amita Sarwal
Tan Hwee Koon
Philip Tatham
Sumitra Visvanathan

DESIGN DIRECTOR
Tan Seok Lui

DESIGNERS
Ahmad Puad bin Aziz
Lee Woon Hong
Theivanai A/P Nadaraju
Felicia Wong
Yong Yoke Lian

PRODUCTION MANAGER
Sin Kam Cheong

VOLUME EDITORIAL TEAM

EDITORS
Kay Lyons
Amita Sarwal

DESIGNERS
Ahmad Puad bin Aziz
Theivanai A/P Nadaraju

ILLUSTRATORS
Anuar bin Abdul Rahim
Osman Asari
Jane Lydbury
Tan Hong Yew

CONTRIBUTORS

Assoc Prof. Abdul Rahman Haji Ismail
Universiti Sains Malaysia

Prof. Dr Barbara Watson Andaya
University of Hawaii at Manoa

Prof. Dr Leonard Y. Andaya
University of Hawai'i at Manoa

Assoc. Prof. Dr Ariffin Omar
Universiti Sains Malaysia

Dr Badriyah Haji Salleh
Universiti Sains Malaysia (retired)

Dr Cheah Boon Kheng
Universiti Sains Malaysia (retired)

Dr Chee Heng Leng
Universiti Putra Malaysia

Dr John H. Drabble
University of Sydney (retired)

Assoc. Prof. Dr Aruna Gopinath
Universiti Malaya

John M. Gullick
Historian

Prof. Dr Amarjit Kaur
University of New England

Dr Khasnor Johan
Australian National University (retired)

Dato' Dr Khoo Kay Kim
Universiti Malaya (retired)

Khoo Khay Jin
Universiti Sains Malaysia (retired)

Dr Kobkua Suwannathat-Pian
Universiti Kebangsaan Malaysia (retired)

Assoc. Prof. Dr Paul H. Kratoska
National Univeristy of Singapore

Dr Leong Yee Fong
Universiti Sains Malaysia

Assoc. Prof. Dr Francis Loh Kok-Wah
Universiti Sains Malaysia

Assoc. Prof. Dr Loh Wei Leng
Universiti Malaya

Assoc. Prof. Dr Maznah Mohamad
Universiti Sains Malaysia

Assoc. Prof. R.H.W. Reece
Murdoch Univerity

Dr Tan Liok Ee
Universiti Sains Malaysia (retired)

Tan Pek Leng
Writer

Prof. Emeritus Dr Nicholas Tarling
University of Auckland

Prof. Dr Carl K. Trocki
Queensland University of Technology

Assoc. Prof. Dr James Warren
Murdoch University

Dr Yeo Kim Wah
National University of Singapore (retired)

THE ENCYCLOPEDIA OF
MALAYSIA

Volume 7

EARLY MODERN HISTORY
[1800–1940]

Volume Editor
Dr Cheah Boon Kheng
Universiti Sains Malaysia (Retired)

ARCHIPELAGO PRESS

Contents

Chronology

1786 A British settlement is established on Penang by Francis Light.

1791 The East India Company (EIC) and Sultan Abdullah of Kedah sign an agreement on the cession of Penang.

1795 Britain takes possession of Melaka for the duration of the Napoleonic wars.

1800

1800 Kedah cedes Province Wellesley to the EIC.

1812 Death of Sultan Mahmud of the Johor–Riau–Lingga sultanate; he is succeeded by his younger son, Tengku Abdul Rahman.

1818 Melaka is returned to the Dutch.

1819 Raffles establishes a free port on Singapore island; Tengku Hussein is recognized as sultan of Singapore.

1821 Siam invades Kedah; Sultan Ahmad Tajuddin flees, first to Penang and later to Melaka.

1824 The Anglo-Dutch Treaty gives British influence over the whole of the Malay Peninsula except the four northern Malay states, and partitions the Johor–Riau sultanate.

1825 Death of Temenggong Abdul Rahman of Johor; he is succeeded by his son Temenggong Daeng Ibrahim.

1826 The Burney Treaty confirms Siamese overlordship of Kedah; guarantees independence for Perak and Selangor, and secures Britain commercial rights in Kelantan and Terengganu.

1826 Formation of the Straits Settlements (Penang, Singapore and Melaka).

1826 Perak cedes the Dindings, including the island of Pangkor, to Britain in return for underwriting its independence from Siam; Britain, however, does not take the Dindings until 1874.

1831–2 Naning War, an uprising led by Dul Said after British officials try to impose Melakan laws and taxes on Naning, an autonomous state.

1835 Death of Sultan Hussein of Singapore; his son Tengku Ali is denied succession to the throne.

Detail of a mural on Muzium Negara depicting the opening of the first railway and the signing of the Pangkor Treaty.

1841 James Brooke becomes rajah of Sarawak.

1842 Siam restores sultanate in Kedah; Perlis is made a separate principality.

1846 Sultan Omar Ali of Brunei cedes Labuan to Britain.

1848 Tin is discovered in Larut, Perak.

1855 Tengku Ali is recognized as sultan of Johor, but with control only over Muar–Kesang district.

1857–63 Pahang civil war over succession dispute between two sons of Bendahara Ali after his death.

1857 Accession of Sultan Abdul Samad as ruler of Selangor.

1858 The Straits Settlements are passed from the control of the EIC to the British government.

1861–74 Larut wars in Perak among Chinese miners and Malay aristocrats.

1862 Death of Temenggong Daeng Ibrahim of Johor; he is succeeded by his son Abu Bakar.

1867–73 Klang war in Selangor between Raja Mahdi of Selangor and Tunku Kudin of Kedah.

1868 Abu Bakar recognized by the British as Maharajah instead of Temenggong.

1868 Death of Rajah James Brooke; he is succeeded by his nephew Charles Brooke.

1874 Pangkor Treaty is signed; Perak is forced to accept a British Resident.

1875 J. W. W. Birch, the first Resident of Perak, is murdered.

1875 J. G. Davidson is appointed as the first British Resident in Selangor.

1877 Death of Sultan Ali of Johor; his son Tengku Alam is denied succession to the throne.

1880 Kuala Lumpur becomes the state capital of Selangor.

1880s Large-scale expansion of tin mining in Perak.

1881 Formation of the British North Borneo Company to administer North Borneo.

1885 The Anglo-Johor Treaty is signed; Maharaja Abu Bakar becomes sultan of Johor.

1885 The first railway line, between Taiping and Port Weld, is opened.

1887 Sultan Idris ascends the throne of Perak.

1888 J. P. Rodger is appointed as the first British Resident in Pahang.

1888 Sarawak, Brunei and North Borneo are placed under British protection.

1800

SIAM

Patani

Kedah

Penang (1786)

Province Wellesley (1800)

Perak

Kelantan

Terengganu

Strait of Melaka

Selangor

Pahang (ruled by the Bendahara)

Minangkabau states

Melaka (1795)

Johor (ruled by the Temenggong)

Sumatra

Siak

Singapore

Riau

South China Sea

Area under the nominal sway of the Johor-Riau sultan
Siamese territory
Bugis area
British territory
Malay states

1890s The first rubber estates are planted in the Malay Peninsula.

1891–5 Rising by Malay chiefs in Pahang against British rule.

1895 The confederation of the Minangkabau states into Negeri Sembilan is completed; Martin Lister is appointed as the first British Resident.

1895 Death of Sultan Abu Bakar of Johor; he is succeeded by his son Ibrahim.

1895 Johor's constitution, the first for a Malay state, is adopted by the State Council.

1896 Selangor, Perak, Negeri Sembilan and Pahang are united as the Federated Malay States, with a Resident-General in Kuala Lumpur, the capital, and a High Commissioner (also the governor of the Straits Settlements) in Singapore.

1897 The first Malay Durbar (meeting of the Malay rulers of the four Federated Malay States, their Residents, the Resident-General and the High Commissioner) is held in Kuala Kangsar.

1898 Death of Sultan Abdul Samad of Selangor; he is succeeded by his grandson Sulaiman.

1900

1900 The Institute of Medical Research is set up in Kuala Lumpur.

1905 The Malay College is established in Kuala Kangsar to provide an English public school style education for sons of the Malay nobility.

Malay Peninsula

1842

Perlis (1842)
SIAM
Kedah
Penang
Perak
Kelantan
Terengganu
South China Sea
Strait of Melaka
Anglo-Dutch Treaty Line of 1824
Pahang
Selangor
Minangkabau states
Melaka
Johor
Sumatra
Singapore (1819)

Area under Siamese suzerainty
Straits Settlements
Area under Dutch control
Independent Malay states

1896

Perlis
SIAM
Kedah
Penang
Perak (1874)
Kelantan
Terengganu
South China Sea
Strait of Melaka
Pahang (1888)
Selangor (1875)
Negeri Sembilan (1895)
Melaka
Johor
Singapore

Note: 1. Negeri Sembilan created from the Minangkabau states in 1895.
2. Dates in brackets refer to appointment of first Resident.

Area under Siamese suzerainty
Straits Settlements
Federated Malay States (1896)
Independent Malay states

1910

Perlis
SIAM
Kedah
Penang
Perak
Kelantan
Terengganu
South China Sea
Strait of Melaka
Pahang
Selangor
Negeri Sembilan
Melaka
Johor
Sumatra
Singapore

Straits Settlements
Federated Malay States
Unfederated Malay States

1909 The Anglo-Siamese Treaty gives Britain control of Kelantan, Terengganu, Kedah and Perlis; British Advisers are appointed in Kelantan, Kedah and Perlis, and a British Agent in Terengganu.

1909 The Federal Council is established as a legislative body for the Federated Malay States.

1909 The rail link from Penang to Johor Bahru is completed, with a ferry service to Singapore.

1910 The indentured labour system is abolished and is replaced with the *kangany* system.

1910 Johor accepts a (British) General Adviser.

1911 The title of Resident-General is changed to Chief Secretary FMS.

1913 The first oil well at Miri produces oil.

1914 Death of Sultan Ahmad of Pahang; he is succeeded by his son Mahmud.

1915 Outbreak of rebellion by Malay peasants in Kelantan against British-imposed taxes.

1916 Death of Sultan Idris of Perak; he is succeeded by his nephew, Abdul Jalil.

1917 Death of Rajah Charles Brooke; he is succeeded by his son Vyner Brooke.

1919 A British Adviser is appointed to Terengganu.

1922 The Sultan Idris Training College is established at Tanjung Malim, Perak.

1923 The Labour Code makes it compulsory for estates to provide schools for the children of their workers.

1933 The Aliens Ordinance limits the number of new male immigrants; as a result, the number of female immigrants increases.

1938 The Indian government places a ban on assisted migration to the Malay Peninsula.

1941 Japanese invasion of the Malay Peninsula.

Miri Well No. 1 in Sarawak, where oil was first struck, propelling the rapid development of the oil industry.

Sarawak and Sabah

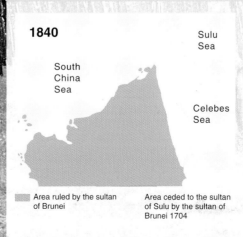

1840

Sulu Sea
South China Sea
Celebes Sea

Area ruled by the sultan of Brunei
Area ceded to the sultan of Sulu by the sultan of Brunei 1704

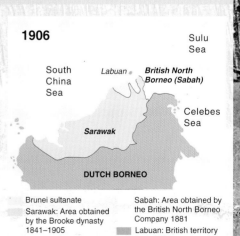

1906

Sulu Sea
South China Sea
Labuan
British North Borneo (Sabah)
Celebes Sea
Sarawak
DUTCH BORNEO

Brunei sultanate
Sarawak: Area obtained by the Brooke dynasty 1841–1905
Sabah: Area obtained by the British North Borneo Company 1881
Labuan: British territory from 1846

Introduction

Steel engraving of Sir Thomas Stamford Raffles, who founded a free port in Singapore for the East India Company in 1819.

TOP RIGHT: A watercolour of Fort Cornwallis in 1853. The fort was built in 1810 to protect the settlement of Penang, and is located at the place where Captain Francis Light, who founded the settlement in 1786, first landed.

This volume is concerned with the history during the period from 1800 until 1940 of the territory which has since 1963 been known as Malaysia. Political and economic transformation as the British established settlements, and later intervened in the administration of the Malay states, is the dominant theme. During this same period, the present-day states of Sarawak and Sabah were acquired, not by the British government but by British citizens. It was a period of remarkable economic development—of particular importance were tin mining and rubber estates—and also of social transformation, with the influx of thousands of foreign workers, many of whom settled in the country.

The early period

The initial focus is on the indigenous societies and their political systems, economies, and cultures, before the process of transformation from the early 19th century. This period 1819–26 was, in many ways, a watershed in the history of modern Malaysia. In 1819, the once great Malay entrepôt system of the Johor–Riau–Lingga–Singapore–Pahang empire, with its capital in Riau–Lingga, began its decline.

Anglo-Dutch rivalry caused the break-up of the empire. The Bugis and the Dutch had supported the succession of Tengku Abdul Rahman, the younger son of Sultan Mahmud, in 1812. However, Stamford Raffles' recognition of his elder brother, Tengku Hussein, who had been displaced from the throne by the Bugis, as ruler of Singapore in 1819 signified the beginning of the end of the empire. His plan was not only to disrupt Dutch trade monopolies, but also to establish a British port to serve the India–China trade routes. Emboldened by British support, Sultan Hussein and Temenggong Abdul Rahman laid claim to the mainland state of Johor. The empire's vassal states, including Selangor, Terengganu, and Perak were initially unable to decide to which Malay ruler they should pay homage. But after the signing in 1824 of the Anglo-Dutch Treaty demarcating the Dutch and British spheres of influence by an imaginary line along the Strait of Melaka, the vassal states began to assert their independence. As Johor, Pahang and Terengganu fell within the British sphere of influence, Sultan Hussein and Temenggong Abdul Rahman eventually retreated from Singapore into Johor, laying claim to it.

A map of the East Indies islands, from Pinkerton's *General Collection of Voyages*, 1811.

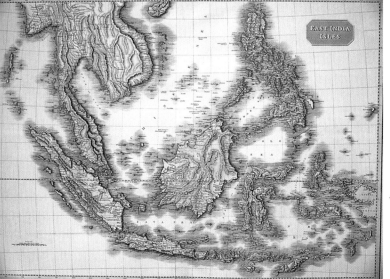

Internal conflicts

The impact of Western imperialism and capitalist penetration in the Malay states in the wake of the 1824 Treaty and the 1826 Burney Treaty weakened their feudal economies and political systems. Several states were brought close to disintegration. The Malay feudal political system was at its most fragile in the 19th century. Internal disputes occurred in all the Malay states. A civil war in Sarawak allowed James Brooke to intervene and become its governor. Internal conflict is a recurring theme in Malay history, but the many conflicts and their escalation to civil wars in this period suggests that they may have been partly triggered by economic factors resulting from the Western impact.

A Murut warrior dressed for battle armed with a spear and wooden shield. His headdress is adorned with hornbill feathers.

Traditional systems

In the Malay feudal political system, the *kerajaan* (monarchy) was dominated by the raja or sultan, but most of his powers were dispersed to ministers and territorial chiefs, who exacted forced labour and military service from their subjects. Those who could not pay taxes or were in debt were forced into debt-bondage. Slavery was practised through the subjugation of local aborigines or the purchase of foreign slaves. The ruler was entitled to monopolies of many trade items, but the chiefs could also acquire wealth. With the expansion of tin mining, rulers and chiefs often competed for the revenue and also became involved in the feuds of rival Chinese secret societies.

The Malay states enjoyed varying degrees of independence before 1909. The northern states—Perlis, Kedah, Kelantan and Terengganu—were subject to the overlordship of Siam. Within these states, the rulers and chiefs usually enjoyed autonomy. Kedah was occupied by a Siamese army from 1821 to 1842, and also exceptional in that it had codes of law and a system of weights and measures for trade similar to those of the Melaka sultanate.

Under the traditional Malay monarchy, power was shared between the ruler and the ministers and chiefs. Two Perak chiefs are shown here with their attendants, who were probably debt-bondsmen or forced labourers.

A sarong of *songket* (handwoven silk textile with a gold thread pattern) woven by Malay women of the east coast.

The lot of the Malay peasants was not always a happy one. They were unable to acquire knowledge or own properties; their boats and houses had to be simple, not elaborately adorned like those of royalty. Their rulers and chiefs could seize their property, or even their wives and daughters. The Malay peasants were, however, industrious. They toiled as farmers, fishermen, navigators and traders, but did not produce sufficient surplus for trade themselves. Trade was largely in the hands of rulers or chiefs and specially appointed traders, such as the royal merchants, who were Indians or Arabs. Many Malay peasant handicrafts were well known: beautifully handcarved weapons and handwoven silk textiles. Kedah was the only Malay state to make a successful transition from entrepôt trade to an agrarian economy. Its rice industry, which had lasted through three centuries, survived into the postcolonial period.

The economy of the Malay Peninsula in the late 19th and early 20th centuries depended on just two industries, tin and rubber, which transformed not only the economy, but also the population as a result of large-scale immigration of workers.

TOP: Rubber estates depended on Indian labourers for their operations.

BOTTOM: Chinese immigrants provided the labour necessary for opencast tin mines.

Foreign intervention

Several Malay states did not give up their independence without a struggle. In Kedah, campaigns to resist Siamese occupation (1821–41) eventually brought about Siamese withdrawal. The small district of Naning, near Melaka, was the first Malay territory to launch anti-British resistance, but it was subjugated in 1832. British intervention in Perak led to a Malay uprising and the assassination of J. W. W. Birch, the first British Resident, in 1875. Malay uprisings after British intervention occurred in Pahang, Kelantan and Terengganu, all led by chiefs. Similarly, in Brunei there was resistance to the efforts of James and Charles Brooke to expand Sarawak's territory.

Unable to prevent British intervention militarily, the Malay ruling classes accepted the inevitable. Their economies were already linked to the Western-dominated global economy. Their political and economic transformation was an evolutionary process. They adjusted to the realities of British military might and economic power as well as British-imposed changes through a system of indirect rule, under which the British Resident or Adviser advised the ruler on how to govern his state. In fact, however, it was the Resident or Adviser who governed and the ruler who advised.

By 1941, all 13 states had identical structures of a modern administration and economy. Their territorial boundaries had already been fixed. All were linked together through a common imperial power, Britain, whose policies affected all these states. However, they were not to form a federation until 1963.

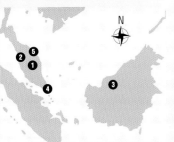

THE INDIGENOUS STATE AND SOCIETY

This study of 19th-century indigenous societies in Malaya begins at a transitional phase of their history, on the eve of colonial rule. Most of these societies flourished as self-sufficient, independent entities, practising their material and social cultures in much the same way as they always had, changing only with the monsoon and dry seasons. The Malay kingdoms (*kerajaan*) in the Malay Peninsula were more advanced than those in northern Borneo, which had been under Brunei rule until the latter part of the 18th century, when a small portion (the northeast and northwest coasts of present-day Sabah) was presented to the sultan of Sulu. European rule came in 1841, when Brunei allowed Sarawak to be governed by James Brooke, the first white rajah of Sarawak (r. 1841–68). In both the Malay Peninsula and Borneo, peasants provided forced labour for the sultans and the chiefs without any wages. They also served as soldiers and ceremonial escorts.

Territorial boundaries were not well demarcated, but all the native peoples and settlements recognized the overlordship of their respective sultans and paid tribute. By the beginning of the 18th century in what is today Sarawak, the Land and Sea Dayak (the Bidayuh and Iban), the Melanau sago cultivators and fishermen and the coastal Malays, comprising Arab traders and retainers of Brunei *pengiran* (nobles), had occupied the Batang Lupar, Rajang, Sarawak, Kalaka and other river systems, forming the nucleus of *negeri* (localized political entities) linked with Brunei. In North Borneo (present-day Sabah), peoples such as the Bajau lived in coastal areas, while the Dusun, Murut and others lived in the interior.

These traditional societies relied on fishing, rice and cash crops as well as the collection and export of forest produce and minerals. The Malays, Bajau and Samal Balangingi were maritime people who had been involved in entrepôt trade since the 14th century, but in the early 19th century this trade declined due to Portuguese, Dutch and English competition, the advent of slave raiding and the frequent insurrections against Brunei rule. With European economic intrusion, the Iranun and Balangingi peoples of present-day Sabah, who were under Sulu rule, indulged in slave raiding to serve the organized slave markets in the Sulu Archipelago and Borneo. Chinese miners from Dutch West Borneo were attracted to Sarawak by antimony mining, which began in the 1820s, after the Dutch imposed controls.

On the Malay Peninsula, Kedah's rice industry was the most advanced, with a modern irrigation system by the end of the 19th century. Perak's tin (which was mined on a large scale in the 19th century) had been known as early as the 17th century, causing Aceh to invade and demand tribute. On the east coast of the Peninsula, textile production was reported to already be a thriving industry in 1838.

However, with European penetration of these societies from the early 19th century, much of the indigenous commercial and social life was soon either disrupted or forced to adapt to the new developments taking place.

1. Houseboats on the Pahang River—a sight which can still be seen today—allowed their owners easy movement from place to place.

2. Elephants, such as these pictured by the Perak River, were widely used in the Malay Peninsula in the 19th century for the transport of both goods and people.

3. Kelabit metalsmiths of Sarawak using piston-bellows and stone hammers for working iron in this 1912 picture taken by the district officer and naturalist Charles Hose.

4. A Malay village of stilt houses at the edge of the sea on Pulau Brani in Singapore Harbour. Many Orang Laut also lived in the area, some in houses and others on their boats.

5. The east coast states, particularly Terengganu, have a long tradition of boat-building to meet the needs of the local Malay fishermen.

Two Dusun women from Sabah at work. The one on the right is wearing a traditional basket on her back, still in use today for the carrying of goods.

The Malay *kerajaan*

The Malay kerajaan *(monarchy) was a political structure in which the ruler, who was vested with supernatural majesty (daulat), was the source of dignity and bestower of high office to members of the Malay ruling class of his state and the embodiment of power and collective welfare to the general body of his subjects. The essential role of the ruler was symbolic and ceremonial, not executive. However, with economic development and British intervention in the 19th century the traditional structure of the Malay* kerajaan *underwent many changes.*

Royal regalia

In each of the Malay states, the royal family has its own regalia, which is passed down from generation to generation. This regalia plays an important role in all the official ceremonies at the palace, but particularly in the enthronement of a new sultan.

As yellow is the colour of royalty in Malaysia it is the colour most often used in the regalia; gold is the favoured metal. The items in the royal regalia may differ a little from state to state. However, the principal articles usually include a *nobat* (ceremonial orchestra); weapons such as a kris, a sword and a spear; a *tepak* (a container for betel nut and its accompanying ingredients); a mace, silk standards and umbrellas.

A long-bladed kris (left) and a gold betel nut container (*tepak*) (right) are considered to be essential items in the royal regalia of the Malay states.

The Malay *states*

Perlis
Kedah
Kelantan
Terengganu
Perak
N
South China Sea
Pahang
Selangor
Negeri Sembilan
Strait of Melaka
Melaka
Johor

10   50   100 km

The monarchy

Throughout Southeast Asia, monarchy was the usual form of government except among primitive communities. Most of the Malay dynasties of the Peninsula derived their status, directly or indirectly, from the sultanate of Melaka, which was the dominant power of the Strait of Melaka until it fell to Portuguese assault in 1511. Members of Melaka's ruling dynasty re-established themselves in Johor, but could hardly hold their own against the Portuguese and later the Dutch, or against native kingdoms such as Aceh and Siak. In Selangor and Negeri Sembilan, however, traditions of the royal families linked them with the Celebes (now Sulawesi) and with the Minangkabau of central Sumatra, respectively.

The monarch was the pre-eminent element of the *kerajaan*. Indigenous conceptions of kingship had adapted and adopted, to some extent, forms and ceremonies of Hindu and, from the 15th century, Islamic monarchy. From the latter came the title of 'Sultan' prefixed to the ruler's name.

Succession

There was no rule of primogeniture giving automatic succession to the eldest son. In theory, any male descendant of a previous ruler was eligible, though in practice the successor was usually a son or a younger brother. Seniority by age, the status of his mother as a royal consort, marriage alliances and holding the title of Raja Muda were all factors in a succession claim. The circle of potentates around the throne chose the successor, typically in formal conclave after the late ruler's funeral. In cases of intense rivalry this was not always a peaceful process. The chosen successor was formally installed and presented with the *kebesaran* (symbols of office), which usually included the *nobat* (royal ceremonial orchestra) and a state seal. At the ceremony of enthronement and on various other occasions, the dignitaries of court and state made *sembah* (obeisance) to the ruler.

Revenue

Until the end of the 18th century, trade, rather than production, was the mainstay of royal revenue, collected through customs and excise duties or monopolies. The ruler sometimes appointed an Indian Muslim trader as his *saudagar raja* (royal merchant) to handle external trade. Wealth was valued as a source of power. Significantly, the office holders were known collectively as Orang-Orang Kaya (literally, men of wealth). Revenue was shared

---

SULTANATE OF MELAKA

The sultanate of Melaka was founded in 1400 by Parameswara, a fugitive (Hindu) Sumatran prince whose son converted to Islam and was responsible for spreading the religion along the trade routes till the sultanate fell to Portuguese assault in 1511. The Melaka sultanate dominated both sides of the Strait of Melaka for a hundred years.

A quarter *penjuru* issued by Sultan Abdul Jalil Shah III of Johor (r. 1623–77).

JOHOR
The first ruler of Johor was Sultan Alauddin Riayat Shah, a son of Sultan Mahmud Shah (d. 1528), the last sultan of Melaka.

The seal of Sultan Muhammad IV of Kelantan (r. 1899–1920).

PAHANG
A vassal of the ruler of the Srivijaya empire during the 13th century. Raja Muhammad, who was a son of Sultan Mansur Shah of Melaka, was made sultan of Pahang in the 15th century.

SELANGOR
Klang, near the coast of Selangor, was, in the 15th century, appanage (land granted by a king for the support of a member of the royal family) of Tun Perak, the great Bendahara of the Melaka sultanate.

The emblem of Selangor.

KEDAH
The present royal family traces its lineage back to 7th- and 8th-century Hindu times when they were vassals of Srivijaya. With the decline of Sumatran power, Kedah came under the influence of the Siamese. The rise of Melaka in the 15th century gave Kedah respite from the Siamese and led to its Islamization.

KELANTAN
A vassal of the ruler of Srivijaya during the 13th century. During the 15th century, the rulers of the state converted to Islam.

PERAK
The present royal family of Perak traces its origins from Sultan Mudzafar Shah (c. 1528–49), the eldest son of Sultan Mahmud Shah, the last sultan of Melaka.

The seal of Sultan Mahmud Shah of Perak.

TERENGGANU
An inscribed stone found at Kuala Berang testifies to the existence of an Islamic state in Terengganu almost a century before the rise of Melaka. It became a vassal of Melaka and subsequently of Johor. The present royal house was founded early in the 18th century by Sultan Zainal Abidin, a brother of Sultan Abdul Jalil of Johor.

between the ruler and lesser magnates, who used it mainly for the support of their households and personal followers (essential for maintaining their status). A subject might petition a ruler for a subsidy to open agricultural land or tin mines, but direct investment in economic projects was not general.

Source of dignity

The control of manpower through debt-bondage and forced labour (see 'Forced labour, debt-bondage and slavery') was more important as a source of royal dignity than were territory rights. Even in the late 19th century, some rulers did not know the exact location of their state boundaries, especially in hilly and uninhabited border land. Undeveloped land has little economic value, but an area with rich tin deposits, or comparatively closely settled by peasant farmers, such as the Krian rice-growing area between Kedah and Perak, could give rise to territorial disputes. It was impossible for a ruler to exert direct authority throughout his state, so he allocated districts to rule by chiefs, who often had hereditary claims to these fiefs. In some cases, they paid a proportion of local tax revenues to the ruler.

Economic and political changes

Events in the first three-quarters of the 19th century slowly altered the balance of political and economic elements of the Malay kerajaan. Western demand for tin led to the rapid expansion of mining in Perak, Selangor and Sungai Ujong. Hence, chiefs of important mining districts such as Larut (Perak) and Lukut (Negeri Sembilan) became wealthier than the ruler, though still professing fealty to him.

Regional trade between states was replaced by direct shipment of produce to the free trade ports of Singapore, Melaka and Penang, thus diminishing the rulers' revenue. The expansion of tin mining led to the import of numerous Chinese labourers, who were difficult to control. Malay rulers and chiefs granted Chinese leaders authority over their own communities in return for a share of the revenue.

Thus, power was dispersed in some Malay states from the royal capital to the outlying districts. Among the ruling class, competition for office became increasingly divisive. Polygamous marriages produced numerous sons for whom there were insufficient jobs. Civil wars in Pahang (1857–63) and Selangor (1867–73) were matched by less bitter struggles in Perak. Conflicts between Chinese groups in these states added to the disorder.

However, there was movement towards consolidation as some rulers, notably those of Johor and Kedah, copied elements of the bureaucratic system of the Straits Settlements government. The ruler remained the temporal head of a Muslim community, though he had no means of exerting such authority. In justifying their intervention, which began in 1874, the British overstated the argument that the kerajaan had disintegrated. It was under pressure, but was in the process of adaptation.

Ruling styles

In favourable circumstances, a ruler who was a strong personality might rule his state with a strong hand, though observing the formalities of consultation. Such a ruler was Bendahara Ahmad of Pahang in the earlier years of his reign. Others such as Sultan Abdul Samad (r. 1857–98) of Selangor, used consultation to agree with everyone, and left the decision-making to be fought out by others. In some states, such as Perak and Kedah, the office of Raja Muda was conferred on a younger brother or son or other kinsman, giving him recognized authority to deputize for the ruler. In the 19th century, the high court offices inherited from Melaka, such as Bendahara, Temenggong, Laksamana and Bendahari, fell into disuse, though these titles were appropriated by ambitious dignitaries. In their place the ruler sometimes appointed a Perdana Menteri (chief minister) and other ministers of his choice. The *budak raja* (royal pages) provided the services of bodyguards and messengers to the ruler and nobles.

Sultan Ahmad (r. 1863–1914) ruled Pahang initially as Bendahara, and was proclaimed sultan in 1884.

Dato Jaafar bin Muhammad, who was appointed the first chief minister of Johor by Sultan Abu Bakar (r. 1862–1895), was from a family whose members had served the Temenggongs of the state for many generations.

Raja Yusuf of Perak (r. 1877–87)—seen here with his two sons (seated) and two retainers—was an unpopular ruler.

ABOVE: Istana Hinggap, a 17th-century Minangkabau-style palace built at Ampang Tinggi in Kuala Pilah, Negeri Sembilan by the Yamtuan for his daughter. It was also a resting place for the Yamtuan on visits to the area; thus its name—*hinggap* means 'to perch'.

LEFT: The Balai Besar (great hall) at Alor Setar, Kedah, used by the sultan for audiences with his subjects, was erected in 1904 to replace an 18th-century structure.

The bodyguards of Tuanku Muhammad, the Yamtuan of Negeri Sembilan, at the second Malay Durbar held in Kuala Lumpur in 1903. Their colourful outfits caused much comment among those attending the Durbar.

The Malay entrepôt state

As the only convenient and safe waterway through Southeast Asia, the Strait of Melaka has long served as a major link between the civilizations to the east and to the west. From the beginning of the Christian era, there is evidence of settlements along the Strait becoming involved in international trade. Communities vied with each other to attract this trade by creating the necessary facilities. Srivijaya, Melaka, Johor and Riau came to epitomize the Malay entrepôt state. Only with the founding of the British-controlled port city of Singapore by Stamford Raffles in 1819 did the Malay entrepôt state succumb to a new system of trade dominated by Western interests.

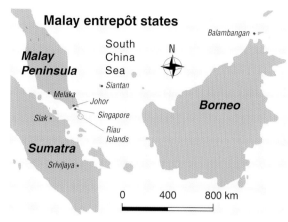

Malay entrepôt states

Characteristics of a Malay entrepôt state

- It was located somewhere on the 'favoured coast' at the southern end of the Strait of Melaka.

- Through its links to the interior groups and the sea peoples (Orang Laut) it gained access to aromatic woods and sea products in demand by foreign merchants.

- It offered a favourable marketplace through orderly government and effective laws.

- It protected traders from pirates and prevented the rise of rival ports by means of its Orang Laut fleet.

- It acquired a reputation for religious scholarship.

An early view of Melaka, in which the walled Portuguese fort can be seen. Melaka was a busy trading port as it lay on the route to Europe for ships sailing from both China and the Spice Islands of the Indonesian Archipelago.

The Malay entrepôt state

The origin of the Malay entrepôt state can be traced to the empire of Srivijaya, which flourished in southern Sumatra between the 7th and 11th centuries. It developed a number of characteristics which became the norm for all succeeding Malay entrepôts. After the 11th century, Srivijaya came under the influence of Central Java and it never regained the prominence of earlier centuries.

Melaka

The rise of the kingdom of Melaka in the early 15th century restored the Malays to the forefront of international trade. Melaka came to share the same features as Srivijaya, setting standards of excellence for subsequent Malay kingdoms. The memory of Srivijaya and, according to Malay tradition, one of its refugee princes, enabled Melaka to be established deliberately as an entrepôt. It not only dominated trade through the Strait of Melaka as Srivijaya had done, but also created norms of Malay behaviour and language, which became acknowledged as the most civilized in the archipelago. The spread of Melaka Malay culture made the Malay language the lingua franca in maritime Southeast Asia.

Like Srivijaya, Melaka also became a centre of religious learning. Islamic tracts were written in Malay, easing the spread of Islam along the trading routes. After the initial conversion of the ruler, the people converted. As in the time of Prophet Muhammad, in the Melaka period trade and religion were intricately linked in the spread of the religion throughout the archipelago.

In 1511, the Portuguese seized Melaka as part of their grand plan to control the ports on the international spice trade route. Melaka had flourished as the redistribution centre of the so-called 'trinity of spices': cloves, nutmeg and mace. After the Portuguese conquest of Melaka, the Malay ruler and his followers fled, eventually settling in Johor where the Malay entrepôt state was re-established. As in the past, the Malays welcomed all traders to their port, and every care was taken to facilitate a profitable exchange.

The Portuguese regarded the restoration of the Malay entrepôt in Johor as a threat to their monopoly and tried to destroy the kingdom. Their efforts to establish a trade monopoly also proved futile because of lack of resources. In time they became part of the local trade network living in an uneasy relationship with their Malay neighbours.

The arrival of the Dutch in the late 16th and early 17th centuries introduced a more dangerous threat to Melaka than the Portuguese had done. In 1602, the newly formed Dutch East India Company (VOC) planned to destroy its competitors and become the leading commercial power in the region. Melaka was seized from the Portuguese by the Dutch in 1641, but they did not attempt to resurrect the glory of Melaka for fear that it would undermine Batavia's importance as an entrepôt.

Buildings constructed in Melaka during each period of foreign rule (Portuguese (1511–1641), Dutch (1641–1824) and British (1824–1957)) are reminders of its long history as an important entrepôt.

TOP: Santiago Gate, part of the A Famosa fortress which was built by the Portuguese to protect the town of Melaka after they had captured it in 1511. This illustration is from James Wathen's *Journal of a Voyage in 1811 and 1812 to Madras and China* (1814).

BOTTOM: The Town Square in Melaka, with the Dutch buildings of Christ Church (completed about 1753) in the centre and the Stadthuys (town hall) (built in the 17th century) on the right are pictured here in a lithograph from Auguste-Nicholas Valliant's *Voyage Autour du Monde* (1852).

Johor

Johor's assistance to the Dutch in the conquest of Portuguese Melaka assured it of special treatment for the rest of the 17th century. Johor's good relationship with Batavia enabled the former to grow in both commercial strength and prestige in the Malay World. During the 17th century, Johor prospered by fulfilling the requirements which had made its predecessors, Srivijaya and Melaka, great.

Johor's wellbeing was undermined by the 1699 murder of Sultan Mahmud, which ended the Melaka dynastic line. The regicide proved divisive, with the Orang Laut withdrawing their support from Johor because their personal link to the Melaka dynasty had ended so brutally. In 1717, Raja Kecil, a Minangkabau adventurer, claimed to be the son of the murdered ruler. In this way, Raja Kecil was able to gain the allegiance of the Orang Laut, who then joined the Minangkabau forces to seize control of the kingdom in 1718.

Raja Kecil deposed the former Bendahara (chief of state) who had been chosen to succeed Sultan Mahmud but remained in Johor for only a brief time. The Bendahara then enlisted the help of Bugis princes and their followers in the Malay region to remove Raja Kecil from the kingdom. After a number of decisive battles, the Malay–Bugis alliance proved superior and the kingdom was again controlled by the Bendahara family.

Raja Sulaiman, son of the Bendahara, became ruler of Johor and the Bugis leader Daeng Marewa became Raja Muda. Unlike the Malay practice of using this title to indicate the heir to the throne, the Bugis considered the Raja Muda as a second king. Under the Bugis Raja Muda, Riau became another entrepôt with all the features which had made Srivijaya, Melaka and Johor great.

English country traders

The late 18th-century arrival of English country (private) traders brought more complications. Though they were more interested in the lucrative China trade than in Southeast Asian trade, the VOC saw these British traders as a threat. Fearful of a Malay alliance with the British, the Dutch enforced restrictive measures against local kingdoms, ending in the seizure of Riau in 1784. However, they were forced to leave the islands in 1787 by Iranun raiders from the southern Philippines who had been invited to Riau by the Malay ruler. Once ensconced, the Iranun refused to leave, and so the Malays and the Bugis abandoned the island—the Malays for Pahang and Terengganu, and the Bugis for Selangor, Siantan and Borneo.

The founding of Singapore

After the British abandoned their trading post on Balambangan (north Borneo) in 1805, they had no strategic port on the India–China trade route. Sir Stamford Raffles was ordered to set up a post in the southern approaches to the Melaka Strait. The Dutch had re-established their post on Riau, the obvious choice, in 1812. Instead, the British created a port in Singapore in 1819. With free trade status and links to the industrial and military might of Britain, Singapore ushered in a new era of entrepôt states. During the 19th century, Malay kingdoms became less competitive and began to serve as feeder ports. Although Singapore resembled the past Malay entrepôts, it differed in that it was controlled by Europeans and was primarily for their benefit. In the words of a Malay scribe, 'a new world was being created and the old world destroyed'.

The spice trade

Spices grown in the Indonesian Archipelago have long been in great demand in Europe. Through a network of Southeast Asian and foreign traders, the precious cargo was transported from the Spice Islands through the Strait of Melaka to Europe. It was because of the ambition to capture this lucrative trade that Portugal invaded and captured Melaka in 1511.

Symbols of foreign rule

The coat of arms of the Portuguese crown (top), the flag of the Dutch East India Company (VOC) (middle) and the coat of arms of the British East India Company (EIC) (bottom) are symbols of the three foreign rulers of the entrepôt of Melaka, beginning from 1511 with the Portuguese seizure of Melaka. The Portuguese ruled until the Dutch took possession of the port in 1641. British rule was established in 1824 after the signing of the Anglo-Dutch Treaty, which gave the British control over the Malay Peninsula.

The most desired of the many spices grown in the Indonesian Archipelago. *LEFT TO RIGHT*: nutmeg (which also supplies mace), cloves and cinnamon.

The Malay diet

British observers in 19th-century Malaya displayed great curiosity about what lay in the hearts and minds of the Malays, but had remarkably little interest in what was in their stomachs. Malay villages usually produced most of what their inhabitants consumed. Rice and locally grown vegetables were the basic essentials of the diet. Villagers living near the coast also obtained fish from the sea, while those in inland villages caught theirs in rivers and streams or ate salted fish. Meat was eaten only occasionally, mainly during festivals.

A 19th-century chromolithograph from John Cameron's *Our Tropical Possessions in Malay an India* of rice fields in Province Wellesley, a district of Kedah which was ceded to the East India Company in 1800.

The common man's diet

James Low, Superintendent of Province Wellesley from 1827 to 1840, observed in his book *The British Settlement of Penang* (1836) that 'a family of five consumed on average about 31/4 chupahs [about 2.7 kilograms] of rice per day', and, in addition 'was abundantly supplied with fish, pulses, plantains, Indian corn, and sweet potatoes, poultry and butcher's meat'. A Malay labourer, he added, needed more than 1.8 pounds (0.85 kilogram) of rice per day, along with some fish, salt, chilli and other condiments, and in addition made use of tobacco and chewed betel. A betel quid consisted of betel leaves (*daun sirih*) (*Piper betle*) wrapped around slithers of areca nut, lime and gambier.

In another account, Isabella Bird describes in *The Golden Chersonese* (1883) how 'the boatmen prepared an elaborate curry for themselves, with salt fish for its basis, and for its tastiest condiment blachang—a Malay preparation much relished by European lovers of durian and decomposed cheese. It is made by trampling a mass of putrefying prawns and shrimps into a paste with bare feet. This is seasoned with salt. The smell is penetrating and lingering.' She herself consumed 'a slim repast of soda water and bananas'. Apart from such snippets, information on Malay foods is sparse.

Rice, the dietary staple, was grown in the Peninsula, but usually for subsistence rather than in commercial quantities. Towns depended on imported rice, as did the mines and estates. The Chinese generally consumed white milled rice imported from Siam, while the Indians mostly ate parboiled rice from Burma or produced locally. Malay farmers ate rice which they pounded in a mortar to remove the husk. Although such rice was perhaps healthier than the products of commercial mills, one of the accomplishments expected of a Malay wife was the ability to pound rice a second time to whiten it by removing the bran.

Although various accounts suggest that many people ate little apart from rice, such statements can be misleading for several reasons. First, the Malay expression '*makan nasi*' (to eat rice) is ambiguous, and can mean either the literal translation or simply 'to eat food'. Thus, when a Malay reports that he ate 'rice' for dinner, it is easy to draw an erroneous conclusion. Second, many meals consisted of rice eaten with small quantities of accompaniments to 'add to the taste', but lacked a 'main course' (*lauk*) of meat or vegetables. However, from a dietary standpoint, those small additions were extremely important. They included *belacan*, the prawn paste described by Isabella Bird, that was often pounded in a mortar together with fresh red chillies to make *sambal belacan*, and supplied both protein and salt. Other condiments included *chinchalok*, a salty liquid

Fruits and vegetables

C. N. Maxwell, a colonial official with extensive experience in Malaya— and a lesser known member of the famous Maxwell family—wrote in 1917 about the forest vegetables collected by the Malays: '... palm cabbages of a dozen varieties, the fruits of rattans, bamboo shoots, the young leaves of many trees, besides fruits and fungi' together with assorted herbs and the leaves of creepers and trees. Along the river banks 'edible ferns and edible water plants' grew in profusion and gardeners produced a wide range of vegetables, which sprang up 'faster than the gardener can weed them out'. People also grew, or collected from the forest, fruits such as durian, bananas, jackfruit, mangoes, rambutans, mangosteens, papayas, chempedak and watermelon.

Boats arriving at Manai fruit market in Terengganu, c. 1912.

Malay women selling vegetables at an open-air market, c. 1926.

The durian

To the Malays, the most highly prized of all fruits is the strong smelling durian. However, the reaction of Europeans to this fruit has been mixed. While some quickly became devotees, others such as Sir Stamford Raffles did not. In the *Hikayat Abdullah*, Munshi Abdullah gives a memorable account of an incident in 1819 when the founder of Singapore reacted strongly to a man who came to his desk to try to sell him six durians. 'As soon as Mr Raffles caught the smell of the durians, he held his nose and ran upstairs.... "The smell of these durians is nauseating and has given me a headache!" From then on, no one dared to bring him any more durians.'

Durians, together with a variety of other local fruits, displayed for sale at a market stall.

containing tiny shrimps. Along with rice, people consumed various leaves (*ulam*) selected to provide contrasting tastes and textures (sweet and moist, astringent, bitter). These were eaten with sambal belacan or chinchalok, and partly met the dietary need for green vegetables. A wide range of vegetables were grown, and many varieties of fruit were grown or collected. In addition, the Malays made cakes from rice or rice flour and coconut milk.

Meat, mostly goat and buffalo, had little part in the regular diet. There was no refrigeration, and so meat could not be kept for any length of time. Meat featured on ceremonial occasions, when a whole animal was ritually slaughtered and prepared for a communal feast. Villagers reared chickens, but ate them only on special occasions. Fish was the principal source of animal protein in the Malay diet.

Improvements in the diet

Surveys in the 1930s suggested that the traditional Malay diet was not nutritionally adequate. These findings were based on League of Nations standards which called for a diet including one gram of protein per kilogram of body weight per day, including at least some animal protein (milk, ghee, eggs, fish or meat), as well as sufficient vegetables and fruit to provide appropriate quantities of vitamins, minerals and carbohydrates.

In Kedah, dietary surveys of Malays living in remote areas indicated that they ate little more than rice supplemented with small quantities of fish. Those near the coast enjoyed a better diet. In Selangor, the Malay diet included a selection of vegetables including onions, sweet potatoes, yams and brinjals, along with chillies and belacan, but few eggs, leafy vegetables or pulses.

During the 1930s, the British administration introduced several initiatives to improve nutrition. The

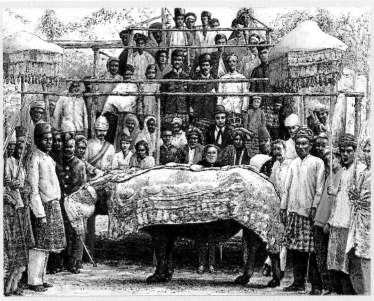

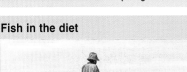

A gift for a princess
'The marriage of his (Prince Datu Klana of Melaka) daughter (was) a very splendid affair. The buffalo was a marriage present from the Straits Government, and its covering was of cloth of gold thick with pearls and precious stones' observed Isabella Bird in *The Golden Chersonese* (1883).

The meat of buffaloes did not play an important role in the Malay diet, being reserved for festivals. However, they were essential to peasants for ploughing the rice fields and pulling bullock carts.

Department of Agriculture encouraged farmers to cultivate vegetables at the edge of their rice fields on bunds made from heaps of decaying weeds coated with mud, and during the dry season to plant groundnuts or other crops in the fallow fields. Farmers were also urged to rear in their rice fields and irrigation canals fish such as *ikan sepat*, a small, oily and nutritionally rich fish that can readily be preserved by drying. When the water was drained from the rice fields, the ponds might contain several hundred kilograms of fish which farmers dried in the sun, storing them for future use or selling them to eke out their meagre income from the rice crop.

Such measures undoubtedly improved rural diets, However, in more recent times double cropping of rice has largely destroyed this agricultural pattern. As the rice fields are flooded at least twice a year, the ground is too wet for growing vegetables. Most of the fish stocks have been killed off by the pesticides and fertilizers now in common usage on the rice crop. Farmers complain that while their income from rice has improved as a result of double cropping, they have benefited little as their extra earnings are mostly spent on purchasing the vegetables and fish they could previously produce or catch in their rice fields themselves.

Fish in the diet

Fishermen with their baskets and nets waiting for the tide to ebb before taking their boats out to sea.

The sea cucumbers, molluscs and crabs which the women could collect on the beach and in shallow water supplemented the catch of the fishermen who went out in boats.

Drying fish in the sun for sale in the interior. Dried fish were also eaten in the monsoon season when fishing was impossible.

The coconut palm was an essential part of the village landscape as it provided many essentials for the Malay diet. From the nut came water for a refreshing drink, milk for making curries and cakes, and coconut flesh. The milk was boiled to produce coconut oil; the sap of the coconut flower was boiled to make sugar. The dried husk was used as fuel for cooking fires, while coconut leaves were used for the weaving of cooking containers and baskets.

Forced labour, debt-bondage and slavery

*Forced labour (*kerah*), debt-bondage and slavery enabled the ruling class, and also some well-to-do commoners, to obtain service or labour from members of the peasant class by compulsion and without payment of wages. Such forced labour sometimes had an economic value, but the main purpose of these exactions was often social or political. Debt-bondage, in particular, had significance as a means of enhancing the prestige of the creditor; this underlay the Malay resistance to British measures for the suppression of this practice.*

Forced labour

Kerah was the most widely used of the three forced labour institutions. In principle, anyone in authority could call on adult male villagers under his control to perform either personal services for him, or public works. He had no obligation to pay for this work, nor even to provide food or rations while it was in progress. A chief might, for example, require peasants to abandon their own holdings during a busy season to cultivate his fields, or to build or repair roads, or clear river obstructions, or work as crew on his boat when he travelled.

In Kedah, where the system was highly developed, some 600 villagers living near the capital provided gangs of about 10 to work for 15 days at a time, by rotation, in domestic duties at the palace. The right to kerah was assignable, so that a chief could pass over to a private landowner the right to call on a village for field workers. Kerah was also the basis of mobilizing peasants for military service. The period of the call-up for any kind of kerah work was unlimited, and often severely disrupted the peasants' own farming operations.

Royalty were always accompanied by bodyguards wherever they went. This service was generally provided by their debt-bondsmen. Creditors provided board and lodging for not only their debtors, but also their debtors' families.

Che Mida of Kuala Kangsar and her third husband, Nakhoda Tiong, with their attendants (both male and female), who were considered necessary for persons of noble birth. These were debt-bondsmen and women who served in the household of the master or mistress to whom they were indebted.

Debt-bondage

Debt-bondsmen (*orang berhutang*) included the wives and children of a debtor, and the debt was often some ancient transaction. Again, the creditor could call on them to work or give service for any period, and did not give credit for the value of their labour

to reduce the debt. In this case, the work was done for the creditor personally. It might be similar to kerah labour, but in many cases male followers gave service simply by attending on the creditor, especially when he was seen in public. It was necessary for a man of high rank to have at least 40 followers in attendance to maintain his status.

The ownership of a large house such as this was a source of prestige and pride for a nobleman (or woman), and many craftsmen were needed for its construction. To have a house built, the noblemen mobilized labour under the *kerah* system. In his household, he depended on debt-bondsmen and women as cooks, nursemaids and general domestics.

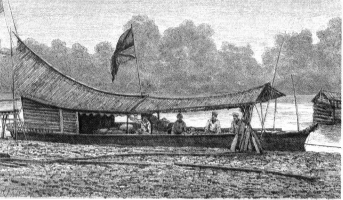
Visiting British officials on tour requisitioned transport such as boats like this for their journeys through the local headman. They utilized the *kerah* system to obtain the necessary boatmen or, for overland journeys, porters.

ABOVE: Sultan Abdul Samad of Selangor (r. 1857–98) and his entourage and other rulers during a visit by Malay sultans to Singapore in 1890 on the occasion of a visit by the Duke of Connaught, a son of Queen Victoria. Among his followers, at least the bodyguards and servants would have been *kerah* labourers or debt-bondsmen. On all their travels, the Malay sultans were accompanied by a large group of followers.

LEFT: As Muslim nobles could not enslave fellow Muslims, their slaves included captured members of Orang Asli tribes (such as the Sakai in this photograph) as well as non-Muslim Batak from Sumatra, and even Africans.

Village women were called upon to work as cooks, nurses, and domestic servants in the creditor's house. Followers and domestics often lived as regular members of the creditor's household and were given free board and lodging. If treated with consideration and affection, a bond was sometimes forged between them and the creditor.

Slavery

Under Islamic law, a Muslim might not enslave another of his own faith. Hence, slaves were captured aborigines, non-Muslim Batak from Sumatra, or even Africans purchased by pilgrims in Arabian slave markets. Slaves had lower status than debt-bondsmen, who were still free men, but they were treated and employed in much the same way.

Resort to these forced labour services was closely associated with differences of rank and status in precolonial Malay society. In Negeri Sembilan, with its egalitarian Minangkabau social system, and in districts where the former local upper class had been dispersed (as in the Klang Valley of Selangor after the civil war), there were few bondsmen or slaves, and kerah service was almost unknown.

Where one person has excessive rights over another, there must be—and there was—abuse. On the other hand, it was not crude economic exploitation, but a complex relationship which modern social historians of Southeast Asia have categorized as 'dependency'. The bondsman who worked in the creditor's house had a patron and protector in his dealings with third parties and the latter's prestige imparted a little reflected glory to his entourage. The upper class, particularly, prized the services of domestic labour. However, the female domestics sometimes complained very bitterly of the harshness of their lot.

The end of forced labour

Under the influence of the British Residents, slavery, which had already declined, came to an end. Debt-bondage presented different problems as debtors attempted to seek refuge with the British. While at first this was granted, later asylum was given only to those suffering from abuse. However, it was the change in the social position of the creditors under the British regime that helped to bring the system to an end, as status was derived from the position held by an aristocrat rather than the number of followers he possessed.

Different considerations made the abolition of kerah service also a gradual process. Service to private individuals rapidly ended, but the colonial government, like its traditional predecessor, needed labour for public works and had little money to pay wages. So the general obligation of adult males to perform kerah work for the state was continued, but with a maximum of six days' work a year, and with exemption for those paying the new land tax (quit rent) on their land. Over time the practice became generally accepted, but with increased government revenue, wage labour replaced kerah. Thus, social change as much as official policy led to the end of compulsory labour in the Malay states.

Peasants had to provide *kerah* labour whenever requested by the chiefs. Thus they often had to defer the planting or harvesting of their own rice fields to perform the same task for a chief.

The British and compulsory labour

The forced labour practices were undeniably Malay custom, in which British Residents were not permitted to interfere. However, Victorian Britain's conscience was haunted by the past horrors of the African slave trade. Hence, any 'slavery' was regarded as an abomination to be drastically suppressed. The abolition of slavery caused no significant problems since there were few slaves and they were not prized assets.

The urgent problem for the colonial administrators in the late 1870s was dealing with debtors, especially women, who sought asylum from unkind creditors. The readiness of J. W. W. Birch, the first Resident of Perak, to afford such refuge was one factor leading to his violent death. Hugh Low, Resident of Perak 1877–89, insisted that

Hugh Low, Resident of Perak 1877–89, who respected the claims of creditors against their bondsmen.

debt-bondage was not merely another form of slavery, and that claims of creditors should be respected unless a runaway bondsman/woman had clearly been maltreated.

While Low worked to achieve a consensus with aggrieved creditors, resistance to the end of debt-bondage crumbled with a change in the position of Malay aristocrats under the Residency System. Most of the nobility could no longer afford to maintain large households, which could only be run with the help of numerous workers. Status now came from government office, rather than the number of followers. Some 'face' was saved by setting off the notional value of a bondsman's future services towards a reduction of his debt. Debt-bondage was abolished by the state councils of Perak, in the 1880s, and of Pahang, in the 1890s.

Early Malay tin mining

As early as the 15th century, alluvial tin was readily accessible from many Malayan river valley floors. Employing simple methods, the part-time Malay miners produced sufficient tin for local use as well as for export. The demand for Malayan tin increased with the development of the tin plate industry in the West. As shallow deposits were exhausted, new methods of mining deeper, requiring more capital and labour, were devised. The Malays failed to adapt to the changes, instead allowing emigrant Chinese to overtake them in the industry.

Tin-mining areas of Perak

N

S. KURAU

Strait of Melaka

Taiping
Blanja

Sayong
Senggang
Perak
Bandar Bahru

Kuala Perak
Balak Rabit
Durian
Sebatang

0   16 km

S. BERNAM

Tin-mining areas

South China Sea

MALAY PENINSULA

Strait of Melaka

Primary tin mining

The history of tin mining prior to 1874 is fragmentary and sometimes conflicting, partly because the scope of early Malay mining itself was limited. Most Malays were cultivators and fishermen living in riverine areas who engaged in mining only after the harvest, and to supplement agricultural income. Hence, well into the 19th century Malay mining techniques remained simple, requiring insignificant investment and labour. Consequently, mining attracted many part-timers but could be conducted only in places where tin was easily accessible, usually at the base of foothills and beside major rivers. A 1768 Dutch survey in Perak showed that mining was concentrated almost solely along the Perak River and its tributaries, and the districts around Kuala Kangsar and Kelian Indah. In 1885, Abraham Hale, the British Inspector of Mines, reported that 350 of almost 500 registered mines in the Kinta district were worked by Malays.

Mining methods

Panning, by using the *dulang*, was the simplest method and was usually carried out in lowland streams after heavy rains had washed the tin-bearing soil down from the hills.

Lampan (ground sluicing) mining involved digging a *parit* (ditch) from the stream to lead the water to the mine. *Karang* (the tin-bearing earth) was thrown into the water and then stirred to break it up. The lighter soil was washed away, leaving the heavier stones and tin ore at the bottom of the ditch. After removing the stones, the remaining mixture was driven downstream with a large wooden spade called a *pengayuh*. The small dams in the ditch collected the tin sand, which was then scooped out with a small wooden tray. The tin sand was then 'dressed' (washed) in a 2.4-metre-long *palong* (a sluice box made from a hollowed-out tree), and sometimes again in a *pandei* (a smaller version of the palong). This lampan method could only be employed in areas where the streams ran downhill to provide the necessary water power. In virgin tin fields, *dulang* washing and lampan mining provided a good revenue for part-time miners.

Ludak and *tebok* mining involved sinking pits when the ore lay above the bedrock. Where the ore was near the surface, ludak mines with 1.5-metre-deep pits were dug. These were kept dry by removing water manually. In tebok mining, the walls of the 3-metre-deep pits were supported by wood and bamboo to prevent subsidence. A simple balance-pole, with a wooden bucket at one end and a weight on the other, was used to remove water

Extracting tin

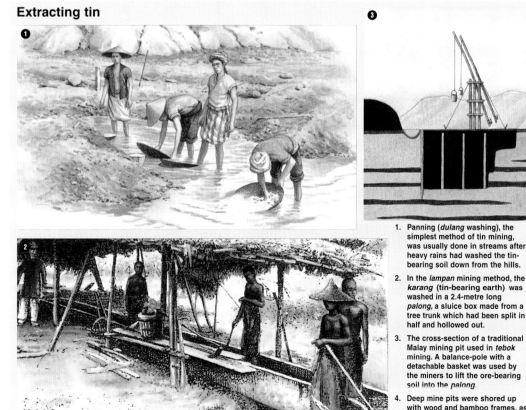

1. Panning (*dulang* washing), the simplest method of tin mining, was usually done in streams after heavy rains had washed the tin-bearing soil down from the hills.

2. In the *lampan* mining method, the *karang* (tin-bearing earth) was washed in a 2.4-metre long *palong*, a sluice box made from a tree trunk which had been split in half and hollowed out.

3. The cross-section of a traditional Malay mining pit used in *tebok* mining. A balance-pole with a detachable basket was used by the miners to lift the ore-bearing soil into the *palong*.

4. Deep mine pits were shored up with wood and bamboo frames, as seen in this 19th-century drawing of Pollock's tin lode in Pahang.

Tin currency

Over the centuries, tin currency in the Malay Peninsula has taken many forms. In Perak, Selangor and Negeri Sembilan, tin ingots in the shape of animals were used as currency. These were originally cast for presentation to royalty and for use in rituals at the opening of new mines. The most popular shape was the crocodile, an animal which features in many Malay legends. In Pahang, the 'tin hat' coins (*tampang*) (below) were inscribed with the sultan's seal. Early Melakan tin coins include the earliest known indigenous Islamic coin (bottom right) issued during the reign of Sultan Muzaffar Shah (1445–9). In the east coast states of Kelantan and Terengganu, coins were broken off tin money trees for use as currency. The money tree at top right is from Terengganu.

Mineral souls, superstitions, charms and taboos

A traditional belief of the Malays was that everything had a soul—humans, animals, vegetables, plants and minerals. The soul of tin was believed to take the shape of a water buffalo, while the soul of gold ore was thought to have the shape of a *kijang* (barking deer).

Mining wizards were considered to be imbued with the power to bring ore to a place where none existed; and to be able to sterilize existing ore and convert it into grains of sand.

At the time of opening of a new mine, a *pawang* (shaman) was called upon to carry out certain ceremonies to appease the spirits and ensure the future success of the mine. The pawang would erect a *genggulang* (altar) and call upon the help of the *hantu* (local spirit). The pawang also hung an *ancha* (sacrificial tray) in the smelting-house.

The soul of tin is believed to take the shape of the water buffalo, used by Malay farmers to plough the rice fields.

from a sump at the bottom. A balance-pole with a detachable basket instead of a bucket was used to lift the ore-bearing soil into the palong for dressing, as in lampan mining.

These mines, usually found in hilly areas with natural drainage, had to be abandoned during the rainy season when flooding and collapse of the walls threatened safety. In this type of mining, the ground was seldom worked out because mining was carried out horizontally, rather than vertically, into deeper layers of the mineral vein.

A related method of mining with still deeper pits was *lombong Siam* (Siamese mines). Abraham Hale reported the existence of 50 of these mines, averaging about 6 metres deep and 2.4 metres in diameter, in the Lahat hills in Kinta in 1885. They had been abandoned, probably due to flooding.

Smelting methods were also simple. The dressed ore was placed with charcoal in a simple clay shaft furnace (*relau*). The melted ore then ran into a hollowed-out mould in the ground.

Traditional uses and trade of tin

Traditionally, tin was rarely used on its own in the Malay Peninsula. As a component metal of bronze, tin was utilized for making weapons and also for musical instruments such as gongs. In some parts of the Peninsula, tin was used as a system of coinage though it did not gain widespread use. Tin was much more widely used in China, Japan and India, which had imported the metal since ancient times.

The trade in tin was sufficiently valuable for the Portuguese, and later the Dutch, to attempt to monopolize it after their conquests of Melaka in 1511 and 1641, respectively. During the 17th and 18th centuries, the Dutch successfully concluded treaties with Malay chiefs to monopolize tin exports. When a large quantity of tin had been collected by the chiefs and their courts from the ancestral mines worked by their followers, the tin was sent downstream to the Dutch Resident. The royal tin, stamped with the ruler's seal, was weighed in the presence of representatives of the court and

the Dutch Resident to prevent disputes over quality or weight. After the chief's delivery was complete, ordinary people would sell their tin, in smaller quantities.

Modern uses and trade of tin

With the emergence of the British tin plate industry in the 19th century, demand for alluvial tin from the Malay Archipelago increased. Purer than the block tin produced by the Cornwall lode mines, Malayan tin was highly suitable for tin plate.

Pressure by the British tin plate manufacturers resulted in the repeal of all duties imposed on tin imports into Britain in 1853. By 1875, stimulated by the expansion of the canning industry and the availability of cheaper alluvial tin from the Malay Archipelago, Britain was the largest producer of tin plate in the world. With Britain as its chief market, the Malay Peninsula was set to become the world's largest producer of alluvial tin.

However, as the shallow deposits of ore were exhausted by the late 1880s, it became necessary to mine below the water table. Better equipment and methods of flood prevention were necessary to exploit these resources. Such equipment required greater capital outlay, and large-scale operations were necessary for economic viability. The Malays possessed neither the new technical knowledge nor the necessary finance. Although both the Chinese and the Europeans had the knowledge and finance, with increased immigration from China only the Chinese businessmen had control of abundant, cheap labour, which allowed them to operate larger mines more economically than the Europeans. In this way, the Chinese displaced the Malays from the Peninsula's tin-mining industry.

The tin ore was smelted in a simple clay shaft furnace (*relau*). Charcoal provided heat to melt the ore, which ran from the furnace into a hollowed-out mould in the ground.

Rice cultivation and Kedah

While traditional Malay society can be identified with agriculture, in particular rice production, the major Malay states were built on regional and interregional trade. Often an associated agrarian hinterland enhanced the attractiveness of the place as a port of call. Kedah was one of the few states which successfully evolved from a trading entrepôt into an agrarian kingdom. This transition was achieved by the 17th century, although the extension and development of rice cultivation continued well into the 20th, with a major spurt in the last quarter of the 19th century.

Kedah

Kedah

South China Sea

Strait of Melaka

N

0   100 km

Factors influencing rice cultivation

Rice cultivation probably started some time in the period 600–1000 CE, around the Kuala Muda–Merbok area. By the early 16th century, Portuguese sources report Kedah as having rice in abundance. This is further confirmed by 17th-century Dutch records for Melaka which record the arrival of ships with rice from Kedah as well as the dispatch of at least one Dutch mission to Kedah in 1642 for the express purpose of purchasing rice for Melaka, then under Dutch control. Kedah sources report a mission to purchase 1250 tonnes of rice during the same period. Such an amount would have fed 50,000 people for one month, calculated on a rate of consumption of 25 kilograms per person per month.

Detail of a flowering rice (*Oryza sativa*) plant, which was so important to the economy of Kedah.

By the 18th century, rice cultivation was an integral part of the Kedah economy, and the export of padi (unhusked grain) and rice (husked grain) was a royal monopoly. During the reign of Sultan Muhammad Jiwa (r. 1723–78), regulations forbade captains of ships to take rice out of the state without the seals of both the sultan and the Laksamana (admiral), on pain of having their ships seized. If a captain who had committed such an offence resisted seizure of his ship, it was permissible to kill him. Such regulations indicated the seriousness of the offence.

Such controls were probably instituted because of the uncertainties associated with this staple crop. Data for the period 1880–1940 suggest that major crop failures occurred about once every ten years, with less drastic shortfalls in between. These failures were primarily the result of drought, together with a regular cycle of buffalo and cattle diseases.

However, it is not clear if rice exports were an important component of Kedah's international trade, and hence of the sultan's revenue, prior to the end of the 18th century and the establishment of the British settlement in Penang in 1786. Padi and rice may have been intended primarily for consumption within the Malay Peninsula and for the provisioning of merchant ships in port, with exports only by request. This is partly indicated by an extant record of a letter of appointment of a *panglima* (chief) in Perlis in the late 17th or early 18th century. The letter states that the export of rice from Perlis should not be allowed as 'all rational people know that if it is permitted, padi and rice will become expensive', and would result in hunger and indebtedness among the people.

Duty on padi and rice

Nevertheless, by the 18th century there was a fixed rate on duty on exports of padi and rice. The rate was reduced after the 1869 Anglo-Siamese Treaty, and was finally abolished after British control of Kedah was established in 1909.

At the end of the 18th century, Kedah was exporting about 3000 tonnes of rice and padi annually. With the establishment of Penang, exports grew in the first quarter of the 19th century to about 4000 tonnes. The duties levied on these exports provided about a third of the state's revenue, compared to only about 10 per cent previously.

By the late 19th century, however, export duty on rice had declined again to about 10 per cent of total revenue. This was not due to a reduction in the importance of rice cultivation in Kedah's economy; rather, it was a result of opium, gambling and spirits becoming more important sources of

Bullfighting

The period after the rice harvest each year in the northern Malay states was a time for fun and games. In addition to the well-known traditional sports of kite-flying, top-spinning and cockfighting, there was also the lesser known sport of bullfighting.

This was not the Spanish version, with man pitted against bull. Rather, this was bull against bull. Owners started training their animals from a young age, and entered them in fights when about three years old.

Two bulls of the same size and age were led on to the field and placed facing each other a few metres apart. (The choice of position for each animal was decided earlier by drawing blades of grass.) When the ropes were cut, the head-to-head fight commenced, and continued until one bull turned away from the contest.

The sport of bullfighting was a test of weight and strength, with little movement around the field. It was extremely popular with the numerous spectators, and was a very serious sport for the owners of the bulls.

revenue. Rice farming was still the largest employer of labour and its importance should be measured by income from the poll, hut and other indirect taxes.

The rice crop was a source of cheap food for both Kedah and Penang, as well as in Kedah's emerging plantation and mining sectors. Indeed, in further reducing the already diminished external trade of Kedah, Penang heightened the role of padi in the economy of Kedah.

This was compounded by obstacles raised by the British in Penang to Kedah's attempts to develop its own tin mining and, subsequently, rubber industries in the 19th century. Both industries required a large labour force, but British rule in Perak and the development of tin mines and rubber estates there encouraged the British in Penang, which was the entry point of many immigrant workers from India and China, to obstruct the flow of labourers to Kedah. This retarded growth in Kedah prior to British rule, though it may have spared Kedah conflicts over mining wealth and territory.

Progress and development in farming

The 18th and 19th centuries, except during the period of Siamese occupation of Kedah, witnessed some major development of waterworks and canals in the state. In addition, a system of land titles was introduced in the 18th century. By the late 19th century, the system was sufficiently widespread that fake titles were being sold to unsuspecting buyers. There was also a market for cultivated land, which could be bought and sold, rented and leased, subject to certain conditions. Indeed, there are hints that in the 19th century there was even cultivation of rice with hired labour in some districts.

British rule in Kedah, not necessarily by design so much as by indirection, entrenched the state's role as a rice producer, establishing Kedah as the 'rice bowl' of the Malay Peninsula.

Drought, disease and recovery

Periodically, rice farmers in the Malay Peninsula have made known the difficulties they face. In the late 19th century, a major drought in Kedah led to an attempted migration to Beruas in Perak. This induced the sultan to suggest that revenue farmer Phuah Hin Leong extend loans to rice cultivators. In the early 1920s, there were numerous petitions, some collective, making requests for exemptions from land tax because of a major epidemic of cattle disease followed by drought. In the latter half of the 1920s, there was at least one demonstration of rice cultivators near Jitra in northern Kedah as a result of hardships arising from crop failure and cattle disease.

In the post-Independence period, the water-control works which were initiated in the 18th century reached their culmination in the massive Muda irrigation scheme covering the central plain of Kedah and southern Perlis. This scheme has ensured that Kedah and Perlis remain, with Kelantan, the rice bowl of the Malay Peninsula.

Revenue earner for Kedah

Rice cultivation
The degree of sophistication of rice cultivation prior to modern times is seen not only in the waterworks and the rules pertaining to their use, but also in the use as fertilizer of guano (bat dung) which was collected and sold under a monopoly arrangement assimilated into the revenue farm system in the 19th century.

Tailings from tin mines were regulated so as not to pollute the padi fields and choke the canals. Laws also regulated relations between cultivators and between landlords and tenants on matters such as the fencing of fields, the grazing of buffaloes, the rental of land, and the abandonment of land.

TOP: Ploughing rice fields near Alor Setar, Kedah.

LEFT: Transplanting rice seedlings in the traditional manner.

Waterworks
The 18th and 19th centuries witnessed a burst of canal and water-control works in central Kedah, mainly by what now might well be called privatization. Individuals, usually with close links to the ruler, would either request or be asked to undertake such works in return for a grant of land adjoining the waterway. An example is Kedah's most famous canal, the Wan Mat Saman canal (more than 35 kilometres long), which was named after the chief minister who undertook to build the canal in the late 19th century. It was constructed in return for a grant of land which he then sold to recover his costs. As was customary, a portion of the land was reserved for the royal family.

A water wheel (above) was used for drawing water from the canal to flood the rice fields (below).

Winnowing and milling
In the early 20th century, milling was undertaken exclusively by the Chinese. There were 10 large power mills in the country. Several large rubber estates also installed small power mills to process the padi which the planters purchased direct from the farmers to supply their own labourers with food.

Winnowing padi in the fields.

Women, weaving and markets

In 1838, Munshi Abdullah bin Abdul Kadir, a Malay writer, visited the east coast states of Terengganu, Kelantan and Pahang and described the production of silk sarongs as a vital and thriving industry. He observed that the rulers were always clad in silk fabrics, which were also a most important export item. Chinese silk yarn for the weaving industry was a principal import commodity. In contrast to most other industries, women played a more prominent role in the weaving industry.

A procession of the Queen of Patani and her followers, the dignitaries riding on elephants. An illustration from *De Bree Voyages*, Frankfurt, 1607.

Weaving centres

Centres of Malay weaving

By the mid-19th century, the export boom resulting from the import of raw silk from China and cotton yarn from England led to greater prosperity for the Malay weavers. In Terengganu, the community of artisans increased around this time and by the late 19th century, towns around the state capital, Kuala Terengganu, and also Kelantan's capital, Kota Bharu, were famous for their weavers.

Female sovereigns, traders and weavers

A special feature of the eastern states of the Malay Peninsula, which possibly spurred the home-based textile weaving industry, was the prominent role played by women as sovereigns—such as the queens of Patani and of Kelantan—and as traders.

Unlike textile production in India, which was dominated by men, almost all aspects of hand loom weaving in the Malay Archipelago were carried out by women. The vendors and purchasers in the Terengganu markets were also all women, a custom prevalent in parts of Java and Sumatra in Indonesia. In Siam, too, women were the principal dealers and traders in the various facets of the textile industry.

The presence of female rulers in weaving centres such as Patani, Kelantan and Java in various historical periods may be one reason why women played a very important role in the economies of these states, which has persisted to the present day.

The queens of Patani

Patani, a Malay kingdom on the coast of the Gulf of Siam (now a province of Thailand), was from early times a vassal of Siam. It was an important trading post on the sea routes between China, Siam and the Indonesian Archipelago. The interest in weaving of the people of Patani began as early as the mid-16th century and received great impetus during the period when the kingdom was ruled by a succession of six queens, from 1584 until about 1688. Prosperity in the region was at its height during the reign of its first two queens, one of whom, Raja Ungu, married the sultan of Pahang.

Division of labour based on gender

In the late 19th century, the weaving industry was characterized by a division of labour based on gender. The weaving process itself was carried out exclusively by women. Other related activities, such as the procurement of plants for dye-making, the processing of natural dyes, the fabrication of weaving tools and the printing and finishing of woven textiles, were the preserve of men. The control over dye-making by men had almost ceased by the beginning of the 20th century, when imported chemical or aniline dyes gradually replaced natural products. Within about 20 years, the knowledge of the traditional dye-making techniques had vanished.

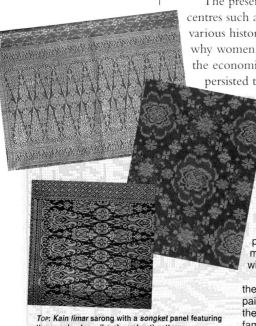

High status Malay textiles

Malay *songket*—supplementary gold (sometimes silver or silk) thread floating across a colourful woven background—is the most sumptuous of all silk textiles. This 'cloth of gold' was an important symbol of prestige and high social status among the royal courts of the Malay Peninsula, as elsewhere in the Malay World. The quality and density of the gold thread brocade, the colour of the silk ground cloth, and the size, complexity, and exclusivity of the motifs and patterns signalled the social status of the wearer. The forms of the cloth—whether stitched at the ends to form a sarong, or left unstitched—were similar for both males and females.

The rich songket brocading was sometimes combined with complex weft *ikat* patterning, achieved by tying the weft (crosswise) threads and dyeing them into multicoloured designs before weaving them into monochrome silk warp (lengthwise) threads. The result was the fabulous *kain limar*.

The weavers of the east coast courts of the Malay Peninsula were among the most skilled in the Malay World. They often resided and worked at the courts, painstakingly producing masterpieces under the protection of the sultans and the supervision of the palace. These fabrics were not only displayed by the royal families during court ceremonies but were also presented as gifts to visiting foreign dignitaries, who were received at the courts with great pomp.

These richly woven silk textiles, worn by a model, are the type of untailored ensemble worn by Che Siti Wan Kembang, a former female ruler of the kingdom of Kelantan. The costume consists of a *kain limar* blouse or bodice wrap, and a *songket* sarong, while a heavy songket stole covers her bare shoulders.

TOP: *Kain limar* sarong with a *songket* panel featuring the *pucuk rebung* (bamboo shoot) pattern.

CENTRE: Close-up of floating *songket* motifs—the corolla of the persimmon fruit—on *kain limar*.

BOTTOM: Songket waist cloth with a back panel of opposing *lawi ayam* (cockerel's tail) motifs.

Another system of division of labour, based not on gender but on specialization, was practised in Terengganu, in the production of the type of printed fabric known as *kain pelangi*. After the pattern had been outlined on the cloth by the artists the fabric was then given to other women who stitched appropriate portions of the fabric to form the pattern, or who tied it with lengths of banana fibre. The cloth was then passed onto the dyers, and after being treated was given to yet another group of people for marketing. The production of woven or printed cloth was thus based on a putting-out system using wage labour paid on a piecework basis according to their rate of production.

Economic livelihood

Economic returns from weaving occupations were low. In Terengganu, where there was stratification of wage rates, rural weavers were paid less—10 cents for an 8-hour day—than their urban counterparts, who earned 13 cents. Between 1913 and 1919, wages ranged from about 30 to 60 cents per sarong, which took about four days to weave. Thus, overall the average daily wage ranged from 7 to 15 cents. There were, obviously, large merchants who made great profit from the utilization of cheap labour.

The living and working conditions of the weavers were dismal. British Agents posted to Terengganu between 1910 and 1919 made reference to the status of local industries in which both men and women worked ceaselessly and where the hand looms of every household were in constant use.

The 1910 Annual Report of Kelantan stated that in Kota Bharu 'almost every house possesses a loom, at which daughters of the house work for long hours daily'. Yet there is no evidence of the existence of slave weavers in the Malay Peninsula. However, the work of weavers in Terengganu—almost all women— was committed to merchants, who were invariably men. Cheap labour was freely available and sold to the merchants on contract.

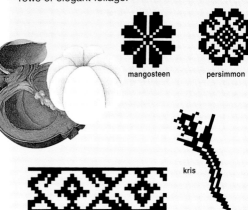
Silk warp threads are tied ready for dyeing in the preparation of a length of *kain limar*.

The status of women

The ubiquitous presence of women in the weaving industry was not necessarily an indicator of their higher status in the community. Women played a vital role only at the intermediate and lower levels of production as master weavers and commission agents, but not as merchants or traders. This 'special' position that women occupied was closely related to the nature of the putting-out system itself, which was largely home-based and therefore dependent on a 'feminized' production network. Personal, woman-to-woman relationships had to be maintained as informal labour contracts involved the employment of women who were confined to their homes.

Motifs from nature

More than a hundred motifs, often with poetic titles, were—and still are—used individually and in combination to ornament the surface of traditional *songket*. Most of these motifs reflected the environment in which the weavers worked, surrounded by flora and fauna, close to the sea, and at the mercy of the monsoons. Objects around the sultans' palaces, such as kris and palisading, and the names of Malay cakes believed to be the sultans' favourites, were other sources of inspiration.

Early Indian influences in the northern parts of the Peninsula are also apparent, for example, in the eight-pointed stars and lotus motifs, the interlocking grids of arabesques and chains, and the triangular rows of elegant foliage.

The east coast weavers of Kelantan and Terengganu continue to manually operate two-harness frame looms for the weaving of silk fabrics, including *songket*.

mangosteen   persimmon   sea horse   rice cake

kris

palace fencing

bamboo shoot with shark's teeth border

cockerel's tail feathers

Female putting-out merchants, master weavers and commissioning agents had specific functions. They maintained an amicable working relationship with workers to ensure that contracts were completed on time. Merchants also depended on female intermediaries to take charge of the basics of production. Thus, women played a more significant role than men in this industry.

The industry's decline

The decline of weaving as a significant source of income for women began in the 1920s, although official reports of that time stated that weaving was still an important occupation in almost all homes in Kota Bharu and Kuala Terengganu. Weavers toiled daily to earn their wages, and the presence of merchants and textile exporters was pervasive. By the 1930s, however, the situation had undergone considerable change. In 1936, the British Adviser in Kelantan noted that, in one instance, the previously thriving weaving industry in a fishing village had ceased production. Weaving implements and hand looms could still be seen under some of the houses, but these were largely unused as a result of stiff competition from cheap, imported textiles.

Iban weavers of Sarawak

Apart from the Malay *songket* weavers of the east coast of the Malay Peninsula, the Iban women of Sarawak are well known for their textile weaving. The patterns, characterized by branching geometric designs and images of animals and anthropomorphic figures, are executed by the warp *ikat* method. In this, selected warp fibres are tied together to form the desired pattern before being dyed—and retied and redyed. The bound sections do not take up the dye. The warp threads are then woven on a back-strap loom, so-called because of the strap that passes around the back of the seated weaver, allowing her to lean back and control the tension of the warp yarns which form a continuous 'loop' in front of her.

Woven Iban skirt decorated with angular whorls.

Iban woman using a back-strap loom attached to a part of the longhouse structure.

Peoples and settlements of Borneo

On the eve of the rule of James Brooke, the first white rajah of Sarawak (r. 1841–68), the peoples of the present-day states of Sarawak and Sabah were a mosaic of semi-autonomous ethnic groups under the overlordship of the sultanate of Brunei, whose political system was reflected at local level in each tributary area. Foremost amongst the indigenous peoples, in numbers and vigour, were the Sea Dayak (Iban). In addition to the native peoples, Sarawak also had a Chinese community comprised of gold miners and more recently arrived traders.

A photograph taken c. 1900 by Charles Hose of a group of young Kenyah from the Long Sibat area of Sarawak. Note the very heavy brass earrings of the women, which resulted in extremely elongated earlobes.

Two young Iban (then popularly known as Sea Dayak) in a photograph taken by Charles Hose about 1900. Elements of their traditional dress included a handwoven skirt and a brass corset for the girl; for the boy, a *parang ilang* (sword) decorated with human hair and a headdress decorated with hornbill feathers.

The migration of the Iban

The migration of the Iban northwards from the Kapuas River, across the watershed between the Kapuas and Batang Lupar or Batang Ai rivers, appears to have begun early in the 16th century. It continued over the next five generations until the beginning of the 18th century when there was a period of consolidation. Resuming again in the early 19th century, by 1841 the Iban dominated the Batang Lupar and Saribas river systems and had also moved eastwards into the Rajang basin. In the process, they encountered two main groups of nomadic hunter-gatherers, the Bukitan and the Seru. The former were largely absorbed through intermarriage; the latter resisted unsuccessfully and those remaining intermarried with the Malays.

Practising swidden agriculture and living in communal longhouses, the Iban were an unstratified society without hereditary chiefs. Status was achieved through warfare, head-hunting and the performance of rituals. From the late 18th century, the Iban of the Batang Lupar and Saribas allied themselves in raiding and slaving expeditions along the Borneo coast and beyond with semi-independent part-Arab chiefs (*sharif*) who were linked to the Brunei sultanate.

The Malays, Bidayuh and Melanau

The Malays first arrived in Sarawak from the Minangkabau region of central Sumatra as Islamic missionaries and traders, and from Brunei as retainers to the nobles (*pengiran*) who had established themselves as the ruling group in the Sarawak River area as early as the 16th century. Through their monopolization of both maritime and upriver trade, access to European technology and claims to magical powers (*ilmu*), the Malays dominated and inter-married with the Bidayuh peoples who had earlier been significantly Hinduized through contact with the Java-based Majapahit empire.

Apart from trade, the other major feature of the Malay economy was fishing. Organized along hierarchical lines and with Islam as a powerful cohesive force, the chieftains (*datu*) of the Sarawak, Kalaka and other river systems formed the nucleus of localized political entities (*negeri*) which were linked with Brunei in a tributary relationship.

In the coastal areas near the estuary of the Rajang lived the Melanau people, who had moved or been pushed down river from the interior. They had become fishermen and sago cultivators. Revenue from the sago trade was controlled by representatives of the Brunei sultan at the mouth of the Oya and Mukah rivers. Many of the Melanau converted to Islam through intermarriage with the Malays, who had a similar hierarchical social system.

The Kayan, Kenyah and others

Like the Iban, the Kayan were swidden cultivators and head-hunters, but unlike the Iban they had a stratified social system of lower, middle and upper classes. Occupying the upper reaches of the Rajang and Baram rivers, they had come from the upper Kayan River in central Borneo. The Kayan resisted Iban expansionism more successfully than other groups. The Kenyah, who were also swidden cultivators and longhouse dwellers, originated from the same area as the Kayan. Although their language and customs were distinct, like the Kayan they also followed a stratified social system.

Ethnic groups of Borneo

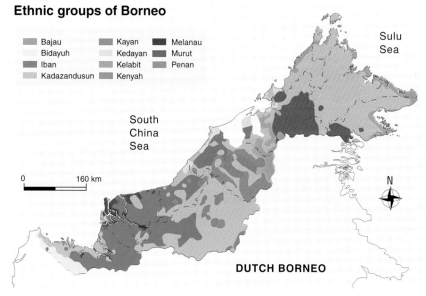

Bajau
Bidayuh
Iban
Kadazandusun

Kayan
Kedayan
Kelabit
Kenyah

Melanau
Murut
Penan

Sulu Sea

South China Sea

0   160 km

N

DUTCH BORNEO

Other ethnic communities in Sarawak include the Bisaya, Kedayan, Kelabit, Murut and Penan and a number of smaller groups. The Bisaya lived mostly around Brunei Bay and on the Limbang River whereas the Kedayan lived near the coast. Most were Muslims. The Kelabit have traditionally inhabited the upland area of north-central Borneo (the Kelabit Plateau), where they were well known for their wet terrace cultivation of rice. They also made their own salt from salt springs on the plateau and sold it to other ethnic groups.

The Penan lived mostly as nomadic hunter-gatherers in the mountainous upper reaches of the Baram, Limbang and Rajang rivers. Here they collected wild sago and jungle fruit and hunted animals and birds with blowpipes. They were famous for making very fine rattan mats.

The Bajau, Dusun and Murut

The Bajau-speaking peoples, a maritime grouping who had converted to Islam in the 16th century, lived in the coastal areas of present-day Sabah. They included the Bajau Laut (sea gypsies), boat dwellers who lived as communally organized fishermen and petty traders along the east coast. The Bajau living along the north-west coast were known for their love of horse riding.

In the interior lived the Dusun (country folk) and the Murut (hill folk), distinctive groups of swidden cultivators. The name Dusun, meaning 'orchard', was considered pejorative, and after Sabah joined Malaysia in 1960 many Dusun groups created for themselves a new ethnic identity—Kadazan—meaning 'town'. In the late 1990s, the group decided to adopt the term Kadazandusun to reflect both their old and new ethnic origins. Like the Iban of Sarawak, they did not possess a social hierarchy and functioned without strong hereditary leaders.

An Iban sword (*parang*) with an ornately carved handle decorated with human hair.

Chinese settlers in Sarawak in the early 19th century were mostly gold miners who had crossed from Dutch West Borneo. A second wave of Chinese immigrants arrived in the late 19th century direct from China.

LEFT: Ong Ewe Hai, the leader of the Hokkien community in Kuching in the 1870s and 1880s, was responsible for the arrival of more Hokkien settlers.

RIGHT: Wong Nai Song, a Fuzhou Methodist minister who, at the invitation of Charles Brooke, the second white rajah, brought in a total of 1,188 men in three groups in 1900 to assist in the development of the lower Rajang.

Sabah was notionally divided by the Brunei sultanate into a number of localized colonized regions (*jajahan*) and negeri for tax-gathering purposes, although Brunei's effective authority did not extend beyond the coastal areas. After dynastic conflict in Brunei in the 17th century provided the sultanate of Sulu with a territorial claim, only the west coastal belt remained under Brunei control, while the northern coast from Marudu Bay belonged to the sultanate of Sulu. The coast between these two areas was ruled by locally based Bajau and part-Arab petty chiefs independent of Brunei and Sulu.

The communal area of a Kayan timber longhouse in Sarawak which was photographed by Charles Hose c. 1900. In the foreground of the picture are bamboo fish traps used for river fishing.

Brunei's authority over the tribes

From the early 16th century, the Brunei sultanate exerted authority over the river systems of north-west Borneo, principally by levying taxes and confirming the status of the local Malay chiefs. However, the extortionate and sometimes cruel behaviour of its officials, as well as disruption caused by internal dynastic disputes, undermined effective control.

The Chinese

Chinese traders are known to have come to the northwestern coast of Borneo as early as the 11th century in search of forest products such as camphor, resins, birds' nests and bezoar stones. Settlements were established in Brunei and at Santubong near the Sarawak River estuary, where locally mined iron ore was smelted and imported goods traded for forest products. Northwest Borneo became a major market for Chinese and Thai ceramics, notably large stoneware jars which the indigenous people came to treasure as heirlooms (*pusaka*) as well as using for practical purposes.

Beginning in the 1820s, when the Dutch took control in west Borneo, Chinese gold and diamond miners in the Montradok area of Dutch West Borneo migrated across the border to the gold mines of the Bau district in Sarawak where they established a settlement with their own autonomous governing body, known as *kongsi*.

Heirloom ceramic jars
From the 13th century, with the beginning of the Yuan dynasty, trade with Southeast Asia increased. Ceramics formed a major portion of the exports to northwest Borneo, notably large stoneware jars which the indigenous people came to treasure as heirlooms (*pusaka*). The jars were used in ceremonies as well as for everyday use. The value of each jar was relative to its colour, shape, size and glaze. Many people still believe that the jars possess supernatural powers. Handed down from one generation to the next, numerous songs, folk tales and legends revolve around the jars.

Charles Hose

Charles Hose spent 23 years as an officer in Sarawak from 1884. A man of insatiable curiosity, he was a keen amateur naturalist and identified many new botanical and zoological species. In addition, he closely studied the ethnic groups of Sarawak and wrote about them in his books *Pagan Tribes of Borneo* and *Natural Man*, Illustrated with his own photographs.

A family heirloom jar with its owner, a Dusun—one of the interior tribes of North Borneo (present-day Sabah).

27

The birds' nests of Borneo

At the end of the 18th century, the Sulu zone and Borneo emerged as a thriving economic region. A number of social, political and historical factors contributed to their prosperity. Foremost among these was the demand from China for edible birds' nests, the procurement of which was dependent upon Borneo's tribal highlanders and rainforest nomads. They were at the lowest level of a complex distribution system for this prized commodity. At the apex of this system was the sultan of Sulu.

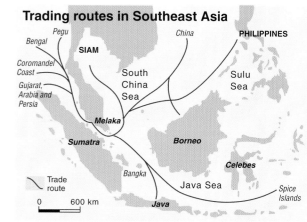

Trading routes in Southeast Asia

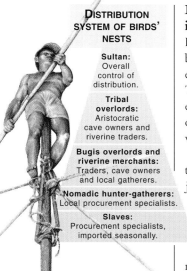

DISTRIBUTION SYSTEM OF BIRDS' NESTS

Sultan: Overall control of distribution.

Tribal overlords: Aristocratic cave owners and riverine traders.

Bugis overlords and riverine merchants: Traders, cave owners and local gatherers.

Nomadic hunter-gatherers: Local procurement specialists.

Slaves: Procurement specialists, imported seasonally.

Birds' nests and the international economy

In terms of the international trade economy and birds' nests, the Sulu region was not important economically until the end of the 18th century. The key unit in this seemingly inconsequential economic network was the strong regional sultanate of Sulu which supplied the larger markets in China with exotic forest products such as birds' nests.

Among the richest sources of birds' nests in the Sulu zone were the remote regions situated just south of the Sulu Archipelago, along Borneo's northeast coast. The economic processes and historical events bound up with the intensifying flow of trade in birds' nests resulted in the more isolated Borneo tribal highlanders and rainforest nomads being drawn into the collecting and processing activities. These people were, in turn, associated with the economic life of the Sulu zone and the global capitalist economy.

The upland agricultural economies of Borneo were essential to the accelerated commercial activity taking place between the entrepôt at Sulu and the Chinese port city of Canton, which was all part of a global market system. In eastern Borneo, cultural and geographical differences and social inequality facilitated procurement between tribal uplanders and nomadic hunter-gatherers in the rainforest.

The China tea trade was centred on the Sulu sultanate after 1768, resulting in the upland rice farmers of the east coast tropical forests being drawn into more extensive trade

A 19th-century sketch of collectors in a birds' nest cave. An 1887 report in *The Illustrated London News* of the bird' nests caves in Borneo reads: 'A bird's nest suggests to an Englishman a mixture of moss, mud and feathers; but an edible nest is a delicate fabric, built like a small bracket against the sides of the cave, and formed of the glutinous saliva of the swift.'

contact with the Taosug and Bugis middlemen along the coastline and at the river mouths. The local economies of these vigorous slash-and-burn agriculturalists were thoroughly commercialized as they sent down the rivers huge volumes of birds' nests in return for tobacco, salt, iron, textiles and other minor manufactured goods.

Economic transformation

Birds' nests were exceptionally valuable to the Chinese. To a large extent, the Chinese need, or greed, for this product changed the face of the ecological history of Borneo and shaped the destinies of thousands of Southeast Asians at a time when radical economic changes were taking place globally. Birds' nests altered the course of cross-cultural trade and historical events. The banquet halls of the emperors of China were, to a great extent, responsible for the economic development.

In *The Head-Hunters of Borneo* (1881), the Norwegian naturalist and explorer Carl Bock writes of the commercial value of birds' nests, 'the whiter kind realizing from 160 to 180 florins per six katties, and the coloured or inferior quality selling for from 110 to 115 florins per six katties'.

Birds' nests and the tea trade

Of particular importance here is how the culinary habits of the Chinese played a role in the global market transactions. In western Europe, there was an insatiable demand for tea from China. To pay for the tea, birds' nests began to flow in huge quantities towards southern China. Traditionally, the nests from

Sulu overlord and Segai-i warrior

The Taosug chiefs of Sulu were wealthy and powerful, partly because of their careful regulation of the Bornean birds' nest trade. The Segai-i Kelai were among the most ardent head-hunters in Borneo. They organized raiding parties to gather nests belonging to tribes hundreds of miles away.

Collecting birds' nests from the sloping roofs of the caves, sometimes 90–120 metres high, was a hazardous task. Thousands of local specialists and slaves harvested these riches for their Sulu overlords who, in turn, attempted to exercise direct authority over the collection of nests from particular cave sites.

LEFT: A Segai-i warrior in war dress. This tribe crippled the Sulu sultanate's birds' nest trade after 1850. RIGHT: A Sulu overlord dressed in high fashion—a headcloth from India, a brightly coloured Chinese silk jacket, satin trousers and several kris—a reflection of his status and prestige.

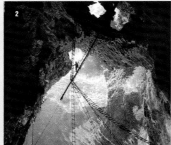

Location of edible nest swiftlets

Sabah
Gomantong Caves
Kuamut Caves
Madai Caves
South China Sea
BRUNEI
Niah Caves
Sarawak
DUTCH BORNEO

Birds' nests: from the cave to the table

The traditional method of collecting swiftlets' nests from caves involved the erection of rattan ladders to reach the high nests (1, 2). The collected nests were then cleaned, weighed and packed for export (3–5). Of the two commercial varieties (there is also a rare, red type), the white nests are thought superior, and thus command a very high price, as they do not contain feathers. The black variety, which is considered to be much inferior to the white, fetches only about one-tenth of the price of white nests.

A bowl of birds' nest soup and prepared birds' nests, as they are sold in the market.

caves in east Borneo were divided among the cave owners, the Sulu riverlord, and the sultan, who was at the apex of the distribution system.

Throughout the late 18th and 19th centuries, the main competitors of the Taosug in the birds' nest trade were the Bugis on the Mahakam River, and their successors on the Berau River. Bugis traders and their predatory Segai-i allies competed fiercely with the Taosug over birds' nest sites.

Birds' nests and violence

The unprecedented demand for this exotic food, especially by the Chinese court, led to a high incidence of violence and warfare, incited by the same competing groups which collected the nests. The prosperity obtained through trading and raiding for birds' nests was most evident among the Segai-i. These slash-and-burn cultivators were among the most ardent head-hunters in Borneo. Fresh heads were required for *mamat* (head feasts) and to accompany purification, funeral and initiation ceremonies. The repercussions of Segai-i raiding were significant; by 1850 they had almost crippled the Sulu's near monopoly of the birds' nests trade.

The headwaters of the major rivers were sparsely populated because of the Segai-i onslaught. Populations which remained unscathed, and who feared for their lives, refused to enter the forests to collect nests for their Sulu overlords and were pressured to move away from the birds' nest caves. Specific knowledge of important caves was lost as the weaker tribes were displaced.

Environmental degradation

The evolution of the China tea trade was also responsible for rapid commodity depletion and environmental degradation on a hitherto unprecedented scale. The rainforests of Borneo were 'open access sites', where natural commodities such as birds' nests were there for the taking. The Taosug

and their rivals tended to overcollect, failing to conserve for the future. Unexpected fortunes and lack of environmental sustainability were contemporary phenomena along with the raiding of caves. Changing global economic demands and Chinese eating habits resulted in the destruction of parts of the natural world of Borneo by the Taosug and Bugis in exchange for other commodities, such as textiles, opium and weapons.

Regional impact

The regional impact created by the integration of the China tea trade in the world capitalist economy, the dramatic effect of Imperial China's cuisine on the fauna and people of Borneo and the associated indigenous violence and environmental degradation can be traced to the need to feed an ever-increasing number of affluent Chinese with extravagant tastes.

Imperial Ch'ing Dynasty

The banquet halls of the last of the Imperial dynasties of China—Ch'ing (also called Manchu)—were to a great extent responsible for altering the course of cross-cultural trade, historical events and economic development during the mid-18th century. Exotic foods from Southeast Asia, including birds' nests, are mentioned as standard fare of Imperial Chinese cuisine. The birds' nests, in particular, seem to have made a considerable impact on the extravagant Manchu court life.

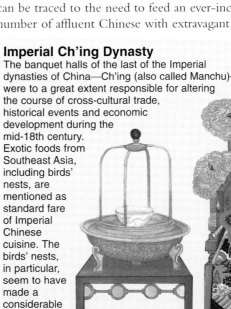

Antimony mining and the sago industry of Sarawak

Antimony (a mineral) and sago flour (an agricultural product) were important export items in the economy of 19th-century Sarawak. After becoming rajah of Sarawak, James Brooke awarded the monopoly of both industries to himself. However, he later passed these monopolies to the Borneo Company, which he charged with the state's economic development. With the export of these two commodities, the state also acquired many of the basic characteristics of the present economy.

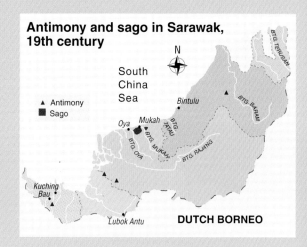

Antimony and sago in Sarawak, 19th century

An antimony mine in the Bau district of Sarawak. In the early days, the ore was sent to Kuching for processing. However, when the Borneo Company was given the mining monopoly they sent the ore to Britain before building their own processing plant near the mine.

Tramways were used to improve access to the antimony mines and to move the mineral from the mines to the smelter.

An antimony processing plant in Jambusan valley in the Bau district of Sarawak, c. 1880s. From the 1820s when the mining began, immigrant miners were attracted to the area.

Antimony

Antimony is a bright silvery white metal which is extremely useful when combined physically or chemically with other substances. Since ancient times it has been used in medicines and cosmetics in Egypt and Asian countries. In the 19th century, it was chiefly used in the manufacture of type metal and other cast alloys, to which it gives hardness. In the 20th century, many more uses were developed, leading to applications in photosensitive substances in colour photography, optical electronics, pigments, as a fire retardant and in medicinal products as an expectorant and nauseant.

Antimony mining

Antimony deposits occurred in the same mineralized belt of Borneo as gold and mercury deposits. Mining began in the Bau area near Kuching in the 1820s when it was realized there was a market for the ore in Singapore. A permanent Chinese (Hakka) mining settlement was founded around 1830, and exports continued to grow until the 1840s when a rebellion by the Chinese labourers led to a temporary halt. It was as a reward for helping to suppress this rebellion that James Brooke was appointed rajah of Sarawak by Sultan Omar Ali of Brunei. On becoming rajah, Brooke awarded himself a monopoly in the trade of antimony ore. However, after the Borneo Company was founded in 1856, Brooke gave the Company the monopoly for the mining of antimony in return for an annual payment of £2,000.

Location of the mines

The principal mines were located in the Bau district near Kuching. The Chinese and the Malays, who had worked the ore initially, sent it to a smelting plant in Kuching. After the Borneo Company took over the production and trade of antimony, the ore was sent to Britain for smelting. However, in the 1860s the Borneo Company erected a smelter near the mines, at Buso, and built roads and tramways to the ore deposits. The company relied mainly on Chinese labour to mine and process the antimony ore.

In the 1860s, annual antimony production averaged about 1,500 tons. The level of output rose rapidly, reaching a peak in 1872, and antimony remained Sarawak's leading mineral export until the mid-1880s. The Borneo Company's antimony exports between 1870 and 1916 totalled Sarawak $1,905,031. Production continued until 1907 when the company's smelting works at Buso were closed down. Thereafter, antimony ore was exported at irregular intervals, and in fluctuating amounts, mainly by Chinese miners.

Monopoly and globalization

In the pioneering phase of antimony mining, Chinese capital and enterprise dominated the industry. However, the establishment of Brooke rule resulted in the monopolization of antimony mining by Rajah James Brooke, and its internationalization. This process was facilitated by Sarawak's links with British trading centres in various parts of the world, the development of communications (notably with the opening of the Suez Canal) and the general lowering of sea freight rates. Thus, private enterprise, government policy and resource endowment dovetailed neatly with the stimuli from the international economy to assist the development of the industry.

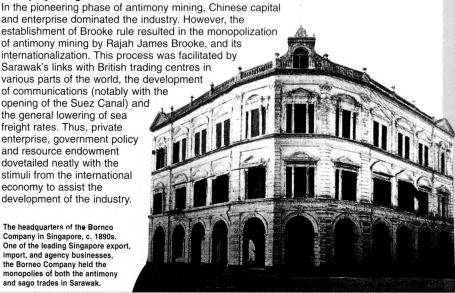

The headquarters of the Borneo Company in Singapore, c. 1890s. One of the leading Singapore export, import, and agency businesses, the Borneo Company held the monopolies of both the antimony and sago trades in Sarawak.

Sago palms grow in swampy areas along rivers. In Sarawak, the palms are cultivated by the Melanau, particularly along the Mukah and Oya rivers.

Sago

Sago flour, which is processed from the stem of the sago palm (*Metroxylon sagu*), was Sarawak's most important agricultural export throughout the 19th century. However, it lost this position in the early 20th century, first to pepper and later to rubber. Sago cultivation was a specialization of the Melanau community, concentrated along the Oya and Mukah rivers.

Prior to the establishment of Brooke rule, the Melanau farmers had exported sago and forest products in return for commodities such as salt, iron, copper and stone. The revenue from the sago trade was controlled by the sultan of Brunei's representatives who were stationed at the mouth of the more important rivers, especially the Oya and the Mukah.

Industrialization

By the 1850s, Singapore's establishment as an international trading centre had led to fundamental changes in the sago trade. Previously, sago had been exported only as a food product in the form of baked biscuits. Later, the demand for cheap industrial starch from the expanding textile industries of Europe and America led to the establishment of sago-processing mills in Kuching by Chinese traders. The raw sago from Mukah and Oya was transported to Kuching for processing instead of being shipped to Singapore, as had been done previously. Sago starch is now in popular demand for industrial use as well as for food products.

The traditional method of softening the sago logs was to tie them into a raft and leave them to soak in the river.

Sago was a staple food in many parts of Southeast Asia, processed in village 'factories' such as this one photographed in Singapore in the 1890s.

Control of sago by Brooke and the Borneo Company

The growing importance of sago and the rivalry among the competing groups over the control of the trade prompted James Brooke to take over the sago-producing districts in 1861. The Borneo Company then moved in, established sago-processing factories, and began to corner the trade. The Company advanced money to 'numerous independent families' to grow sago palms and supply its mills. The sago flour was refined for export to the British market. By virtue of its monopoly in the marketing of sago, the company practically displaced the Muslim and Chinese middlemen who had earlier built up the trade.

Both James Brooke and the Borneo Company had similar objectives—to control the export of sago, regulate prices, and profit from the venture. As a first step, the Borneo Company and the Chinese mill owners moved their mills from Kuching to the Oya and Mukah rivers. They also introduced new technology which led to a reduction in the number of employees required. Nevertheless, the Borneo Company incurred substantial overhead costs and gradually withdrew from flour production to concentrate on exporting refined flour bought from the Chinese mills. By 1900, the Chinese middlemen had an almost complete monopoly in the purchase of wet sago flour, its refining and export, and also the retail trade of the product. The Brooke government enforced the use of standard weights and measures and attempted to regulate Chinese trade practices by requiring them to live in centrally located bazaar settlements. The great expansion of sago cultivation resulted in Sarawak becoming the leading exporter of sago flour. By the late 1880s, Sarawak was producing more than half the world output.

The first step in processing sago is to shred the sago log, done here by rasping. The pith is then leached and left to settle in sedimentation troughs.

Prosperity for the Melanau

The expansion in sago production led to marked changes in the social and economic life of the Melanau people. By 1900, they had virtually abandoned their former semi-subsistence economy for one based on a single export commodity—sago. Their former longhouse organization also broke down, and was replaced by ribbon settlements of individual houses lining the river banks.

Processing methods

The initial processing step of shredding the sago logs can be done in a number of ways. Traditionally, the Melanau used a small wooden adze. The Borneo Company used steam engines to turn a nail-studded drum for rasping, and mechanically shook the pith on to trays flooded with water. Later, the Chinese used a long, nail-studded plane.

SAGO FLOUR EXPORTS (TONS)	
1887	8,700
1897	14,330
1907	20,400

In the final process, the pellets or grains of sago starch are baked over the traditional wood-fired clay hearth.

In the 19th century, the naturalist Alfred Russel Wallace witnessed the traditional method of washing the shredded sago pith using leaves of the sago palm as containers.

Slave trading and markets of Borneo

The impact of European commercial intrusion in China towards the end of the 18th century with the increased demand for tea had a significant bearing on the growth of the slave trade in Southeast Asia. The Iranun and Balangingi seafarers of the Sulu region raided from New Guinea in the east, as far west as the Bay of Bengal. Organized slave markets in the Sulu Archipelago and Borneo provided not only labour for the collection of valuable forest products, but also victims for ritual sacrifice.

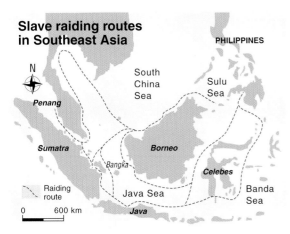

Slave raiding routes in Southeast Asia

PHILIPPINES
South China Sea
Sulu Sea
Penang
Sumatra
Borneo
Bangka
Celebes
Raiding route
Java Sea
Banda Sea
0   600 km
Java

'Dampier, who in 1686–7 lived for six months among the Illanuns, in later years the most formidable of all Malay pirates, subsequently wrote a detailed account for them and made no mention of any piratical propensities, and described them as a peaceable people, who bought such foreign commodities as they needed with the products of their gold mines. What was it, then, that caused these people and their neighbours to revert from peace to piracy. The answer is: the greed of European powers who traded in the Eastern Sea.'

– Owen Rutter,
The Pirate Wind: Tales of the Sea Robbers of Malaya (1930)

32

Cross-cultural trade

Sulu's ascendancy in the late 18th century developed from the expanding cross-cultural trade between India, Southeast Asia and China. Indirectly, it was an insatiable demand for tea which prompted European interest in the marine and forest products of Sulu, especially sea cucumbers and birds' nests, and which spurred Sulu's sudden rise to regional dominance. During this period, China was the sole supplier of aromatic tea, which had replaced ale as the national beverage in Britain.

The British quickly recognized the potential of participation in the Sino-Sulu trade as a means of redressing the one-way trade imbalance from Europe to China. Marine and forest products—highly valued in China—were needed. Commercial and tributary activity became linked with both long-distance maritime slave raiding and the systematic use of slaves to collect trading produce. It was these factors which made Sulu the key redistributive centre of natural commodities for the China trade.

Just as sugar 'demanded' slaves and resulted in the Atlantic slave trade, tea also 'demanded' slaves in the Sulu region to gather the desired trading items. This led to the advent of Iranun and Samal Balangingi slave raiding. Since the British primarily wanted exotic items such as birds' nests and sea cucumber for the China tea trade, the issue of slavery in Sulu and Borneo suddenly became a priority. The demand for local commodities in return for imported goods affected the allocation of labour power and an increased demand for people in the Sulu Archipelago and Borneo.

The lords of the eastern seas

The need for a reliable source of labour was met by the Iranun and Samal Balangingi, slave raiders of the Sulu sultanate. Rapid growth in slave raiding was inevitable to keep

The sea warriors and their boats

The need for a reliable source of labour was met by the Iranun and Samal Balangingi, the slave raiders of the Sulu sultanate. The slaving flotillas which conducted annual raids on the Straits Settlements in the Melaka Strait contained the large *lanong* or *joanga*, an Iranun warship of the late 18th century. More than 30 metres long, these boats had three sails which could be swiftly raised or lowered. The crew consisted of 150–200 men, with the warrior sailors on the upper platform of the boat. At the bow were mounted a long gun and several swivel cannon.

By 1830, the swift, lightly armed Balangingi *garay* had replaced the lanong. The garay was up to 24 metres long, with an enormous rectangular sail. Like the lanong, it was powered by oarsmen; the smaller boats had 25–30 men while the largest held 100 men. The advantage of using the garay was its better manoeuvrability and striking power, which was necessary for inshore raiding.

An Iranun sea warrior of the early 1840s, dressed in the distinctive thick red quilted vest and armed with a kris, a long spear and a kampilan (a heavy sword ornamented with human hair).

A lanong, an Iranun pirate warship, pictured on the northwest Borneo coast with Mount Kinabalu in the background, from Narrative of Events in Borneo and Celebes by Rodney Mundy (1848).

A garay, the boat used for slave raids by the Samal Balangingi people. The largest of these boats was manned by more than 100 oarsmen.

pace with Sulu's global trade by providing the essential labour for natural commodity collection and processing. One extraordinary feature of the interconnections between Sulu slave raiding and the advent of the world capitalist economy was the rapid movement of slave raiders across the entire region as one Southeast Asian coastal population after another was hunted down by the slave traders.

From the late 18th century to the mid-19th, Southeast Asia felt the full force of the slave raiders of the Sulu Archipelago. Their harsh exploits were carried out on a large scale. Manning fleets of large, swift boats, they navigated along the west coast of Borneo and crossed the South China Sea to the

Strait of Melaka and the Bay of Bengal. In the south, their raiding vessels thrust through the Makassar Strait and fanned out over the Indonesian world. They crossed the Banda Sea to New Guinea, made raids along the coasts of Java, and circum-navigated Borneo. In pursuit of captives, the slave raiders terrorized the Philippine Archipelago.

The Iranun and Balangingi earned a reputation as daring, fierce marauders who jeopardized the sea routes of Southeast Asia and dominated the capture and transport of slaves to the Sulu sultanate. Tens of thousands of captive people from across Southeast Asia were seized and put to work in Sulu's fisheries, in the birds' nest caves of Borneo, in the rice fields or in the transport of goods to local markets. Some slavers also took their captives to seasonal markets and trading posts in Mindanao, as well as Marudu, Sandakan and Gunung Tabor on the north coast of Borneo. Many slaves transported to Marudu in repayment for the food, powder, arms and salt supplied to the Balangingi under the credit system of the local leaders were employed in farming and in the collection of forest produce.

Slave markets and exchange

Slave trading and raiding were not restricted to the sea, but were also conducted in the interior of Borneo, Celebes (Sulawesi) and Luzon. In this context, slave raiding and indigenous violence provide insights into the pioneer migrations, lifestyles and world views of vigorous, proud tribal peoples who were slash-and-burn farmers and ardent head-hunters, such as the Kenyah and Iban. Less fortunate slaves were sold on the east coast of Borneo, where riverine groups were involved in the slave trade with Taosug and Bugis middlemen, who acquired birds' nests and wax for global trade in return for slaves. Some captives were sold as victims for ritual sacrifice. Others fulfilled important economic roles among interior groups, such as collecting forest produce.

After 1858, however, it became increasingly difficult for the Balangingi to sell their slaves at Sulu because of the increased naval pressure of European powers—the Spanish, the British and the Dutch. The eastern coast of Borneo became the chief market for slaves after the Spanish blockade of Sulu.

Attacks on foreign vessels were common in waters around Borneo during the 19th century. This is a depiction of an Iranun attack on the *Jolly Bachelor*, a British ship, in 1843.

An Iban war cap, with pheasant and hornbill feathers.

As global trade and monetization affected local social systems and regional trade networks in the 19th century, and because the very survival of slavery in Southeast Asia, as elsewhere in the world, was doubtful, debt-bondage developed. The main slave-raiding zones in the South China Sea and the eastern Indonesian Archipelago attracted intense naval pressure from Britain, Spain and the Netherlands for more than 25 years. By the 1880s, the number of slaves moving across the region had been reduced to a trickle.

The abolition of slave traffic in the region was a mortal blow to the economy of Sulu. When the Taosug and others could no longer rely on slave raids for labour, the amount of tribute collected greatly increased. Fines also became far more prohibitive as the local rulers derived greatest advantage from extending the various forced labour systems.

Human sacrifice

The ritual sacrifice of the Kenyah and Kayan peoples of Borneo, known as *surmungup*, accounted for much of the demand for captives by these two indigenous groups. Their religious beliefs required the sacrifice of outsiders. These beliefs were connected with the taking of heads on the occasion of festivals, and also after the death of a chief or other person of rank.

The development of the slave trade along the Bornean rivers altered ceremonial practice surrounding ritual sacrifice. In earlier times, preference had been given to the killing of young warriors or slaves captured from rival groups in warfare. The coming of the Taosug traders enabled the widespread purchase of out-siders, particularly the elderly and infirm, for ritual sacrifice. The ready availability of cheap slaves, who could be purchased for forest produce, made it easier for commoners to participate in the traditional ceremonies.

TOP RIGHT: Skulls of victims were evidence of a community's prowess in head-hunting. These skulls were photographed in a Kayan longhouse, c. 1900.

BOTTOM RIGHT: Iban women of Sarawak dancing with heads.

The sultan of Gunung Tabor, a state on the eastern coast of Borneo, and his entourage. Some of the captives seized by the Iranun and Balangingi slave raiders provided labour to work in the sultan's coal mines.

'View of the North Point of the Prince of Wales's Island & the Ceremony of Christening It', a 1786 engraving by Captain Elisha Trapaud of the flag-raising ceremony on 11 August 1786 after the founding of a British settlement on Penang (named Prince of Wales Island by the British) by Francis Light on behalf of the East India Company.

An aquatint by J. Clark after James Warren of George Town, Penang, in 1811, with coastal trading boats in the foreground. George Town was already a busy centre for both coastal and international trade.

A view of Taiping in the 1890s. After the town was established in the 1870s near the old tin-mining village of Kelian Pauh by Captain Speedy, the Assistant Resident of Perak, it grew rapidly as a supply centre for the tin mines. After Taiping became the administrative capital of the state in 1889, many impressive government buildings were constructed. The first railway in the Malay Peninsula, opened in 1885, linked Taiping with Port Weld on the coast.

LEFT: The berries of pepper (*Piper nigrum*), an evergreen vine native to the southwest coast of India, provides the world's most important spice. Pepper was an important early export of Kedah, and played a vital role in the development of 19th-century Johor. Planters from Singapore moved to the state to establish pepper and gambier estates under the *kangchu* system.

THE BEGINNINGS OF A MODERN EXPORT ECONOMY

Captain Francis Light, a country trader, suggested Penang as the site of a new port on the Strait of Melaka to the East India Company, and negotiated with Sultan Abdullah of Kedah for a lease of the island. He landed on Penang to establish a settlement on 16 July 1786.

This view of Singapore from Mount Wallich in 1856 shows how the town and the port had grown rapidly since its founding by Stamford Raffles in 1819. It can be seen that forests had been cleared to make way for the development. Mount Wallich was flattened in 1879 to provide material for the filling in of Telok Ayer. Tanjong Pagar MRT now stands on the site.

The Singapore headquarters of Boustead & Co., one of the earliest agency houses (established in 1828), which developed an import and export business as well as acting as agents for others, such as rubber estates and shipping companies.

The founding of the British port city of Singapore in 1819 ended the Malay entrepôt empire of Johor–Riau–Lingga–Pahang at the southern tip of the Strait of Melaka. The Malay entrepôt had begun to decline as a result of the new trading system introduced by the Portuguese, Dutch and English traders. The northern Malay entrepôts such as Kuala Kedah, Kuala Perlis and Pulau Pangkor were all affected by the opening in 1786 of the British East India Company's free trade centre on Penang, which quickly attracted foreign traders. Though Penang provided a market for Kedah's exports, it was a competitor for ports in Kedah, which demanded to be compensated for lost revenue. Kedah was forced to concentrate on its rice industry.

Singapore's strategic location and its policy of free trade enabled the new port to overtake Penang as the main focus of regional trading networks. From 1819 to 1821, 3,000 ships (both European and Asian) visited the port and generated trade worth $8 million. By the time of the first census in 1824, the population was nearly 11,000. Melaka's role as an entrepôt had also declined, partly because the harbour was silted up. European mercantile firms engaged in the export of local products found it convenient to appoint agents in Singapore. These agency houses sold imported manufactured goods, such as textiles, on commission and provided return cargoes of local products. They also handled shipping lines and banking facilities.

In Johor, gambier and pepper were the first cash crops grown. The ruler allowed Chinese from land-scarce Singapore to establish plantations under the *kangchu* system. Temenggong Daeng Ibrahim and his son Temenggong Abu Bakar laid the foundation of the modern state, establishing the capital of Johor Bahru.

Chinese immigrants also became involved in tin mining, first in Melaka and Negeri Sembilan and later in Selangor and Perak. The best example of Sino-Malay partnership in tin mining was Long Jaafar of Perak and Chinese tin miners of the Larut district. Long Jaafar obtained capital from Chinese merchants in Penang to mine tin and recruited Chinese workers of various origins and secret society affiliations. His success led to the bestowal on him by Sultan Jafar Muadzam Shah of Perak the title of Mentri Larut (Minister of Larut), giving him the right to govern Larut and its dependencies. rights later passed to his son, Ngah Ibrahim.

By the 1880s, the role of the Straits Settlements ports (Singapore, Penang and Melaka) had changed from that of an entrepôt to that of a staple port as a result of the growth of tin and rubber exports from the Malay Peninsula. Throughout the 19th century, the economy of the Straits Settlements was such that it drastically influenced and transformed the economy of the other states on the west coast of the Malay Peninsula (Johor, Negeri Sembilan, Selangor, Perak and Kedah).

A statue of Sir Stamford Raffles stands at the Padang in Singapore, close to the place where he is believed to have first landed.

The impact of Penang on Kedah's economy

Kedah was among the earliest states in the Malay Peninsula to develop agricultural production for export, notably rice. The establishment of Penang in 1786, and the rapid growth of the island's population and trade stimulated the Kedah economy in the first and third quarters of the 19th century. However, external influences—Siamese invasion and British political hegemony—and internal factors such as the calibre of the rulers restrained the state's development at other times.

Penang and Kedah

Strait of Melaka

Alor Setar

Kedah

SUNGAI MUDA

George Town

Penang

Province Wellesley

N

South China Sea

MALAY PENINSULA

Strait of Melaka

Kedah's economy in the pre-Penang era

Settlement in the Malay Peninsula developed earliest near rivers where irrigated rice cultivation (*sawah*) was most feasible. Kedah possessed three such river systems: the Kedah, Muda and Yan. The plough (*tenggala*), which is almost certainly of Indian origin, reached Kedah possibly by the 8th or 9th century, facilitating the development of farming. Settled farming communities developed and a surplus of rice was available for export to rice-deficit areas, such as Melaka, in the 15th and early 16th centuries. Rice output benefited from several phases of canal building in the flat coastal plain during 1660–80, 1738 and 1771. Other exports from Kedah included pepper, tin and elephants.

In 1772, Francis Light estimated Kedah's annual trade at Spanish $4 million. Rice exports in 1785 totalled some 80,000 piculs (about 5000 tonnes). There are no accurate figures for population, which was variously reported as between 40,000 and 100,000 in the late 18th century and including, besides the indigenous Malays, immigrant communities of Indians (Chulias) and Chinese. The population figures could fluctuate widely according to political stability. Kedah, like the other Malay states, was subject to external assault from time to time. The state was attacked by the Acehnese in 1619 and by the Bugis in 1770. Such attacks caused population loss and widespread destruction of productive resources, such as pepper vines.

Revenue farming in Kedah

In Kedah, revenue farming was well established by the beginning of the 19th century. Hokkien merchants from Penang had a virtual monopoly of all the revenue farms in Kedah. The sultan awarded Che Seong and Che Toah the monopoly on trade and navigation of the Muda River; they imposed and collected duty on all goods shipped along the river, which led to the main transit port of Kota Kuala Kedah, where fees were levied on all imports and exports. Other Chinese received revenue farming licences from members of the nobility, who had been awarded the right to collect duty on a commodity as *ampun kernia* (royal gifts) by the sultan in lieu of salary. Most preferred to farm out these rights. Among the best known of these revenue farmers were Lee Yok Siew, his brother Lee Yok Cheng and Chiu Ah Cheoh, the Kapitan China of Kulim.

By 1900, revenue farming accounted for 90 per cent of the state's revenue. The opium and *chandu* farm was by far the most lucrative of the 28 major types of farms, most held by Chinese merchants from Kedah and Penang. Farms held by Malays tended to be of lower value. Leases, which were auctioned, were for a specific period; the average was four years. The successful bidder had to sign a contract known as a *surat kecil* (literally, small letter). Conditions included paying a deposit in advance, for at least six months (some for a much longer period); the deposit was refunded on a monthly basis. The farmers also could not vary from the established, fixed rates of duty or service charge. Rentals had to be paid promptly; a defaulter could have his farm confiscated.

The opium and *chandu* farm was the most important of the revenue farms in Kedah. Between 1895 and 1905, the average annual value of this farm was $250,000.

REVENUE FARMS IN KEDAH 1900	
FARM	ANNUAL VALUE ($)
Opium & *chandu*	212,400
Rice & padi	102,500
Gambling	129,750
Customs	62,000
Spirits	58,848
Tobacco	48,040
Multiple farms	64,900
Tin	33,250
Tapioca	23,300
Timber & wood	18,640
Pawnbroking	10,650
Poultry	8,160
Langkawi	6,500
Pigs	5,200
Cattle	3,000
Ferry	2,144
Eggs	2,000
Market	2,000
Boat licensing	1,650
Vehicle licensing	1,520
Pearl oysters	1,000
Hides & horns	780
Four islands	300
Measurement	240
Fishing stakes	104
Guano	100

The impact of Penang

The British East India Company (EIC) was primarily interested in establishing a foothold in the Malay Peninsula to act as a naval station on the trade route to China and also as a centre for the conduct of trade with neighbouring areas. Apart from its potential as a harbour, Penang offered little to the British by way of economic resources. Under the EIC administration from 1786, the population of Penang began to grow rapidly. By 1818, the total had reached nearly 29,000, with the numbers in the Malay, Chinese and Indian communities roughly balanced at around 8,000 each.

The Company encouraged the Penang inhabitants to produce their own food, but non-Malays were more interested in commercial agriculture such as spices and pepper, and so the demand for rice quickly exceeded local supplies. This had a positive impact on the Kedah economy as Penang provided an expanding market for products such as rice, cattle and poultry from Kedah. More canals to irrigate the rice fields were built in Kedah between 1816 and 1818.

The close proximity of the island of Penang to Kedah on the mainland is clearly seen in this early 19th-century view of Kedah from Penang.

However, the development of Penang also had a negative effect on Kedah as the island proved to be a competitor for international trade, and took commerce away from Kedah ports. Successive sultans demanded compensation for lost revenue.

In 1821, Kedah was invaded by Siam, which occupied the state for the next two decades. The population fell to around 20,000 by the late 1830s. Towns and villages were destroyed, and large tracts of rice land were abandoned. Many people fled to the neighbouring Province Wellesley (now Seberang Perai), which had been gained by the EIC from Kedah in 1800. In 1838, the Siamese suppressed the export trade in rice and poultry. Penang was adversely affected, but it is not clear to what extent the shortfall was made good from other suppliers.

Prosperity in Kedah

After the restoration of Sultan Ahmad Tajuddin to the throne in 1842, both the population and the economy of Kedah began to recover. In particular, Kedah regained prosperity during the long reign of Sultan Ahmad Tajuddin II (1852–79). Many Malays returned, and the total population rose to around 50,000. The most active sector of the economy was agriculture, primarily rice, and again the Penang market provided much of the impetus to growth. New settlements sprang up along the rivers. The sultan took measures to improve the transport of goods, including the building of short stretches of road which could be used by bullock carts. The major example was the building in the 1860s of a road 110 kilometres long from central Kedah to the border with Siam, though this exacted a heavy price in terms of forced labour (*kerah*) which the peasants had to provide for such projects.

During Ahmad Tajuddin II's reign, Kedah's links with Penang strengthened. Chinese and Indian merchants settled in the new towns, such as Baling and Kuala Muda, as well as Alor Setar, the capital. Chinese agriculturalists were granted land for new crops, including coffee and sugar cane.

Prosperity falters

In the late 19th century and early 20th, growth of the Kedah economy was slow, in marked contrast to the rapid economic growth in the adjacent areas of Penang, whose population rose by 40 per cent between 1881 and 1901, and the other Malay states.

Agriculture continued to be the mainstay of the economy, but rice exports in 1888 were estimated at only 7000 tonnes, little more than a century earlier. More canal building was begun in 1885 by the chief minister, Wan Mat Saman, with a 35-kilometre stretch from Alor Setar to the base of Kedah Peak. Smaller projects followed. During this period, tapioca was the main estate crop, together with some coffee and sugar, but there was no significant increase in terms of cultivated area and output.

Causes of the economic slowdown

Both internal and external factors accounted for this slowing in the Kedah economy. Internally, the long reign of Sultan Abdul Hamid (1882–1943) saw the emergence of acute financial problems by the early 20th century as the ruler's personal expenditure outstripped the state's revenue. As a result, little was spent on the general development of the state.

Externally, expansion of British colonial power in the Peninsula after 1874 put pressure on Siam, the suzerain of Kedah, not to allow the granting of land or other concessions to any third power, such as Germany or France. This policy was even used to restrain British merchants in Penang from investing in Kedah. Finally, in 1909, the transfer of suzerainty to Britain (see 'The 1909 Anglo-Siamese Treaty') opened up Kedah to foreign investment in rubber and tin production, but not to the same extent as other areas. By the early 20th century, the economic relationship between Penang and Kedah was not as positive as it had been a century earlier.

Canal building

The extent of rice cultivation in Kedah never failed to impress visitors to the state. When Frank Swettenham, then British Resident of Perak, visited Kedah in 1889, he remarked that 'the padi fields are of greater extent than any that I have seen elsewhere in the Peninsula. The whole country up to Perlis for some distance from the coast is one vast padi plain.' Much of the land inland was useless swampland.

The importance of rice cultivation in Kedah is seen in the emphasis on canals. In other states, irrigation works were simple and temporary, but in Kedah the canals were vital for successful rice growing. The first major canal is believed to have been built in the 17th century.

In 1885, Wan Mat Saman, the chief minister, built a canal from Alor Setar to the foot of Kedah Peak. With no special training for the task, he faced enormous physical and financial difficulties. The 35-kilometre-long canal (7 metres wide and 1.5 metres deep) benefited the state—and Wan Mat Saman—greatly. He was allowed by the sultan to sell strips of land on both sides of the canal to intending settlers. The success of the canal attracted other canal builders to the state.

The Wan Saman Canal in Kedah.

The British entrepôt of Singapore

The establishment of a British-controlled port on the small island of Singapore in 1819 was one of the most significant developments in the history of modern Malaysia. The Strait of Melaka had always been an international waterway, and its importance was enhanced as Singapore, on the India–China trade route, became the region's new commercial hub. In addition to its economic importance, Singapore soon became an important centre for education and publishing.

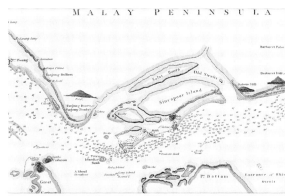

Horsburgh's 1806 chart of the Straits of Singapore which Raffles and Farquhar used on their expedition to Singapore. Although the most up-to-date available, it was not without its inaccuracies.

Singapore in 1819

In 1819, Singapore, which was then part of the Riau–Lingga kingdom, was under the control of Temenggong Abdul Rahman of Johor. About 1,000 people lived on the island, consisting of small numbers of Malays and Chinese and several Orang Laut communities. The Orang Laut generally frequented the coastal swamps and the banks of the Kallang River, collecting marine and jungle produce, while other sea-going groups used the island as a base for raiding. Singapore was not known as a trading centre, although it had about 20 gambier plantations worked by both Chinese and Malays to supply the trade with China.

Raffles and a new entrepôt

The rise of modern Singapore is intimately linked with Sir Thomas Stamford Raffles (1781–1826), a former clerk in the British East India Company who had risen to become Lieutenant-Governor of Java in 1811. Raffles vigorously opposed the expansion of Dutch influence in the region, and from 1818, when he was appointed Lieutenant-Governor of Bencoolen in west Sumatra, he urged his superiors to establish a new post somewhere in the Strait of Melaka. Although other islands were initially preferred, Raffles finally decided on Singapore, primarily because it was on the sea trade route to China and was ideally located to serve as a trading centre for the entire archipelago. He was also attracted by Singapore's mythical past, and the idea of restoring what he believed was once a 'great emporium of these seas'.

To legitimatize his project, Raffles recognized the elder son of the late ruler of Riau–Lingga as Sultan Hussein Shah of Singapore. In 1819, Raffles negotiated an agreement allowing the British East India Company to

A diorama depicting the historic meeting of Sir Stamford Raffles and Major William Farquhar with Temenggong Abdul Rahman on 29 January 1819.

establish a trading settlement in return for annual payments to Sultan Hussein and Temenggong Abdul Rahman. William Farquhar was appointed Resident, answerable to Raffles at Bencoolen.

Raffles left for England in 1823; in the same year, John Crawfurd became the new Resident of Singapore. A significant stage in the development of Singapore came in 1824 with the signing of the Anglo-Dutch Treaty, which divided the Malay World down the Melaka Strait. The Malay Peninsula and Singapore came within the British 'sphere of influence' and the Dutch left Melaka permanently. In the same year, Crawfurd also negotiated an agreement with Sultan Hussein and Temenggong Abdul Rahman in which they acknowledged the whole island of Singapore as a British possession.

Commercial success

Despite initial opposition from the Dutch, as well as British doubts, Singapore's commercial potential was soon evident. Its convenient location and free trade policy quickly made the island the focus of regional trade networks, notably of the Bugis. Thriving local trade attracted Chinese junks as well as European ships. In the first three years, the arrival of around 3,000 vessels generated trade worth $8 million.

A master plan for the settlement's development was drawn up in 1822, which helped to ensure Singapore's early success as a focus for regional trade. This plan allowed for the original settlement to be enlarged for the government quarter, the extension of the European section, the construction of a public esplanade along the waterfront and the allocation of districts for the various ethnic groups.

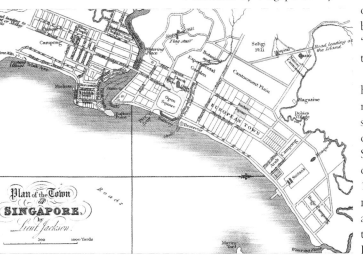

Plan of the Town of SINGAPORE by Lieut Jackson.

The commercial centre was carefully planned, with specific areas reserved for official buildings. Ordinances specified the width of roads, and the construction of superior commercial buildings was encouraged. Raffles' modest official residence on Bukit Larangan (Fort Canning) was built in Malay style of timber and *atap*, recognition that indigenous buildings were suited to the tropical climate.

Under Crawfurd's administration, a new prison was built, the Singapore River dredged, roads were widened and, in 1824, the first street lights appeared, using coconut oil. While adding to the physical attractiveness of the new town, these measures also interfered with residents' lives. The Temenggong's settlement, for example, which was located in the government quarter, was moved to Teluk Belanga.

Despite its rapid development, five years after its founding the settlement was still surrounded by thick rainforest where tigers roamed. Nonetheless, there were indications that the island was destined to become a regional literary and educational centre. Missionaries introduced printing presses in 1822 and a fortnightly newspaper, the *Singapore Chronicle*, began publication in 1824. The first schools were also established by missionaries, and an institution for the children of the local élite was envisioned by Raffles. Established in 1823, this institution struggled initially but eventually became the famous Raffles Institution.

This is the earliest known view of Singapore (c. 1824) and shows shipping in the harbour, the Padang and the Singapore River. In 1821, Raffles assigned Lieut. Jackson to design and build a drawbridge across the river, which is shown unfinished in this print.

In 1823, just before Raffles left Singapore for the last time, he laid the foundation stone for the Singapore Institution (later renamed Raffles Institution), the object of which was 'the cultivation of Chinese and Malayan literature, with the improvement of the moral and intellectual condition of the People....' This 1841 drawing shows the main building.

Early migration

From its inception, Singapore's population was cosmopolitan. New settlers were encouraged, even though it was some time before the East India Company was convinced the settlement was viable. By 1821, there were about 5,000 inhabitants, including around 3,000 Malays and other Indonesian groups, and 1,000 Chinese. Many Chinese were long-standing inhabitants of the region who had moved from Melaka, Penang and elsewhere; others were poor coolie labourers from southern China.

By 1824, the year of the first census, there were nearly 11,000 residents in Singapore. The Malays, including migrants from all over the Archipelago, numbered about 4,580, the Bugis 1,925 and the Chinese 3,317. Each ethnic community generally lived in its own residential district, with the area west of the Singapore River allocated to the Chinese. However, the more fashionable areas were open to wealthy homeowners of all races.

The administration challenge

Developing infrastructure was not easy as there were few sources of revenue for administration. Because Farquhar was not able to charge duty on imports, he was forced to defy Raffles and introduce a tax farming system, selling the franchise for the sale of pork, opium and liquor as well as the right to maintain pawnbrokers' shops and gambling dens.

Largely because of this revenue, the financial position of the colony improved. Though Crawfurd argued in favour of controlled gambling, which he saw as one of the few amusements for the local population, it was eventually abolished in 1829.

The relationship between the British and Sultan Hussein and Temenggong Abdul Rahman was ambiguous. Despite expectations of a partnership, disagreements soon forced the Malay chiefs into the background. At first, the most powerful community leaders were 12 European magistrates who advised the Resident and presided over their own courts. These were later replaced with a new court under an Assistant Resident. There were inevitably cases of cultural insensitivity, but in principle it was accepted that all individuals were equal in the eyes of the law.

LEFT: A letter dated 25 August 1824 from Temenggong Abdul Rahman, ruler of Johor, to Sir Stamford Raffles (then in Bencoolen) discussing who should succeed Sultan Hussein of Singapore.

Mediation by a Chinese clan society in a dispute between immigrant workers.

Many poor male Chinese migrants indulged in opium smoking, gambling and prostitution.

Opium pots and a pipe (right and far right) used for smoking the drug.

Early social problems

A major problem in early Singapore was the gender imbalance in the population. Because of the preponderance of poor male migrants, it was difficult to limit the spread of gambling, opium smoking and prostitution. The importing of women and girls from the region, particularly by Bugis traders, led Raffles to prohibit the slave trade in 1823. The practice of debt-bondage, however, continued. The arrival of large numbers of Chinese men also brought secret societies which, while offering protection in an alien environment, provided an umbrella for crime and extortion. Disputes also occurred among the Malays because of rivalries between Malay migrants from Melaka and Malay followers of the Temenggong and the Sultan, These disputes were a principal reason behind the government's efforts to discourage Malays from wearing their customary kris.

The export economy of the Straits Settlements

The Straits Settlements—Penang, Melaka and Singapore—were established between 1786 and 1824 as free ports. Initially, they were naval bases and centres for international trade, particularly between India and China, and also a counterpoise to the power of the Dutch East India Company (VOC) in the Malay Peninsula. Later, these ports served as leading regional entrepôts, as prime collection and distribution points, and as entry points for the foreign entrepreneurs and immigrant labourers who hastened the economic development of the region.

A group of wealthy Chinese merchants. Businessmen such as these played an important role in the economy of the Straits Settlements as plantation owners, manufacturers and exporters.

A European overseer and Chinese workers, c. 1900. Immigrant labour provided the workforce for the tin mines and rubber plantations, the products of which were exported through the Straits Settlement ports.

The Straits Settlements

South China Sea

Penang

Strait of Melaka

N

Melaka

0   100 km

Singapore

King Edward VII and Queen Victoria on the obverse of coins minted in the Straits Settlements. The first series of coins bearing the inscription 'Straits Settlements' was issued in 1871.

Links with earlier centuries

Entrepôt ports had long been a feature of the Malay region because of the China–India trade route. In the 15th and early 16th centuries, Melaka was the pre-eminent entrepôt in maritime Southeast Asia for Asian traders (see 'The Malay entrepôt state'). During the Portuguese and Dutch occupations of Melaka from 1511 to 1824, its importance as an entrepôt declined, but it remained a significant port of call as increased numbers of Chinese migrants came to the region after China lifted restrictions on overseas trade in the early 18th century.

The creation of free ports

The initial aim of the British East India Company (EIC) in seeking a territorial base in the Malayan region in the late 18th century was to provide a sheltered port of call for ships engaged in 'country trade' (that is, private merchants operating under licence from the EIC), principally with China. It was also envisaged that such a base would encourage trade with the surrounding region to obtain desired commodities, such as pepper and other spices, for the trade with China.

The first acquisition was the island of Penang under an agreement with Sultan Abdullah of Kedah in 1786. From the outset, the port of George Town was a free trade centre with no import or export duties charged. The island quickly attracted a multi-ethnic mercantile community of Chinese, Indians, Malays and Europeans, and offered for export pepper and spices from Penang plantations.

However, Penang's geographical location was not best suited for the entrepôt role envisaged by the EIC. Lying at the northern end of the Melaka Strait, it was somewhat removed from the more natural meeting point between the sea routes of the trade networks of both the region and the long-distance route to China. A more suitable site was provided by Singapore, which the EIC acquired from Temenggong Abdul Rahman of Johor in 1819.

Singapore rapidly overtook Penang as the main entrepôt of the region. The free trade regime attracted Asian, European and local merchants to the island. European mercantile

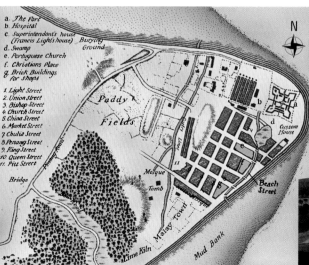

a. The Fort
b. Hospital
c. Superintendent's house (Francis Light's house)
d. Swamp
e. Portuguese Church
f. Christians Place
g. Brick Buildings for shops

1. Light Street
2. Union Street
3. Bishop Street
4. Church Street
5. China Street
6. Market Street
7. Chulia Street
8. Penang Street
9. King Street
10. Queen Street
11. Pitt Street

Bridge

Burying Ground

Paddy Fields

N

Custom House

Mosque

Tomb

Beach Street

Malay Town

Lime Kiln

Mud Bank

LEFT: The town plan of George Town (Penang's port) which was prepared by Francis Light, who founded the settlement for the EIC in 1786.

RIGHT: A 19th-century hand-coloured aquatint by William Daniell of Glugor House and spice plantation in Penang.

firms, the agency houses (see 'European agency houses and the Malay states'), dominated the import–export trade with the West, while Asian firms, principally Chinese-owned, operated a regional network known as bazaar trade. The growth of international trade was facilitated by reductions in the import duty charged in industrialized countries on primary products. Britain, for example, adopted free trade policies from the mid-19th century.

Penang's role was that of an entrepôt for the region around the northern Strait, while Melaka experienced a decline, partly due to the progressive silting of the harbour. It became mainly a feeder port to its larger neighbours, but retained its importance as the domicile of the Melaka Chinese, a long-established mercantile community who had links with other Straits ports as well as investments in mining and agriculture in the Malay states.

The growth of staple exports

In the late 19th and early 20th centuries, the main function of the Straits Settlement ports changed from entrepôts to staple ports. This was due to the growth of tin and rubber exports from the Peninsula, as well as petroleum from the Dutch East Indies. As staple ports they provided a location for the bulking together of the output from the scattered estates and

Advertisements announcing products and services, such as those of the Shell and Straits Steamship companies, appeared regularly in newspapers and magazines during the 19th century.

This view of Boat Quay in Singapore in about 1890 clearly shows how much the port had developed since the settlement was begun in 1819.

The town of Melaka in the period around 1870, showing the homes of the Chinese merchants lining the waterfront.

mines. The tin ore underwent smelting to remove impurities and produce tin of a guaranteed level of refinement. The smelting industry was originally in Chinese hands. However, in 1887 two European merchants, James Sword and Herman Muhlinghaus, set up the Straits Trading Company. With official monopolies on the export of tin ore from Selangor and Sungai Ujong, the company set up a smelter on Pulau Brani in Singapore. In 1895, the company smelted 30–45 per cent of the tin exported from Perak, Selangor and Negeri Sembilan.

Rubber was also exported through these three ports. Facilities were established for sorting and classifying the various grades, and in the early 20th century regular auctions held in Singapore and Penang were attended by buyers from major Western rubber manufacturers. The Straits ports also helped to popularize rubber growing in the region. Chinese merchants distributed seeds to pilgrims returning from Mecca who subsequently planted smallholdings in the Dutch East Indies (Borneo and Sumatra). Their output, together with that from smallholdings in Malaya, was channelled through Singapore where a substantial processing industry flourished in the 1920s, turning the impure rubber into grades saleable on the world market.

Petroleum exports began early in the 20th century, after discoveries in Sumatra and Borneo. Major oil companies such as Shell, Royal Dutch and Standard Oil used Singapore as a centre for blending and storage. All these activities, in addition to the traditional entrepôt trades, combined to make the Straits Settlement ports, especially Singapore, a magnet for global shipping. The British agency houses handled the international shipping lines. Chinese-owned shipping competed in the regional markets, but lost its position to locally established European interests (for example, the Straits Steamship Company) in the 1920s and the 1930s.

Trade was the lifeline of the Straits Settlements and the bulk of employment was in the services sector: commerce, port operations and transport. A small manufacturing sector produced food, clothes and furniture to supply local demand. Like all economies heavily dependent on the maintenance of a high volume of trade, material conditions fluctuated according to the strength of international demand for staple products. The early 1900s were a period of rising prosperity, but the 1920s and the 1930s saw severe slumps which led to heavy unemployment and social distress.

The Straits Trading Company, which broke the Chinese monopoly on tin smelting, was founded in 1887 by James Sword (top left) and Herman Muhlinghaus (top right). Below their portraits is a photograph of the Straits Trading Company office in Kuala Lumpur at the beginning of the 20th century.

Top: The latex collected and processed in rubber estates was sent for further processing in rubber factories before being transported to the Straits Settlement ports for export.

Bottom: An oil store in Penang, c. 1890, belonging to C. S. Seng & Co., a leading Chinese importing house and an agent for the Standard Oil Company.

41

The Temenggongs of Johor

In 1784, the Temenggongs of Johor were a threatened, virtually disinherited minor lineage of the Johor–Riau aristocracy. By 1885, the heir to that title became the sultan of the Malay state of Johor. Today, their descendants occupy an important position as state rulers and participants in the Malaysian constitutional monarchy. Although they began the 19th century with a reputation for involvement in piracy, Temenggong Daeng Ibrahim (r. 1825–62) and his son, Abu Bakar (r. 1862–95), gained wealth and legitimacy, winning respect from the British rulers of Malaya and ultimately from other Malay royal houses.

LEFT: Temenggong Daeng Ibrahim (r. 1825–62) developed the state with the revenue from pepper and gambier estates.

RIGHT: Temenggong Abu Bakar (r. 1862–95) assumed the title of sultan after he was recognized by the British as sovereign ruler in 1885.

The Temenggongs' domain, 1818–23

SUNGAI JOHOR
South China Sea
Singapore
--- Estimated boundary

The state of Johor, 1885

Johor

SUNGAI JOHOR

South China Sea

Singapore

--- Estimated boundary

'The view from Government Hill' (1846), a painting by John Turnbull Thomson, shows the development of the town of Singapore 25 years after its founding. It depicts the occasion on 31 August 1846 at which the Governor of the Straits Settlements, Colonel William Butterworth, honoured Temenggong Daeng Ibrahim for his role in checking piracy in the Strait of Melaka.

The Malay World

Prior to the 19th century, the Malays of Johor–Riau were primarily rulers of the sea. The members of royalty sought to dominate the maritime world of the Strait of Melaka. Referred to as *dibawah angin* (below the winds, indicating it was outside the monsoon belt), the entire area—from Penang in the Malay Peninsula to Palembang in Sumatra, to Pontianak in Borneo and the Natuna Islands in the South China Sea—was the domain of the maritime Malays. Within it lay the main China–Europe trade routes. From the 8th century, Malay rulers set up trading cities and maritime kingdoms in this region. When powerful and unified, the rulers promoted trade and grew wealthy. When weak and divided, trade, and consequently their wealth, suffered.

The Temenggongs

The office of Temenggong had been a part of the Malay royal court since the time of the Melaka sultanate. The Temenggongs were always key officials of the maritime Malay state, usually ranking just below the Bendahara (prime minister) and, in many cases, were related to the ruling family. As well as status in the court, these officials also had claims to certain territories within the state, and thus ruled over the local people. The most important of these were the Orang Laut, who inhabited the islands of the Riau–Lingga Archipelago. However, by the 18th century the family of the Temenggong, related by

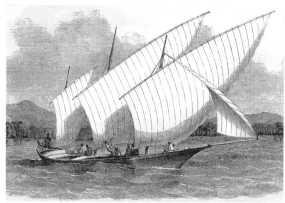

This pleasure boat belonging to Temenggong Daeng Ibrahim, built in India to the very latest in boat design, is an indication of the wealth he derived from the economic development of the state.

blood to Sultan Abdul Jalil Riayat Shah IV (r. 1700–19), the first sultan from the Bendahara family, had been displaced from the centre of power in the Johor–Riau empire by the Bugis.

The fortunes of the family were at a low ebb in 1819 when Temenggong Abdul Rahman took refuge in Singapore. These improved after the Temenggong brokered the meeting between Stamford Raffles and Tengku Hussein, the elder son of Sultan Mahmud of Riau, who had also been ousted by the Bugis. Raffles recognized Hussein as the sultan of Singapore, and both Hussein and the Temenggong signed the treaties which gave the British East India Company (EIC) control of Singapore (see 'The British entrepôt of Singapore').

In 1824, the Anglo-Dutch Treaty divided the Johor–Riau territory between the British and the Dutch. The Malay Peninsula and Singapore came under British authority, and Sumatra and the Riau–Lingga Archipelago under the Dutch. The British recognized the Temenggong as the ruler of Johor, and with the expansion of British rule, the family became increasingly powerful. In contrast, Sultan Hussein and his descendants lost their status in Singapore, and by 1855 found themselves excluded from the throne of Johor.

Piracy

Some European traders and officials claimed the Temenggong was in league with the pirates in the Strait of Melaka (see 'Slave trading and markets of Borneo'). Such accusations continued to affect the

Johor ruler's relations with British governors until the mid-19th century. Part of the problem lay in the definition of the term 'piracy'. The seafaring people whom the Europeans called 'pirates' were considered the navies of the various Malay chiefs by the local people, and their activities were considered naval warfare and tax collection, not murder and robbery. Ultimately, the piracy suppression campaigns of the 1830s and 1840s eradicated the Orang Laut around Singapore. In 1846, the EIC presented a Johor state sword to the Temenggong in appreciation of his help in the suppression of piracy.

Modernization and education

Temenggong Daeng Ibrahim invited the Rev. Benjamin Peach Keasberry, an American missionary, to establish a school in his settlement at Teluk Belanga, Singapore, for his sons and also those of his followers. Munshi Abdullah bin Abdul Kadir, the renowned Malay scribe, was a teacher in this school, which educated the young Abu Bakar and the first generation of Johor's Malay administrators. Thus, when he succeeded his father in 1862, Abu Bakar was well prepared to guide his new Malay state through a period when colonial governance was gaining strength. In the 1860s and 1870s, Johor's Malay and Chinese population increased considerably, and Abu Bakar also organized a corps of able Malay administrators.

In 1885, the British government recognized Abu Bakar as the sovereign ruler of the State and Territory of Johor, and he assumed the title of sultan, dispensing with that of Temenggong (see 'British mediation and the new sultanate in Johor').

Gambier and pepper

The end to piracy made it necessary for the Temenggongs to obtain revenue from the relatively empty territory of Johor. The solution lay in allowing Singapore Chinese pepper and gambier growers to establish plantations in Johor.

Malay farmers had long cultivated pepper and gambier for export to China. By the early 18th century, the Chinese demand for both products had increased. The use of gambier for tanning hides had been discovered as was, later, its use as a dye.

In the 1730s, Malay rulers invited Chinese labourers to their territories to cultivate these two crops, which were well-suited to growing together. Gambier, a low-value product, needed only seasonal labour, while pepper, a high-value product, could be fertilized with the waste from the gambier extraction process. Also, pepper provided labourers with employment during the gambier off-season, enabling employment of a full-time labour force.

This cultivation system, first used in the Riau–Lingga Archipelago, was based on groups of planters settled in small river valleys, organized around the *kangchu* (lord of the river) system. It was later replicated in Singapore and Johor.

The *kangchu* system

The *kangchu* system was a clever combination of traditional Malay governance and Chinese clan entrepreneurial practice. The Chinese terms used in the system reflect its origins. The Chinese headman (kangchu) to whom the concession was issued was responsible for bringing in settlers, fostering cultivation, maintaining law and order in the settlement and collecting the taxes for the ruler.

His headquarters, usually at the mouth of the river, were known as the *kangkar* or *chukang*. The town of Tebrau, for example, was known as Kangkar Tebrau or Tan Chukang after Tan Kye Soon, its founder. Such headquarters usually developed into small towns comprising a row of shophouses, a temple, an opium den, a gambling house and other necessary services. Coolies and planters arrived, bankrolled by merchants in Singapore, and later by some in Johor Bahru, and soon gambier and pepper plantations dotted the river valleys.

The *surat sungai* show that the kangchu concessions were divided into shares and owned by a corporate group known as a *kongsi*. Usually the kongsi included the kangchu and one or two wealthy Chinese merchants.

Top: One of the *surat sungai* issued by the Temenggong of Johor granting permission to Chinese planters to establish gambier and pepper estates.

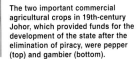

Right: Tan Yeok Nee (1827–1902), one of several Teochew towkays who amassed considerable wealth from gambier plantations in Johor during the late 19th century. He aided Sultan Abu Bakar of Johor in gambier cultivation.

Gambier and pepper planters were established in Singapore before 1819, and estates spread rapidly after the arrival of the British as planters from Riau moved to escape Dutch taxes. By the 1840s, there were conflicts among various secret societies. With the permission of Temenggong Daeng Ibrahim, the headman of Ngee Heng Kongsi moved to Johor.

The first *surat sungai* (literally, river letter), issued by the Temenggong in 1844, gave a Chinese headman permission to cultivate pepper and gambier along Sungai Sekudai. Planting grew at a moderate rate during the 1850s, with a major spurt in the 1860s after Temenggong Abu Bakar succeeded his father. He was aided by Tan Yeok Nee, a Teochew towkay who became the mayor of the new town of Johor Bahru. By the 1870s, there were almost 100,000 Chinese gambier planters.

However, the Johor ruler was able to control the operations, even as the leases were fragmented into shares and sold, resold and leased. By the second half of the 19th century, profits from gambier and pepper made Johor wealthy. In the early 20th century, the land was converted to rubber and other crops.

Gambier and pepper were Johor's most significant exports in the mid-19th century. The two crops thus provided an economic foundation for the first Chinese settlers; an income for the ruler; and, as Johor's first commercial crop, prepared the way for 20th-century capitalism.

The two important commercial agricultural crops in 19th-century Johor, which provided funds for the development of the state after the elimination of piracy, were pepper (top) and gambier (bottom).

European agency houses and the Malay states

The agency house was a particular type of mercantile firm which evolved to engage in the business of international trade. The origin of the agency houses lay in the late 18th and 19th centuries with British merchants trading in Asia, principally in India and China, dealing in the export of local products. As the Industrial Revolution in the West gathered pace, British companies found it convenient to also use these agencies in the East to sell manufactured goods on commission.

The early agency houses

The Straits ports of Penang and Singapore attracted merchants of many nationalities (see 'The export economy of the Straits Settlements'). Those from Europe realized the trade potential of these ports as transhipment points through which manufactured goods could be imported and distributed in the region. At the same time, return cargoes of local products, such as pepper, spices and tea, and also forest produce like aromatic woods were collected for re-export to world markets. Some agencies also provided banking facilities before the establishment of local branches of international banks.

Later, when major expansion occurred in the mining of tin, followed by the cultivation of rubber in large estates, the agencies played a crucial role in organizing the raising of capital overseas in markets such as the London Stock Exchange.

Founders of agency houses

1. John Buttery who, together with G. M. Sandilands, founded Sandilands, Buttery & Co.
2. Alexander Guthrie, who founded Guthrie & Co. in Singapore in 1821.
3. William Adamson, Samuel Gilfillan and H. W. Wood, who together set up Gilfillan, Wood & Co.
4. John Middleton Sime, who was responsible for the establishment and growth of Sime Darby.
5. A. A. Anthony's company represented insurance agencies such as Commercial Union from 1882.

Financial structure

In Singapore, by 1827 there were 14 agency houses, of which all but one were British. By 1846, the number had risen to 43, of which 20 were British. Among the earliest were Guthrie & Co. (1821) and Boustead & Co. (1828) which both went on to achieve lasting prominence. The agency houses were organized as private partnerships with each member contributing to a pool of working capital, which was invariably small, and withdrawing it at retirement. Thus there was a heavy reliance upon credit provided by manufacturers in the West which was, in turn, extended to the Chinese merchants who had set up and controlled a network of retail outlets throughout the region. These merchants also supplied the agencies with primary products for export.

Agency houses tried to keep their financial resources as liquid as possible to cope with sharp fluctuations in trade. However, some did invest directly in production at an early date. Guthrie & Co., for example, started nutmeg cultivation in Singapore in the 1830s.

Sime Darby

Immigrant coolies and their European overseer (seated, centre) in one of Sime Darby's rubber plantations. Rubber, oil palm and cocoa plantations continue to be the company's prime agricultural activities.

Sime Darby's first office in Melaka. In 1902, the agency house started as a small British company which managed 200 hectares of rubber estates in Melaka. It has since grown into one of the largest multinational corporations in ASEAN. The parent company and base, now Malaysian, are located in Kuala Lumpur.

LEFT: The first Sime Darby logo had a set of scales to symbolize its trading activities.

Conditions in the Malay states

For much of the 19th century, the interior of the Malay Peninsula was largely covered by indisturbed rainforest. Settlement was concentrated along the coastline and up the rivers, which were virtually the only means of access. In each of the Malay states, the ruler (sultan) had a seat of power usually located at, or near, the river mouth. This was a convenient location from which to control the flow of trade and to extract the revenue which the sultan needed to maintain his household and armed retinue.

The pace of development began to gather momentum from around the middle of the 19th century when the discovery of tin deposits in Melaka, Sungai Ujong and Perak brought an influx of immigrant Chinese miners, as well as Malays from other parts of the Peninsula and from Sumatra. Chinese planters were also engaged in export-oriented commercial agriculture, such as gambier, pepper and tapioca cultivation.

The increase in population created a larger demand for food and manufactured products, as well as an increase in the volume of exports. The heightened flow of trade with the interior attracted the attention of merchants in the Straits ports. European agency houses in Singapore and Penang were keen to persuade the sultans to allow development. The rulers, with an eye on increased revenue, were not unwilling, but generally lacked the capital resources needed to improve facilities such as transportation. Thus, commercial capital began to flow into the Malay states in the form of advances to the sultan. In return for the capital, the agency handled his financial affairs as well as benefiting from the increased flow of trade. A good example was Ker, Rawson & Co. of Singapore who assisted and represented Temenggong Daeng Ibrahim of Johor during the 1860s and 1870s.

Security

However, considerable insecurity accompanied the business of investment. Internal conditions in the states where tin mining was expanding most rapidly (Sungai Ujong, Selangor and Perak) were disturbed by civil strife in the 1860s and early 1870s, involving in each case Malay factions around the ruler of the state and the Chinese secret societies (see 'Long Jaafar and the tin miners in Larut').

The spread of British hegemony in Malaya brought settled conditions (see 'Civil wars and British intervention'). Further expansion of tin mining—after major discoveries in the Kinta district of Perak in the 1880s—and of commercial agriculture (sugar in Province Wellesley, gambier and tapioca in Negeri Sembilan and coffee in Selangor) generated rapid growth in trade and population. However, in the early stages of this expansion the limited resources of the agency houses prevented them playing a leading role in the development of export production in the Malay states. Previously, the driving force behind agriculture and mining had been Chinese enterprise, except for sugar and coffee in which European planters played a significant role.

The agency houses at their zenith

The advent of rubber cultivation in the early 20th century (see 'The rubber industry and Indian immigration'), and the technical developments in tin mining introduced by European companies— a switch from labour-intensive methods to the use of water power and dredges—gave the agencies an opportunity to establish a dominant position in the economic life of the Malay states, particularly those along the west coast of the peninsula.

The capital requirements of these industries for large-scale production far exceeded local resources. The agency houses used their connections with major financial centres such as London to organize the raising of funds through the public flotation of foreign-registered public joint-stock companies to operate in the tin and rubber industries. This led to an increase in the number of agency houses opening branches in the new urban centres such as Kuala Lumpur, Seremban and Ipoh (see 'The development of urban centres'). Many of the agencies changed their corporate status from private partnerships to private companies with limited liability.

AGENCY HOUSES IN BRITISH MALAYA FROM THE 19TH CENTURY			
FIRM	FIELDS INVOLVED	ESTABLISHED	BRANCHES
Guthrie & Co.Ltd	coffee, rubber	1821 Singapore	1910 Kuala Lumpur
Boustead & Co. Ltd	sugar, rubber, tin	1828 Singapore	
Sandilands, Buttery & Co. (taken over by Antah Holdings)	rubber	London	1830s Penang 1854 Singapore
Harrisons & Crosfield Ltd	rubber	1844 Liverpool	1907 Kuala Lumpur
Paterson, Simons & Co. Ltd	rubber	England	1861 Singapore
Adamson, Gilfillan & Co. Ltd (later Harper & Gilfillan)	tin	England	1867 Singapore
A. C. Harper & Co. Ltd	rubber	FMS	
W. Mansfield & Co. Ltd	shipping	England	1876 Penang
Borneo Co. Ltd (later Inchcape Timuran Bhd)	tin, rubber	1856 London	
McAlister & Co. Ltd	insurance, shipping	1857 Singapore	
Sime Darby & Co. Ltd	tin, rubber	1902 Melaka	
Behn, Meyer & Co.	insurance, shipping	1840 Singapore	

In return for their services, the leading agency houses were usually appointed as secretaries and managing agents for these new companies. The agency houses also obtained the exclusive rights for the supply of equipment to the mines and estates as well as the sale of their output on the world markets, all on commission. This brought profitable growth in allied lines of business, for example insurance agencies and shipping companies. By World War I, the European agency houses had established a controlling position in Malayan foreign trade which was to last for the next 50 years.

This period also saw the emergence in the agency houses and associated businesses of personalities who greatly influenced Malayan economic and political life. Notable among these were Sir Frank Swettenham (who had retired in 1904 as Governor–High Commissioner) and Sir Eric Macfayden (Harrisons & Crosfield), and Sir John G. Hay (Guthrie).

A Borneo Company boat used for the transportation of goods. Established in London in 1856, the Borneo Company was one of the leading agency houses in Singapore and Borneo.

Although the majority of the agency houses in the Malay Peninsula were British, there were also foreign-owned agencies. These included the German agency house Behn, Meyer & Co., which was founded in Singapore in 1840. Shown here is its office on Weld Quay in Penang, c. 1890.

Long Jaafar and the Chinese tin miners in Larut

Large-scale tin mining in Perak introduced a period of Sino-Malay partnership in the industry, exemplified by Long bin Jaafar and the Chinese miners of Larut. Chinese capitalists advanced finance to the chiefs in return for the right to trade in the tin produced. The use of thousands of Chinese immigrant labourers belonging to various secret societies to work the mines unfortunately resulted in violent clashes, known as the Larut wars, and eventually led to British intervention and the appointment of a British Resident.

One version of the story of the discovery of tin in Perak is that a runaway elephant belonging to Long Jaafar returned home with traces of the precious mineral on its body.

Larut district in the 1860s

Sungai Krian
Sungai Kurau
Sungai Sepetang
• Ijok
• Kelian Bahru
• Kelian Pauh
• Matang

N

Strait of Melaka

Perak

0   20 km

South China Sea

□ **MALAY PENINSULA**

Strait of Melaka

CHINESE POPULATION OF LARUT

Year	Population
1862	4,000
1873	25,000
1874	40,000
1880	80,000

With the development of opencast tin mines in Larut, the number of Chinese coolies arriving to find work rapidly increased.

Long Jaafar, the Malay miner

It is believed that in 1848, Long Jaafar, the son of a minor chief in Perak, was bathing in a stream in the Larut valley when his attention was caught by some black sand. When examined, this 'sand' was found to be tin. Long Jaafar had no lack of enterprise, but he lacked the capital to make use of his find. He approached merchants in Penang for funds to develop a mine. Long Jaafar's modus operandi was typical of those times before the Chinese had obtained a firm hold over tin mining. Chinese merchants merely advanced the necessary capital to the Malay chiefs who worked the mines with Chinese labour, on the understanding that all the tin produced would then be traded through them.

From his first mines in Kelian Pauh (present-day Taiping), Long Jaafar extended his mines to Kelian Bahru (Kamunting). Unfortunately, the two groups of Chinese labourers he recruited to work the mines in the two districts had different dialect origins and secret society affiliations (see 'Chinese secret societies')—Hakka of the Hai San society in Kelian Pauh and Cantonese of the Ghee Hin society in Kelian Bahru—thus sowing the seeds for the turmoil that subsequently engulfed Larut.

Despite the difficulties, Long Jaafar's resounding success as a tin-mining entrepreneur was echoed in the political sphere. In 1850, Sultan Jafar Muadzam Shah conferred on Long Jaafar 'the Government of Larut and its dependencies ... to be managed by him at his own expense, to be his own property, and the inheritance of his children'. A similar proclamation in 1856 designated more clearly the boundaries of this fiefdom and confirmed the rights of governance on Ngah Ibrahim, Long Jaafar's son, who was awarded the title Mentri Larut (Minister of Larut) in 1863. This unprecedented ascendance of a virtual commoner to a high position of power within the political hierarchy of Perak signalled the entry of a new variable in the power equation—wealth.

The Chinese coolies

Attracted by the opportunities in the newly opened tin mines, Chinese labourers began to flock to the Larut district, each hoping to collect his pot of 'black gold'. By 1874, the mining population had grown to 40,000. However, many did not fulfil their dreams as the mortality rate was very high, and for those who survived, the riches were not theirs. The system they laboured under was not developed for their gain.

The Chinese capitalists

Perak

Kapitan Chung Keng Kwee (1829–1901)—merchant, entrepreneur, opium farmer and secret society leader—is best personified as 'the enterprising spirit of the era'. Not satisfied with merely financing tin mines from afar, in the traditional manner, Chung proceeded to invest in them directly. This involvement was made possible when Ngah Ibrahim abandoned the policy of his father, Long Jaafar, and allowed capitalists from Penang to open tin mines in Larut. Chung's involvement as the headman of the Hakka secret society, the Hai San society (which fought against the Cantonese Ghee Hin society), gained him the unsavoury title of 'the most famous *capitan* of the Larut Wars'. At left is Chung's family residence on Church Street in Penang.

Selangor

In the state of Selangor, tin mining, the mainstay of the economy for most of the 19th century, passed from Malay to Chinese ownership in the middle of the century. Yap Ah Loy (1837–85), appointed Kapitan China in 1858, was by far the largest mining entrepreneur. In the final years of his prosperity, he owned about half the tin mines in the state and employed about 4,000 men. He was also the largest property owner and landlord in Kuala Lumpur, and the leader of the local 'tax farm' consortium.

Yap Ah Loy was responsible for building the first brick shophouses in Kuala Lumpur, in 1884, on the edge of Market Square.

Almost without exception, the tin mines in Larut worked on the 'truck system', which stipulated that 90 per cent of the tin produced in a mine belonged to the coolies and the other 10 per cent to the towkay who supplied the coolies to the mine owner and was also responsible for supplying their food and other stores. The accounting was done annually, during the Chinese New Year, when the coolies were credited with nine-tenths of the proceeds from the sale of the tin during the previous year, minus the amount of the stores they had consumed. Although the coolies' share allocation appeared on paper to be very generous, they were charged double the usual market price for their supplies, and deductions were also made to repay the coolies' debt for their fare from China. As a result, it was not unusual for a coolie to find himself still in debt at the end of a year of hard labour, and thus forced to continue his toil.

The Larut wars

The coming together of the Malay miners, the Chinese capitalists and the Chinese coolies laid the foundation for the prospering of the tin industry, but it also set the stage for the incessant conflicts that plagued Larut for several decades. The root cause of the conflict was control over the richest tin deposits. The mines at Kelian Pauh worked by the Hai San society members were less rich than those of the Ghee Hin society at Kelian Bahru, which led to Hai San encroachment on the Ghee Hin holdings. This scramble was made worse because the mining permits granted by Ngah Ibrahim did not clearly demarcate the boundaries of the leases.

Animosity between the rival clans and secret societies turned these disputes into bloody feuds. Moreover, Ngah Ibrahim did not have the means to govern the large Chinese population, with the result that when the Chinese started to fight for the tin mines, he was forced to side with whichever faction was winning at that time. There were also power struggles between the rival claimants to the Perak throne in which the Chinese miners took sides. When gang warfare became intertwined with political intrigues, an explosive end was inevitable.

This see-saw battle between the Chinese societies for the control of the Larut mines lasted from July 1861 until 20 January 1874, when the Chinese leaders were compelled to sign an undertaking to maintain peace among themselves and to accept a commission appointed by the Straits government to settle the dispute concerning the ownership of the mines and other matters related to the disturbances. This was the Chinese section of the Pangkor Treaty, officially designated the Chinese Engagement, to which 26 Chinese headmen put their signatures, with Chung Keng Kwee as the representative of the Hai San society and Chin Ah Yam for the Ghee Hin society. Chung Keng Kwee's Kong Loon Kongsi, which was reputed to own the largest mine in the country, employed about 300 coolies.

The Pangkor Treaty

The Pangkor Treaty was signed on 20 January 1874 on Pulau Pangkor, off the coast of Perak. Prior to the signing, Governor Sir Andrew Clarke sent his officer W. A. Pickering to meet rival Chinese leaders in Penang to find out whether they were ready to reach an agreement and accept the Straits Governor acting as arbitrator. Pickering's mission was successful and Clarke invited the leading Malay chiefs in Perak to meet him at the island of Pangkor, near the estuary of the Perak River, to settle the problems of Perak.

The Pangkor Treaty incorporated two documents:
1. The Chinese Engagement: The mining areas were divided between the two rival groups—Ghee Hin and Hai San. Their leaders undertook to keep peace or to pay a penalty of $50,000. While this was not the end of secret society rivalries, it did mark the beginning of a period of comparative peace and prosperity achieved through the production of tin.
2. The Pangkor Engagement, which contained the following important provisions:
   a. 'That the Sultan receive and provide a suitable residence for a British officer, to be called Resident, who shall be accredited to his Court, and whose advice must be asked and acted upon in all questions other than those touching Malay religion and custom.'
   b. 'That the collection and control of all revenues and the general administration of the country be regulated under the advice of these Residents.'

Proclamation concerning the Pangkor Engagement.

A photograph taken at Bandar Bahru in Lower Perak, probably on 15 September 1875, of the British officials involved in enforcing the provisions of the Pangkor Treaty. There is some disagreement about the identity of the officers, though they are believed to be, from left to right: Captain Anderson; W. Innes; H. E. McCallum (private secretary to the governor); Sir William Jervois, the governor of the Straits Settlements; H. F. P. Plow; J. W. W. Birch (with walking stick), the first British Resident of Perak, who was murdered in November 1875; Major J. F. A. McNair (partly obscured by Birch); Captain F. Stirling; T. C. S. Speedy; and Frank Swettenham.

The importance in Malaysian history of the signing of the Pangkor Treaty in 1874 is reflected in the inclusion of its depiction in the mural on the front wall of the Muzium Negara, Kuala Lumpur.

Allowing the Chinese direct investment in the mines also meant increasing their stake in procuring choice pieces of tin-mining land and, hence, the potential for clashes over land grants—precisely what unfolded in the Larut wars.

A similar drama, with different characters, was happening in another tin-rich state, Selangor. In both places, rampant civil strife was brought under control by British intervention (see 'Civil wars and British intervention'). The disorder in both states reflected the inability of the Malay polity to deal with the new Chinese elements in its economic and political set-up and the tensions that new sources of wealth and new power alignments had wrought among the Malay ruling class. British intervention to resolve these disputes signified not only their imminent involvement in tin mining, but also in the governance of the Malay states.

The table used for the signing of the Pangkor Treaty can still be seen in Muzium Negara.

Chinese secret societies

In the Malay Peninsula, kongsi, more popularly known as Chinese secret societies, were cooperative associations whose members pooled resources for a venture and shared the profits. However, their character changed over time as they were able to enrol immigrant labourers even before they left China. They were able to keep the coolies in perpetual debt, not only for their passage but also for the supplies and services offered through revenue farms. These included gambling, alcohol and opium. Such practices eventually led to a British ban on the societies.

A row of 19th-century *kongsi* houses on King Street, Penang, which served as the headquarters of the Chinese secret societies on the island.

Were they secret?

The Penang office of the Chinese Protectorate, the government body concerned with the welfare of the Chinese immigrant labourers.

'Secret societies' was a Western label, for there was little that was not known about these groups. Annual reports of the Chinese Protectorate (the colonial department of Chinese affairs) listed these societies, their headmen and their membership numbers. The Chinese term *kongsi*, meaning 'public shares', reflects more accurately the nature of these partnerships set up for economic enterprise and social regulation.

Early *kongsi*

The *kongsi* had their origins in the illegal mining communities and sea-merchant kingdoms of southern China which based their brotherhood governments on principles of partnership and democratic self-government. This egalitarian system was practised in its purest and most idealized form in the gold mines of western Borneo, from where it spread to other pioneering Chinese communities of Southeast Asia. However, the kongsi in these other locations may not have adhered so strictly to democratic principles.

Even if they did not embody all its substance, the forms of these kongsi began to make their appearance in the Malay Peninsula towards the end of the 18th century. Triad lodges were set up in Penang around 1790 and in Singapore by 1825. The better known Hai San and Toa Peh Kong were founded in Penang in 1820 and 1844 respectively. By the 1860s, kongsi had also opened in Sungai Ujong, Selangor and Perak after the migration there of Chinese mining communities.

The term 'kongsi' reflects the collective spirit which bound together these various early mining communities. Each venture was capitalized by a kongsi in which the members were entitled to a share of the profits based on their contribution to the enterprise. If new members lacked capital, they could earn these rights through the input of their labour. The kongsi thus facilitated a pooling of resources as well as the sharing of profits. This enabled immigrants to pursue their primary purpose of making a living and supporting their families in China through their remittances home.

Guan Di, the God of War and the patron deity of Chinese secret societies, is flanked by his two sworn brothers, Liu Bei and Zhang Fei. In front of the idol is an altar on which are placed items used in the initiation ceremonies of secret society members.

Clan members could place their gilt ancestral tablets in the temple of their *kongsi* to fulfil their ancestor worship obligations.

In these frontier territories where there was no effective formal governance, the kongsi also played the crucial role of arbitrator, settling disputes and mediating social relations, ensuring that a viable community could be sustained. The rituals of sworn brotherhood hence served to seal the ties which had been forged on more functional foundations.

The bonds of brotherhood were important for rallying together members of the kongsi when they were faced with external threats or incursions. Many of the 'secret society riots' were protests against the impositions of the colonial authorities: the Hawkers Riot of 1872 against proposals to restrict hawking on the streets; the Post Office Riot of 1876 against the move to intercede in the trade of sending letters and remittances to China; and the Taiping Riot of 1879 against the proposal to introduce *chandu* (processed opium) farming.

Conglomerates

The purported egalitarianism of the kongsi was, however, often breached in practice. This was especially true after the initial partnerships had evolved into huge conglomerates or secret societies, such as the Ghee Hin, Hai San and Toa Peh Kong, which were dominated by a coterie of luminaries including Yap Ah Loy, Chung Keng Kwee, Khoo Thean Teik, Loke Yew and Tan Kim Cheng.

From their strongholds in Singapore and Penang, these societies branched out into the Malay states, especially Perak and Selangor, as they became increasingly populated by Chinese tin-mining coolies. The societies controlled the tin mines, the recruitment and deployment of labour, the opium and other revenue farms, prostitution and gambling—in fact, practically everything connected with Chinese coolie life in the 19th century.

The coolies were already in the grasp of the kongsi before they boarded the ships in China, as their passages had been arranged and paid for by syndicates linked to the labour recruiters, who were society members. The workers' names were often entered on the membership roll of the societies by the recruiters without their knowledge.

Control over labour recruitment was of crucial importance in swelling the ranks of a kongsi, and hence in ensuring a steady supply of labour, a ready market for the opium, alcohol and other goods and services it farmed, and a guaranteed clientele for its gambling dens and brothels. Thus there was a direct correlation between the extent of control over recruitment of members and the size—and, hence, the power—of the societies. The largest of the societies, the Ghee Hin, also controlled the greatest number of labour recruitment agencies.

With such extensive interests to safeguard, the kongsi increasingly took on the form of armed bands to protect the interests of their towkays and headmen, and society clashes were often no more than battles over their spoils. Force, coercion and exploitation became very much a part of the scene. Ironically, the leaders of these rival gangs who were often the instigators of public disorder had titles such as Justice of the Peace and Kapitan China, and enjoyed high social status.

The colonial administration faced a dilemma when dealing with the kongsi. Although the power wielded by these societies threatened the authority of the colonial state, the government officials possessed neither the means nor the ability to rule the Chinese immigrants who, to them, remained an 'inscrutable race'. Hence, they were forced to surrender the governing of the Chinese population to their own leaders and to resign themselves to co-existence with this 'empire within an empire'.

Suppression

The situation changed towards the end of the 19th century when the colonial state had become better consolidated, buttressed by an established administration, an expanded police force and an array of restrictive legislation. The Societies Ordinance of 1890 proscribed the activities of secret societies in the Straits Settlements and the Malay states. This suppression reflected the increasing competition between Western enterprises and the Chinese capitalists. The Chinese hold over the economy, via the secret societies, had to be broken to allow the penetration of Western capital.

The societies were also losing their grip over the coolies due to a number of demographic changes: increasing numbers, greater dispersal and the replacement of bonded workers by free labour. The closed society which had allowed the kongsi to function so effectively no longer existed, and as their control waned so did their power and prestige. By the time they were finally banned, the societies had already become pale shadows of their former selves. Many towkays also found that it served their purpose better to reorganize their businesses in the mould of Western corporations.

Shorn of its social function of brotherhood and its political function of self-government, the term 'kongsi' came to denote no more than a commercial company. The 'secret societies' that remained assumed the form that the colonial state had defined for them—clandestine criminal organizations—as they are generally regarded today.

The three main societies

Ghee Hin

The members of the Cantonese Ghee Hin were involved in the Larut wars of 1872–4. By building stockades on the Larut River, which blockaded the area and severely hampered the movement of tin, they were able to raid passing vessels.

RIGHT: Headquarters of the society at 29 Church Street, Penang, which was once used by the Hai San Society.

LEFT: Khaw Boo Aun assumed the post of coolie broker in the late 1860s. He was the financier of Raja Abdullah in the Perak Civil War in the early 1870s.

Membership certificate of the Ghee Hin society.

Hai San

The Hai San society was founded in Penang in 1823. Like the other *kongsi*, it first operated as an economic and social organization for the welfare of Chinese immigrants. Its members were involved in the Post Office Riot of 1876. The society members turned themselves in during the 1890 suppression of secret societies after the Societies Ordinance had proscribed their activities.

ABOVE: Headquarters of the society in Penang.

RIGHT: Kapitan Chung Keng Kwee was the acknowledged headman of the Hai San society, and was one of the signatories of the Pangkor Treaty in 1874.

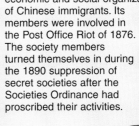

Toa Peh Kong

This *kongsi*, also known as Kien Tek Tong, was established in 1854 in Penang. Its members comprised Hokkien and Straits-born Chinese. It was founded by men from the Fujian province of China who had always been antagonistic to the Cantonese of the Ghee Hin society. The members were mostly wealthy merchants and shopkeepers, including manufacturers and sellers of firearms and ammunition.

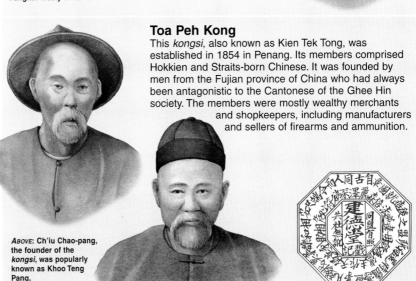

ABOVE: Ch'iu Chao-pang, the founder of the *kongsi*, was popularly known as Khoo Teng Pang.

RIGHT: Khoo Thean Teik, who became the leader of the society in the 1860s.

Membership certificate of the Toa Peh Kong society.

A hand-coloured engraving from a drawing of Melaka in 1807 by E. H. Locker. Melaka was placed under British control by the Dutch from 1795–1818 to prevent a possible takeover by the French during the Napoleonic wars. It became British territory in 1824.

HMS *Rinaldo*, which took part in the Klang war of 1867–73. This was a dispute over the control of Klang, and its available revenue, between Raja Mahdi of Selangor and Tunku Kudin of Kedah, the son-in-law of Sultan Abdul Samad of Selangor. Both men enlisted the aid of Chinese secret societies. The British supported Tunku Kudin, who was eventually the victor.

Sultan Sulaiman of Selangor (r. 1898–1938) with his followers in front of the old wooden palace at Jugra, Kuala Langat, in 1898. This had been the favourite home of his grandfather, Sultan Abdul Samad, whom he had recently succeeded. A new palace was built for Sultan Sulaiman in Klang.

THE IMPACT OF BRITISH IMPERIALISM

The view from Strawberry Hill on Penang looking towards the mainland. Province Wellesley (now Seberang Perai), the coastal area of Kedah facing Penang, was ceded to the East India Company by Kedah in 1800.

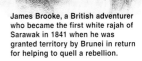

James Brooke, a British adventurer who became the first white rajah of Sarawak in 1841 when he was granted territory by Brunei in return for helping to quell a rebellion.

By 1826, the whole of the Malay Peninsula had been brought within the British sphere of influence, while it was two more decades before areas of northern Borneo were included. In the early 19th century, British imperial policy was determined by a variety of strategic, political and economic factors, but after the 1870s economic factors played a major role.

The establishment of Singapore as a British free port was aimed at checking the Dutch policy of trade monopoly in the Strait of Melaka and also at safeguarding the India–China trade routes. However, only in 1824 with the signing of the Anglo-Dutch Treaty, which demarcated British and Dutch spheres of influence with an imaginary line down the Strait of Melaka, did the Dutch threat in the Strait of Melaka come to an end.

The British settlement on Penang in 1786 was the initial step in the spread of British power through the northern states of Kedah (then including Perlis), Kelantan and Terengganu, all under Siam's overlordship. In 1821 when Siam attacked Kedah, Sultan Ahmad Tajuddin Halim Shah fled first to Penang where he was protected by the British, who also prevented Siam bringing Perak and Selangor under its control. The Burney Treaty of 1824 guaranteed the independence of these two states.

James Brooke's acquisition of Sarawak in 1841 and the British government's acquisition of Labuan as a naval base in 1846, both territories from Sultan Omar Ali of Brunei, brought these areas under the British sphere of influence.

British imperial policy was essentially confined to taking islands to meet naval and strategic needs. The British avoided large-scale annexation of territory or intervention in local affairs unless necessary as these actions could prove expensive. However, they interfered in the affairs of the district of Naning, which they had taken over from the Dutch after the Anglo-Dutch Treaty of 1824. British attempts to impose Melaka taxes on the Naning people led to the first instance of Malay resistance against the British; it ended with Naning's subjugation in 1832.

In 1855, the British again interfered in the affairs of Johor when they settled the territorial dispute between Tengku Ali and Temenggong Daeng Ibrahim. Tengku Ali was finally recognized as sultan of Johor, but was given control over only the territory of Muar–Kesang, while the rest of Johor was ruled by Temenggong Daeng Ibrahim. In 1885, the British recognized the Temenggong's son, Abu Bakar (who had succeeded him in 1862), as sultan, thus creating a new sultanate in Johor from the Temenggong lineage of the former Johor–Riau–Lingga–Pahang dynasty.

Succession disputes and violent disturbances in Perak, Selangor and Negeri Sembilan led to the abandonment of the policy of non-interference in 1874. The British government intervened first in Perak, then in Selangor and Sungai Ujong, a small kingdom in Negeri Sembilan. The rulers of these Malay states each agreed to the appointment of a British Resident whose advice had to be accepted in all matters except those of Malay custom and the Islamic religion. In 1888, the British intervened in Pahang because of internal disputes, and the Bendahara agreed to accept a British Resident in return for being allowed to adopt the title of sultan.

Abu Bakar, ruler of Johor from 1862 until 1895, originally carried the title of Temenggong. He adopted the title of maharajah in 1866, and was granted the title of sultan by the British in 1885. His close ties with Queen Victoria forestalled British intervention in Johor until after his death.

The Burney Treaty, Siam and the northern Malay states

With the signing of the Burney Treaty in 1826, Siam and Britain became joint guardians of law and order in the Malay states until 1909, when Siam relinquished its claim over its northern Malay tributaries. Siam was predominant in the northern states of Kedah (and, from 1841, Perlis), Kelantan and Terengganu, while British influence extended implicitly through the remaining area of the Malay Peninsula. Siam also gave commercial concessions to British agents in its Malay tributaries and undertook not to extend its power beyond Perak.

Siamese princes and Kedah nobles at Chakrabong House, the residence of the high commissioner for Phuket in Penang, in the late 19th century.

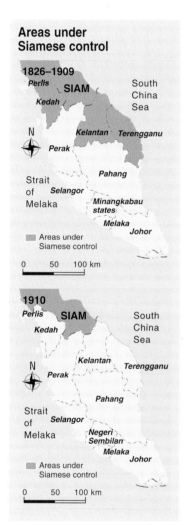

Areas under Siamese control

1826–1909

1910

The Penang headquarters of the East India Company, which ruled the island from 1786, when Francis Light founded a settlement there, until 1858, when power passed to the British government.

The northern Malay states in the 19th century

Though Siamese–Malay relations can be traced back to the 15th century, it was not until the 17th century that Siam focused its attention on the northern Malay states—Perak, Kedah, Kelantan, Terengganu and Patani. However, by the beginning of the 19th century, Patani had been incorporated as a frontier region within the Siamese kingdom. The Siamese authorities considered it no longer a tributary, but subject to the direct authority of the king.

In the 1820s, the governor-general of British India sent a mission to negotiate a treaty of friendship and commerce with Siam, which was the only local power in Southeast Asia capable of contesting British activities in the Malay Peninsula. The northern states involved in any possible conflict of interest between the British, which was the powerful newcomer, and Siam, the traditional regional power, were Perak, which had been forced to accept Siamese suzerainty in 1818; Kedah, which had been governed directly by the Siamese since 1821; and Kelantan and Terengganu, both of which had submitted to the Siamese resurgence of power in the early years of the 19th century.

The British presence in the Malay Peninsula, especially after the signing of the Anglo-Dutch Treaty in 1824 which made the whole Peninsula a British sphere of influence, gave Malay rulers an alternative to Siamese overlordship which they were quick to exploit, much to the frustration and alarm of Bangkok. For example, the three-cornered relationship between Kedah, the British in Penang, and Bangkok led eventually to the Siamese invasion and occupation of Kedah in 1821. Perak, Kelantan and Terengganu likewise

exploited the presence of the British East India Company (EIC) administration in Penang in the hope of shaking off Siamese overlordship.

From the 17th century, the response by the Malay rulers to the Siamese tributary claims arose from the necessity of smaller and weaker states surviving and achieving peaceful coexistence with their more powerful and aggressive neighbour. This was done without the Malay rulers sacrificing their own authority and freedom of action within their own states. Acquiescence to the tributary relations with Siam was the price to be paid to preserve their domestic supreme position and/or the autonomy of their state. Naturally, the system was not to be endured any longer than necessary. Whenever an opportunity arose to end these obligations, Malay rulers seized upon it without any compunction.

During the 19th century, Malay rulers or aspirants to the throne requested Siamese assistance when it was necessary to strengthen their position or to get rid of domestic rivals in return for absolute loyalty and the obligations of a Siamese tributary.

Seal on a letter, 1835, from the Chau Paya of Ligor (Siam) to the governor of Penang.

The Siamese tributary system

Siam's tributary system towards the various small principalities close to the kingdom was based on the state's political philosophy inherited from Buddhism and from historical contacts with the civilization of Angkor. It was a means of regulating the relationship between the Siamese king and his counterparts in these areas. For the northern Malay states, the symbols of this traditional diplomatic tie were the *bunga mas* (gold flowers) and *bunga perak* (silver flowers) which the Malay rulers were required to present to Bangkok every three years.

In return for this sociopolitical acceptance, Bangkok undertook to give protection to its Malay vassals against all threats as well as other kinds of assistance requested. Originally, the tributary system allowed much latitude in the suzerain–vassal relationship, whereby a loss or gain of a tributary was deemed a natural consequence of the rise and fall of the political and military fortune of the suzerain's state. However, after 1767 and the founding of Bangkok, the loss of a tributary came to be regarded as evidence of the ruler's weakened legitimacy to rule. The guiding principle appears to have been 'once a tributary, always a tributary'. Thus, revolts or attempts to be released of tributary obligations could never be entertained as they undermined the suzerain-king's political and ideological strength.

Besides the inherent sociopolitical value in the Siamese–Malay relations, the northern Malay states were also of genuine value to Siam's security and stability as a major power in the region. Siam regarded the principalities within its outer circle as buffers, cushioning it from threats from other powerful and hostile states. Thus, both Laos and Cambodia acted as a buffer against Vietnam; the Shan and Mon states were a buffer against Burma. The northern Malay states, especially Kedah and Patani, had since the 15th century been regarded not only as a possible gateway or as a base for launching hostile attacks against Siam, but also as a potential source of trouble in the southern region which could endanger the kingdom's sociopolitical stability. From Bangkok's perspective, the strategic significance of the northern Malay states could not be underestimated.

An example of the *bunga mas* (gold flowers) which the northern Malay states were required to present as tribute to the Siamese ruler every three years.

British objectives in the Malay Peninsula

The paramount objectives of the British in the Malay Peninsula after the surrender of Penang by Sultan Abdullah of Kedah to the EIC were economic gains, the safety of the trade route between India and China, and the security of the British empire in Asia. It was thus important to maintain the peaceful transaction of commerce and to cultivate congenial relations with all the local states, in particular with powerful ones such as Siam. Kedah suffered most unjustly from this British policy of non-intervention when, in spite of agreements, territorial leasing and cession, it failed to obtain British support against Siamese invasion.

In 1822, the first mission sent by the British government of India to Siam, under the leadership of John Crawfurd, to establish a politico-economic understanding failed. However, this did not deter them from sending a second mission three years later. This was the successful Burney mission, under the leadership of Henry Burney, the Military Secretary at Penang. After about six months of negotiations, the treaty was signed in June 1826.

The Burney Treaty of 1826

The success of the Burney mission, which dealt primarily with commercial concessions, was based on three factors: first, the British victory in Burma, which had caused a fundamental shift of mind-set among the Siamese ruling élite, especially King Rama III; second, Britain's moderate demands for economic and diplomatic ties; and third, the personal approach of Captain Henry Burney.

The Treaty dealt mainly with commercial concessions and the Anglo–Siamese understanding over their spheres of influence in the Peninsula, in order to avoid future hostility and armed conflicts.

In spite of strong opposition to the Burney Treaty by the British authorities in Penang, it was generally considered a diplomatic success for both Siam and Britain, with both parties obtaining their principal objectives. The compromise struck in 1826 was realistic, timely and enduring. Its success can be gauged from the fact that between 1826 and 1909, in spite of disturbances and rivalries arising from the displeasure of the Malay rulers with Siam's tributary system and Singapore's design on the Siamese–Malay tributaries, there were no outbreaks of hostility between Bangkok and London.

However, from the viewpoint of the Malay rulers, the compromise was unsatisfactory. The repeated efforts by the rulers to be released from their obligations to Siam, as well as to be freed from British political and economic claims, were examples of their dissatisfaction.

King Rama III (1824–51) was the third ruler of the Chakri Dynasty. Under his leadership, Siam signed the Burney Treaty in 1826.

Features of the Burney Treaty

An Anglo-Siamese understanding was reached over respective spheres of influence in the Malay Peninsula, to avoid future hostility and armed conflicts.

The British:
- unconditionally admitted that Kedah was under Siamese authority.

- accepted the status quo in Kelantan and Terengganu, which were claimed by Siam, by undertaking not to interfere in Siam's internal affairs.

- were ceded the Dindings, including Pulau Pangkor, by Perak for driving Siamese troops from Perak territory. The offer was not taken up until 1874.

In return, Siam:
- granted commercial concessions to British agents in her Malay tributaries.

- undertook not to extend its power beyond Perak, which had acted as a buffer between Siamese and British spheres of influence.

- accepted the friendship of, and official relations with, Britain and agreed to grant better commercial terms.

James Brooke:
The white rajah of Sarawak

James Brooke was an English adventurer who was rewarded with land and a title in return for helping to suppress a rebellion in Sarawak. He established a private colony under a dynasty of white rajahs which was to rule the state of Sarawak until World War II under an authoritarian system utilizing both indigenous chieftains and British district officers. Revenue for the administration of the state was obtained from a system of monopolies on minerals and agricultural products.

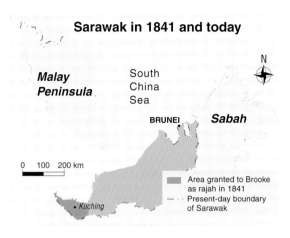

Sarawak in 1841 and today

Malay Peninsula

South China Sea

BRUNEI

Sabah

N

0 100 200 km

• Kuching

■ Area granted to Brooke as rajah in 1841
--- Present-day boundary of Sarawak

James Brooke (1803–68) was born in Benares (Varanasi), India, the son of an East India Company official. He was sent to England to be educated but ran away from school and returned to India. At the age of 16, he became a cadet in the Bengal Army and was promoted to lieutenant two years later.

Raja Muda Hassim

The Raja Muda Hassim is a remarkably short man, and slightly built, about 45 years of age; active and intelligent, but apparently little inclined to business. His disposition I formed the highest estimate of, not only from his kindness of myself, but from the testimony of many witnesses, all of whom spoke of him with affection, and gave him the character of a mild and gentle master....

— From *Journal of James Brooke*, on his first meeting with Raja Muda Hassim in 1840.

Brooke's arrival in Sarawak

James Brooke, influenced by Sir Stamford Raffles's idea of a strong British presence in the Indonesian Archipelago, sailed to Sarawak in August 1839 after learning that Sultan Omar Ali of Brunei, of which Sarawak was a dependency, was favourably disposed towards the British. On his second trip in 1840, Sarawak's mineral and forest resources were a decisive factor in Brooke's decision to help Raja Muda Hassim, the governor, suppress an uprising by the Malays of Sarawak against the sultan of Brunei. In return for his assistance, James Brooke was bestowed the title of rajah of Sarawak in 1841 and was granted the area later known as the First division for a modest annual payment.

Brooke established his capital at Kuching on the Sarawak River. After consolidating his authority, he rapidly moved to extend his territory by penetrating areas nominally under the authority of Brunei. He attempted to establish a British colonial presence, but was unsuccessful. However, he survived the initial military campaigns against him, primarily because of British naval support, but also because he coopted the local Malay élite and made use of Iban warriors to quell opposition. In the 1850s and 1860s, the weak Brunei sultanate accepted major Brooke annexations of the principal Iban-occupied districts in return for further annual payments.

The document from Raja Muda Hassim (left) ceding the territory of Sarawak to James Brooke in 1841. The agreement was later ratified by Sultan Omar Ali of Brunei.

Government and administration

The government established in Sarawak by James Brooke was personal and authoritarian. He set up small forts in tribal territory, where the rule of force was gradually replaced by the rule of law. These forts, which were permanent structures built at the river mouths, helped to maintain peace so that the Brooke administration could establish a virtual trading monopoly over its realm. The forts permitted the stationing of European officers in dangerous, outlying districts, enabled the control of war fleets by means of a few cannon and, at the same time, facilitated the collection of duties on riverine trade and taxes on the local population.

As more territory was ceded to Brooke, Sarawak was divided into three divisions for administrative purposes. Senior administrators were recruited from Britain. In governing the indigenous people, the Brookes either adopted and reinforced existing chieftaincies, in the case of the Malays, or created new political authorities, in the case of the Iban.

There thus arose two parallel systems of administration which were both obedient to the rajah's authority. One was a hierarchical ranking of government-appointed indigenous chieftains whose duties were to administer traditional law and to levy tax for the rajah. The other was a system of district officers—regional residents recruited in Britain—whose duty was to administer the introduced Western system of justice, land ownership and taxation, and to intervene in local affairs when it was considered necessary to do so to keep the peace.

For administrative convenience, the three major ethnic groups in the territory—Malays, Iban and Chinese—were each assigned roles which were perceived as appropriate to their cultural attributes. The Malay role was that of administration, the Iban role was military, while the Chinese role was economic. Intermingling among the groups on a social level was forbidden. To facilitate enforcement, Chinese traders were confined to the town bazaars, Malay kampongs were located in the towns, and the Iban needed the Resident's permission to travel outside their districts.

The HMS *Dido* (734 tons, 18 guns), captained by the Hon. Charles Keppel on his first commission, paid two brief, but memorable, visits to Borneo. During the first, in 1843, Keppel led a raid which destroyed the Iban strongholds along the Saribas River. In 1844, he undertook a similar raid on the Iban along the Sekrang River. These two expeditions were essential to the consolidation of James Brooke's position in Sarawak.

Economic framework

From the beginning, James Brooke adopted a policy of monopolization of the mineral resources of Sarawak, reserving for himself a monopoly in the trade of antimony ore (see 'Antimony mining and the sago industry of Sarawak'). As governor of Labuan, he kept Western interests out of Bintulu and obtained for himself exclusive rights to mine coal along the northwest coast of Borneo. His main rivals were Chinese miners who had been mining gold near Pangkalan Tebang just north of the Indonesian border since the early 19th century. Later, they moved to Bau where, through their *kongsi* (cooperative business concerns), they pioneered gold and antimony production (see 'Petroleum and mineral resources in Borneo'). Their autonomous existence was ultimately challenged by Brooke, resulting in the Chinese uprising of 1857. This led to the collapse of the Chinese mining industry in Sarawak and a strengthening of Brooke's position. It also led to the taking over of mineral exploitation in the state by the Borneo Company, subsequently the most powerful business concern in Sarawak.

Under Brooke rule, control of land also became a key issue. Traditionally, land had been communally held and the concept of private ownership was virtually unknown. James Brooke claimed sovereignty over all land, but allowed the indigenous people to claim ownership on the basis of sublease and native customary law. The first major piece of legislation, the Land Code of 1842, prohibited interference with native customary law. Immigrants were allowed to settle only on land not occupied by indigenous groups.

Sarawak's main commercial agricultural crop in the 19th century was sago, grown by the Melanau on the Mukah and Oya rivers (see 'Antimony mining and the sago industry of Sarawak'). In the late 1850s, the sago trade was severely affected by troubles in the producing districts. James Brooke quelled the rebellion and took over the districts in 1861. The Borneo Company, with government encouragement, then moved in. It established sago processing factories and monopolized the trade in sago, previously controlled by Malay traders and Chinese middlemen.

Development

As a private colony, Sarawak had a unique colonial history. The administrative machinery was tiny and financial assistance to the indigenous population was kept to a minimum. Very few developmental initiatives were undertaken. The Borneo Company was given the task of developing Sarawak's agricultural and mineral resources to provide the necessary revenue for the administration of the state. There was no intention of revolutionizing the territory. Consequently, while James Brooke's administration precipitated change, it was intended to be only in a small degree planned change.

A drawing by Arthur Adams, c. 1843, of Sultan Omar Ali, who ruled Brunei from 1828 until 1852.

Baroness Angela Burdett-Coutts (1814–1906) was Britain's wealthiest woman in the mid-19th century. Through her financial support, as James Brooke's patron, she played a decisive role in Sarawak's dynastic politics in the 1860s.

Kuching, the capital of Sarawak, on the banks of the Sarawak River, with Mount Santubong in the background, taken from F. S. Marryat, *Borneo and the Indian Archipelago* (1848).

Dul Said and the Naning War

The Naning War was an uprising resulting from unwelcome interference in the local customs of Naning, a small autonomous state adjacent to Melaka. Dul Said, a respected local chieftain, resented British attempts to rob himself and the local clan chiefs of their traditional authority and to impose Melaka's law and taxation systems in Naning. His refusal to submit to their authority angered the British, who launched a long and costly military battle against Dul Said.

A map of the Malay Peninsula showing the 1826 boundaries of the Straits Settlements (Singapore, Melaka and Penang) and the political affiliations of the Malay states. Naning is clearly marked 'N' on the border of Melaka.

Naning and the Dutch

When the Dutch conquered Melaka in 1641, they came into conflict with the small neighbouring state of Naning, then nominally under the authority of Johor. Naning had been settled by Minangkabau migrants, and divided into four *suku* (clans). From 1643, the Naning administration was subject to Dutch approval, and was required to submit a tenth of its produce to Melaka annually. However, the Dutch were unable to collect this tribute even after Johor ceded its nominal suzerainty in 1758. In about 1765, the tribute was commuted to a payment of rice and other gifts. Although the Dutch regularly confirmed the *penghulu* (chief) of Naning in office, they rarely interfered in local affairs and Naning remained essentially autonomous.

Naning and the British

During the Napoleonic Wars, the British occupied Melaka, and in 1801 they reaffirmed the earlier Dutch treaties with Naning. The Naning chiefs agreed to be loyal to Melaka, to submit tribute and to pay annual homage, but there is no evidence that these agreements were enforced. However, one significant step came in 1807 when Melaka's British Resident decreed that the Naning penghulu could no longer impose the death penalty. In future, all capital offences were to be tried in Melaka.

British interference in Naning affairs increased markedly after the Anglo-Dutch Treaty in 1824, by which the control of Melaka passed from the Dutch to the British East India Company. The governor of the Straits Settlements, Robert Fullerton, who was resident in Penang, assumed that Naning was part of Melaka and failed to understand that past treaties had never been enforced. Critics pointed out the ambiguity of the historical records, and argued that Naning's economy was not sufficient to justify imposing English 'rights'. Although debates continued, W. T. Lewis, the Resident Councillor of Melaka, strongly favoured the extension of British control. In 1827, he submitted a report criticizing Naning's administration. Fullerton therefore decided that the tribute of a tenth of the local produce should be collected and Naning should become subject to Melaka's land laws and jurisdiction. The penghulu and suku heads should be given small pensions and appointed revenue collectors for the Company. The stage was set for confrontation.

Dul Said

The penghulu of Naning, Abdul Said, who was popularly known as Dul Said, was descended from a line of Minangkabau chiefs. He had succeeded his uncle in 1801, and his appointment had been confirmed by the Resident of Melaka.

As he had been the penghulu for more than 20 years, Dul Said's standing as a local leader was very high, and he was commonly believed to possess supernatural powers. His status was enhanced even further because he had adopted titles linking him to the great rulers of Melaka, invoking memories of a time when Malays were supreme. Far from being a

The destruction of the Portuguese fort at Melaka in 1807 was carried out by William Farquhar on the orders of the governor of Penang. Several hundred workers toiled unsuccessfully for three months on the demolition before Farquhar resorted to the use of gunpowder. The destruction was finally stopped by the timely arrival of Stamford Raffles. The demolition is said to have cost £70,000, an enormous sum at that time.

Government House at Melaka, from which Governor Fullerton tried to impose Melaka's law and taxation system in Naning. At left is the Porta de Santiago, the remnant of the Portuguese fortress built in 1512 which was destroyed by William Farquhar under orders from the governor of Penang in 1807.

tyrant, as imagined by British officers, Dul Said was a respected chief in the traditional Malay style. He was well aware that neither the Dutch nor the English had made any real effort to collect the tribute to which they were theoretically entitled, despite the treaties signed more than a century earlier. Already annoyed by the limitations on his judicial powers, he saw Fullerton's new demands as a gross infringement on his authority. In December 1828, he defiantly issued a judgment in a murder case instead of referring it to Melaka.

Delicate negotiations

Governor Fullerton was mistakenly convinced that the people of Naning would welcome British troops and accept incorporation into Melaka's territory. He also believed that any authority which Dul Said claimed was not traditional or hereditary, but usurped. However, when agents were sent to collect the tribute they met with such fierce opposition that they asked for soldiers to protect them. Because several influential Penang councillors still maintained that the British demands were unlawful, it was decided to leave affairs in abeyance until after the death of the elderly Dul Said.

In Naning, opposition to the British was growing. In 1829, Dul Said refused to go to Melaka to meet Governor Fullerton, as this would be seen as a sign of submission. He resented the presence of British officials sent to take a census in Naning, suspecting plans for a takeover. Fuelled by rumours in Melaka, his suspicions were not laid to rest despite British conciliatory missions, especially when it was known that troops were being maintained in Melaka in readiness for any hostilities. A clear act of defiance came in October 1830 when Dul Said seized the fruit from an orchard in Melaka territory, claiming that the land fell within his jurisdiction.

A collection of traditional Malay swords and daggers including the kris, *lading*, *sundong* and *sabit*. The wavy-bladed kris always had an uneven number of waves, never an even number.

Aware that he would need allies if he were to oppose the British, Dul Said sought assistance from neighbouring chiefs, notably the ruler of Rembau. The latter was concerned that the British might give authority over Rembau to Sultan Ahmad Tajuddin of Kedah, who had been deposed by the Siamese in 1821 and had recently arrived in Melaka. By mid-1831, it was apparent that any compromise with the British over Naning was impossible. The Melaka administration believed that if Dul Said were permitted to continue in his defiance they would have difficulty in maintaining control. Many Melaka citizens still resented the transfer from Dutch authority after the signing of the Anglo-Dutch Treaty of 1824. For his part, Dul Said said he would be satisfied with nothing less than a recognition of Naning's full autonomy.

Local correspondence

Dul Said, as *penghulu* of Naning, would have become well acquainted with William Farquhar during Farquhar's long term as Resident of Melaka (1803–18). On 23 January 1820, Dul Said wrote to Farquhar 'in the new state' (Singapore), sending a goat and three capons and asking for $50 and some gunpowder. Farquhar replied on 15 February, refusing to meet Dul Said's requests and telling him that he should write only with the permission of the Dutch, as they had taken back control of Melaka. The seal used (upside down) by Dul Said on his letter was locally made, and imprinted with the letters VEIC, the logo of the Dutch East India Company.

FAR LEFT: A letter dated 23 January 1820 from Dul Said, the *penghulu* of Naning, to William Farquhar, Resident of Singapore.

LEFT: A copy of Farquhar's reply to Dul Said, dated 15 February 1820.

The outbreak of hostilities

Expecting little resistance, the English dispatched a small force of 150 sepoys to Tabuh, Dul Said's stronghold, in July 1831. The expedition was a disaster because of swamps and thick jungle. Melaka had been left unguarded, and it was now feared that Dul Said might attack. Even the retreat path was blocked by giant trees, and after three weeks the expedition returned ignominiously to find the citizens of Melaka in panic and preparing for battle.

Despite this fiasco, the English felt it was necessary to force Dul Said to acknowledge their superiority, and in March 1832 another expedition set out. This time, the Melaka authorities had been successful in undermining the alliance between Dul Said and Rembau by promising to observe the latter's independence. Determined to avoid the mistakes of the previous campaign, the English commander used convict labour to cut a road 180 metres wide through the jungle from Melaka to Tabuh, 55 kilometres away.

Again, there were no pitched battles, although the Malays harassed the protecting parties and the road diggers from the cover of the rainforest. Neither side enjoyed a great advantage, even though the English troops, around 1,300 men, far outnumbered Dul Said's followers.

The situation changed with the arrival of a force of Malays led by Sayid Saban, the son-in-law of the Rembau ruler. Because of their knowledge of the terrain, the tide rapidly turned, and in June 1832 Tabuh was captured. Dul Said and his chiefs fled, and the Naning resistance came to an end.

The Naning War was a battle between the British and Dul Said, the *penghulu* of Naning, a semi-autonomous state, resulting from British attempts to collect tribute from the residents of Naning and to impose the laws of Melaka on the state. The war was eventually won by the British, but at very heavy financial cost.

British mediation and the new sultanate in Johor

The Johor sultans of the 16th and 17th centuries were direct descendants of the Melaka dynasty. However, this lineage came to an end in 1699 with the assassination of Sultan Mahmud, who had no heirs. He was succeeded by the Bendahara (prime minister), and the capital was moved to Riau–Lingga. Thus it was one of his descendants, Sultan Abdul Rahman, who was ruling the Johor–Riau–Lingga sultanate when the British established a free port in Singapore in 1819. Subsequently, British mediation, which favoured the Temenggongs, largely determined the lineage of the new sultanate of Johor.

The large, thatch-roofed house in this illustration, c. 1836, is believed to have been the home of Temenggong Abdul Rahman at the foot of Teluk Belanga Hill (Mount Faber).

British and Dutch colonies

Istana Kampung Glam, the palace in Singapore built by the British for Sultan Hussein Shah in exchange for signing the 1819 Treaty with the Temenggong, which allowed the British to establish an EIC settlement on the island.

A postcard showing the palace which was built by Temenggong Abu Bakar in Johor Bahru, on the shore of the Tebrau Strait, after he had moved the capital of the state of Johor from Singapore to Johor Bahru.

Temenggong Daeng Ibrahim

Daeng Ibrahim, who succeeded his father as territorial chief of Johor in 1825, was the founder of his family's political and material fortunes. Able and intelligent, he spent much of his time in Singapore where he lived comfortably on the revenues from gambier and pepper plantations in Johor established by Chinese who had migrated from Singapore, and mixed freely with European merchants and administrators.

The rulers, 1812–1862

At the time Sir Stamford Raffles established the British settlement in Singapore in 1819, Singapore was the fief of Temenggong Abdul Rahman of Johor, who was willing to allow the British to occupy the island (see 'The British entrepôt of Singapore'). However, without the sanction of Sultan Abdul Rahman of Riau–Johor, Britain would have no legal standing in Singapore.

Raffles found that there had been a succession dispute after Sultan Mahmud passed away in 1812. The elder son, Tengku Hussein Shah, who was away in Pahang when his father died, was not elected; instead, his younger brother Abdul Rahman ascended the throne. Applying the principle of primogeniture, which was at that time applicable in Britain but not in the Malay states, Raffles decided that the British should recognize Hussein as the legitimate ruler. In return, on 6 February 1819 Sultan Hussein signed a treaty allowing the British to occupy Singapore.

The British subsequently neglected Sultan Hussein, and looked to Temenggong Abdul Rahman as the de facto ruler. When Abdul Rahman passed away in 1825, he was succeeded by his second son Temenggong Daeng Ibrahim, who had close relations with the British merchants in Singapore. Daeng Ibrahim opened up Johor to Chinese pepper and gambier cultivators from Singapore, and Johor's ensuing economic success greatly impressed the British administrators of Singapore (see 'The Temenggongs of Johor').

Meanwhile, after the death of Sultan Hussein in 1835, the British did not consider it necessary to acknowledge his son Tengku Ali as the new ruler, though he appealed repeatedly for such recognition. It was not until 1855 that the British relented, but only after Ali had agreed not to interfere in the affairs of Johor, which would continue to come under the Temenggong's administration.

On 10 March 1855, Tengku Ali signed a treaty with Temenggong Ibrahim and the British Resident Councillor of Singapore agreeing to the conditions laid down by the British and was installed as the new sultan of Johor, but he was to have control only over the territory of Muar–Kesang adjacent to Melaka, while the rest of Johor came under the control of Temenggong Ibrahim.

From Temenggong to Maharaja

Temenggong Ibrahim was succeeded in 1862 by his son Abu Bakar, who established even closer ties with the British. On his first visit to Europe in 1866, Abu Bakar was granted an audience by Queen Victoria, met the Prince of Wales and toured England. He became enamoured of Western ways and adopted Western political culture. He felt that the title of Temenggong did not befit his standing and obtained British sanction in 1868 to use the title of Maharaja, which was used by rulers in India.

Johor faced another crisis when Sultan Ali, Abu Bakar's uncle, passed away in 1877. Tengku Alam, Sultan Ali's son, laid claim to the throne. However, as in 1835, the British refused to entertain the claimant's request to be named sultan. By that time, Abu Bakar's stature had grown considerably and some British officials considered him the model ruler to be emulated by other Malay rulers.

JOHOR LINEAGE

CHRONOLOGY OF EVENTS	LINE OF SUCCESSION

CHRONOLOGY OF EVENTS

1812　Death of Sultan Mahmud; succeeded by his younger son Tengku Abdul Rahman

1819　Tengku Hussein (elder son of Sultan Mahmud) declared sultan of Singapore by Stamford Raffles

1825　Death of Temenggong Abdul Rahman; succeeded by his son Temenggong Daeng Ibrahim

1835　Death of Sultan Hussein; his son Tengku Ali denied claim to throne by Britain

1855　Ali recognized by British as sultan of Johor, with control only over Muar–Kesang

1862　Death of Temenggong Daeng Ibrahim; succeeded by his son Abu Bakar

1868　Abu Bakar recognized by the British as Maharaja instead of Temenggong

1877　Death of Sultan Ali; his son Tengku Alam denied claim to throne by Britain

1880　Sir Frederick A. Weld appointed governor of Straits Settlements

1885　Anglo-Johor treaty signed, and Abu Bakar recognized as sultan of Johor

LINE OF SUCCESSION

Sultan Abdul Jalil (r. 1699–1718)
- Sultan Sulaiman (r. 1728–1759)
  - Sultan Abdul Jalil (r. 1759–1760)
    - Sultan Mahmud (r. 1762–1812)
      - Sultan Hussein of Singapore (r. 1819–1835)
        - Sultan Ali (r. 1855–1877)
          - Tengku Alam
      - Sultan Rahman of Lingga (r. 1812–1830)
- Bendahara Tun Abbas (d. c. 1736)
  - Temenggong Abdul Jamal (d. c. 1765)
    - Daeng Kechil
      - Temenggong Abdul Rahman (d. 1825)
        - Temenggong Daeng Ibrahim (r. 1825–1862)
          - Temenggong Abu Bakar (r. 1862–1895) [Maharaja 1868–1885, Sultan after 1885]

Sir Frederick Weld, Governor of the FMS from 1880 to 1887, who was determined to bring all the Malay states under British tutelage.

From Maharaja to Sultan

By the early 1870s, the British experimented with the strategy of getting Abu Bakar involved in trying to solve the disputes in the Malay states. They even toyed with the idea of acknowledging him as the ruler of Johor and some of the adjoining territories.

After Sultan Ali's death, Abu Bakar tried to gain control of Muar–Kesang, with the support of the acting governor, A. E. H. Anson. As Tengku Alam also had a claim to the district, the local chieftains met to elect the new ruler. However, as most at the meeting were supporters of Abu Bakar he was elected and recognized as the overall ruler of Johor.

Alam and his supporters, not satisfied with this decision, had gained the support of W. H. Read, an influential Singapore merchant who had helped to place Raja Abdullah on the Perak throne. In 1879, disturbances broke out between the supporters of the two rivals. Though the Colonial Office felt that Anson had given undue support to Abu Bakar, they helped to restore order to the Maharaja's advantage.

British policy towards the Malay states changed significantly when Sir Frederick A. Weld arrived as the new governor in 1880. He persuaded the Colonial Office to play a more direct role in the affairs of the Malay states. As a result, Maharaja Abu Bakar was discouraged from involving himself too deeply in the affairs of the Malay states which lay adjacent to Johor, such as Negeri Sembilan.

By 1884, Weld also urged the Colonial Office to revise British policy towards Johor on three grounds: maladministration; Abu Bakar's inclination to accept the irresponsible advice of his European lawyers; and the danger of foreign influence.

Weld's suggestion of the appointment of a Resident to Johor was supported by junior officials in the Colonial Office, which was about to appoint a Resident in Pahang. However, Sir Robert Herbert, the Permanent Under-Secretary, and Lord Derby, the Secretary of State for the Colonies, both disagreed. Nevertheless, British intervention seemed likely, and Abu Bakar met Sir Cecil Clementi Smith, the acting governor, who reassured Herbert and Lord Derby about the quality of Abu Bakar's rule.

During his visit to London in May 1885, Abu Bakar was assured Britain would not intervene, but that a new treaty was needed. This December 1885 treaty, negotiated by Abu Bakar, declared relations between him and Queen Victoria were those of alliance and not of suzerainty or dependence, and acknowledged Abu Bakar as the sultan of Johor.

Abu Bakar

Abu Bakar, known as the 'father of modern Johor', was born and brought up in Singapore where his father, Temenggong Daeng Ibrahim, made sure he received an English education. A year after succeeding his father, Abu Bakar built a new capital on the mainland, at Tanjung Puteri (now Johor Bahru). During his long reign, Abu Bakar was able to preserve Johor's independence from the British by giving them no reason to intervene in Johor's affairs. He did this by encouraging economic development and opening up Johor to foreign investment and commerce. He was also instrumental in making Johor the first Malay state in the Peninsula to have a modern civil service and a written constitution (in 1895).

Abu Bakar's charm and grace captivated all. He was popular with the British authorities in Singapore and the Colonial Office. He also made a number of overseas trips, meeting the sovereigns of several European states and people such as the Pope and the Emperor of China.

Painting of Sultan Abu Bakar by Louis Fleishmann, 1892.

Civil wars and British intervention

In the 19th century, civil wars occurred in several Malay states because of the rapidly changing social order which accompanied the expansion in tin mining. Pressure on the Malay rulers to increase production to supply British trading companies in the Straits Settlements resulted in increased Chinese immigration to work the mines. It also greatly increased the revenue of the Malay rulers, resulting in squabbles among royal family members who hoped to succeed to the position of ruler.

The compound at Klang of Tunku Kudin, son-in-law of Sultan Abdul Samad, who was fighting Raja Mahdi for control of the town. Note the cannon in the doorway, and cannonballs against the walls.

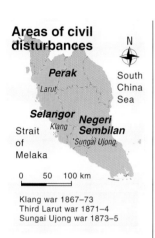

Areas of civil disturbances

Klang war 1867–73
Third Larut war 1871–4
Sungai Ujong war 1873–5

Tin mining

The Dutch monopoly of tin trading in the Malay states came to an end with the 1824 Anglo-Dutch Treaty. With British traders purchasing tin directly from the Malay states, the ruling class began to increase tin production, employing mostly Chinese workers who introduced more efficient technology (see 'Long Jaafar and the Chinese tin miners in Larut'). Territories which saw a significant increase in mining activities were Klang in Selangor, as well as Sungai Ujong and Lukut in Negeri Sembilan.

Even more rapid expansion of tin mining occurred in the 1840s when the Malay ruling class began to grant concessions to merchants in the Straits Settlements to work the mines. Growth was most noticeable in Larut in Perak, although mining activities also expanded in Klang, Sungai Ujong and Lukut, although in Lukut only until the 1860s.

By the mid-19th century, increased production was also due to the demand from the growing tin plate industry in Britain as supplies from the Cornish tin mines were exhausted.

Civil disturbances

The changing economic scene had serious political repercussions on the Malay states. Control over territory increased in importance for chiefs as Straits merchants sought more concessions to work tin. The Malay rulers taxed all tin exports and so greatly augmented their income. Disturbances and civil wars increased because of succession disputes and attempts to gain control of tin-producing districts.

The Klang war of 1867–73 was a contest over Klang between Raja Mahdi of Selangor and Tunku Kudin of Kedah, son-in-law of Sultan Abdul Samad. Both enlisted the aid of Chinese secret societies.

In Larut, the position of Ngah Ibrahim, the Mentri Larut, became untenable after the death of Sultan Ali in 1871. Raja Abdullah, with support from Straits merchants, tried to dislodge Ngah Ibrahim, who was supported by opposing Chinese merchants. This led to the third Larut war.

In Sungai Ujong, disturbances occurred with the succession of a new Dato Kelana in 1873. However, he was ineffective because the Dato Bandar proved to be more influential as he controlled the mines and enjoyed the support of the Chinese.

Civil disturbances had adverse effects on the development of the mining industry, and thus affected the interests of Straits merchants with large investments in the tin mines. The Colonial Office quickly responded to their requests for assistance as the Straits Settlements had become a British crown colony by 1867 and the government was therefore obliged to protect the interests of British subjects.

British intervention

In late 1873, the Colonial Office instructed Sir Andrew Clarke, the new governor, to submit a report on whether it was necessary to appoint British officers to advise the Malay rulers.

Clarke, influenced by Singapore merchants, acted immediately instead of waiting for further instructions. In early 1874, he named Raja Abdullah as sultan of Perak and forced him to sign the Pangkor Treaty (see 'Long Jaafar and the Chinese tin miners in Larut'), which required him to accept a British Resident whose advice had to be followed.

In the course of 1874, Sultan Abdul Samad of Selangor and the Dato Kelana of Sungai Ujong also accepted Residents. In each instance, the British openly supported one faction. In Selangor, Tunku Kudin was confirmed as the Viceroy. In Sungai Ujong, British forces subjugated the Dato Bandar.

British intervention saw the introduction of the Western concept of 'the rule of law' in the Malay states to replace the absolute power of the ruler.

The sequel

Malay society did not immediately adapt well to the new system of government. Disturbances broke out in Perak and Sungai Ujong. In Perak, J. W. W. Birch, the first Resident, was assassinated on 2 November 1875; in Sungai Ujong, war broke out between the British and Yamtuan Antah, who claimed to rule all the districts of Negeri Sembilan. But an attempted uprising in Selangor was aborted. British control over the entire Peninsula was completed only in 1919 when Terengganu accepted a British Adviser.

The Pangkor Treaty, which was signed on 20 January 1874 on Pulau Pangkor, was an attempt by the British authorities in Singapore to end the disputes in Perak both among the Malay chiefs and those between the rival Chinese secret societies. The Treaty recognized Abdullah as sultan of Perak, and provided for the appointment of a British Resident. However, Raja Ismail, Abdullah's rival claimant to the throne, and his chiefs did not sign the Treaty. A major point of dissatisfaction to the chiefs was that the Treaty gave the British officials the right to collect all taxes, which had been the chiefs' major source of income.

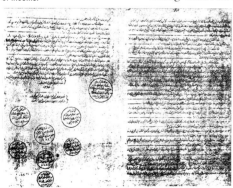

The Perak war

Events in Perak 1875–6

With the benefit of hindsight, it is clear enough that the Malay uprisings in Perak, Selangor and Sungai Ujong in late 1875 were unplanned and uncoordinated responses to British intervention, and so presented no serious threat to British control. But the violent death of J. W. W. Birch, the first Resident of Perak, on 2 November 1875, caused much alarm—and indignation—at the time, leading to overreaction by the colonial regime. Birch had assumed office barely a year before his death and was zealously carrying out his duties, causing much disquiet and restlessness among the Malay chiefs.

In response to requests from Governor Jervois (1875–7), 300 British troops were dispatched from Hong Kong under the command of Major General Colborne. This force, with naval and other contingents, went up the Perak River in boats as far as Belanja. An entire brigade, with artillery, was sent from India, under Brigadier General Ross. This force landed at Larut and advanced overland into the valley at Kuala Kangsar. In early 1876, the British military force in Malaya totalled 2,750, with six small warships in support.

At no stage was there any more than brief resistance by small numbers of Malays. But Ross, exasperated by his inability to win a famous victory, summarily executed a Malay villager, Panjang Meru. He then launched a needless full-scale assault on Kota Lama, but his tactical incompetence led to unnecessary casualties. The war correspondent who accompanied Ross's force later wrote a satirical account entitled 'Needs Explaining'. Meanwhile, Swettenham recruited the services of Raja Mahmud, a Selangor prince and warrior, to support him in the British campaign in Perak. They made a marauding affray up the Kinta valley, but their quarry, ex-Sultan Ismail, had fled to Kedah; he later gave himself up at Penang.

It was not until March 1876 that the British had run their chief opponents to ground, and yet another year before Perak's ruler, Sultan Abdullah, was arrested, deposed and exiled for his complicity in events.

The British force ascending the Perak River towards Belanja. The flotilla of 45 vessels comprised large square boats which carried the guns and provisions.

A view of the encampment at Bandar Bahru from the back of the Residency which Birch had occupied.

The British army camp at Pasir Salak, home of the Maharaja Lela and the place where Birch was killed, on the Perak River.

An attack by British naval ratings on the village of Kota Lama, on the Perak River, in retaliation for the villagers' attack on the followers of Raja Muda Yusuf.

Kemunting
Larut River • Larut Taiping
Matang Bukit
Bukit Gantang
Bukit Berapit Pass
• Kota Lama
Kuala Kangsar
• Sayong

Blanja

Kampong Didap Kampong Kota Pagar
Kampong Pala
Padang Tangala
Bota
Pasir Telor

DINGINGS

Pulau Pangkor Dinding River

Pasir Salak
Scene of Birch's murder

Bandar Baru and Residency

Perak River
Kota River

▬▬ Hills
‒ ‒ ‒ Political boundary
······ Pathway

The controversy

J. W. W Birch, the first British Resident of Perak, who was killed on 2 November 1875.

Sultan Abdullah, who was implicated in the killing of Birch, was removed by the British as the ruler of Perak and in July 1877 was banished to the Seychelles, along with several other Perak chiefs. Abdullah's main rival to the throne, Sultan Ismail, and the latter's loyal supporters, were banished to Johor.

J. W. W. Birch showed intolerant zeal in reforms which abrogated some traditional privileges of the Malay ruler and territorial chiefs of Perak, especially their rights to collect taxes and to retain large numbers of followers under a system of debt-bondage (slavery), which was sociopolitical rather than economic in its effect.

Because the centres of Malay power were scattered and the territorial chiefs totally disunited, the British had been able to intervene in the Malay states and impose the Pangkor Treaty in 1874. Even though the Treaty stated that the British would not interfere in Malay custom and Islam, British pressure to reverse their 'hands-off' policy intensified in 1875. In response to Birch's high-handed actions in stopping the chiefs from collecting taxes—before even a compensatory allowance was decided upon—the chiefs decided to temporarily sink their differences and rivalries. To that extent they shared a resolve, though not a plan, to eliminate the British 'interloper'. In a society in which resort to violence against an opposition was a norm, they had in varying and uncertain degree complicity in the death of Birch, which was instigated by the Maharaja Lela, the territorial chief of Pasir Salak, where Birch's murder occurred. The Maharaja Lela had personal grievances against Birch, including an incident of public humiliation by the Resident,

For this complicity the chiefs suffered execution or exile at the hands of the British regime. However, modern opinion in Malaysia depicts them in its school books as champions of independence. In Kuala Lumpur, Birch Road has been renamed Jalan Maharaja Lela, and the tune which the deposed Sultan Abdullah brought back from his exile in the Seychelles (1877–93) has become the musical accompaniment of the national anthem (*Negara Ku*).

Maharaja Lela

The Pasir Salak Historical Complex, situated on the banks of the Perak River at the site where Birch was killed and fighting between Malay and British troops occurred.

The role of the Maharaja Lela, the chieftain of Pasir Salak who led a group of Malay warriors in the slaying of Birch, needs to be viewed within the context of the Malay feudal structure and the intense factional politics among the Perak Malay chiefs in 1874–5. The Maharaja Lela's involvement in the killing was provoked not only by Birch's tactless manner, and with the question of his allowances, but also by the ambivalent character of Sultan Abdullah, whom the British recognized as the ruler of Perak, and his responsibility in the appointment of Birch as British Resident. The Maharaja Lela distrusted Sultan Abdullah and regarded Sultan Ismail, another claimant to the throne and leader of the Upper Perak faction, as his real ruler.

In response to strong nationalist feelings on the Perak rebellion, the Perak government has built a Historical Complex at Pasir Salak. Here, a group of traditional Malay houses display weapons and other memorabilia from the rebellion. The grave of Maharaja Lela bears a plaque extolling him for his deeds in fighting against colonialism. A monument in memory of Birch and his gravesite, erected by the British, is nearby.

The new sultanate of Pahang

Dutch influence in Pahang, which had declined in 1795, came to an end in 1824 with the signing of the Anglo-Dutch Treaty, thus paving the way for the Bendahara of Pahang to consolidate his position. This process received a setback with the Pahang civil war of 1857–63, and it was not until 1884 that Bendahara Ahmad was declared sultan. However, the continuation of domestic turmoil eventually led to the appointment of a British Resident in 1888.

Bendahara Ali

In Pahang, 1801–2 was marked by a power struggle among the four sons of Bendahara Abdul Majid. Court intrigues led to the death of the Bendahara and two sons. The title of Bendahara passed to Tun Kuris, the third son, in 1803 and later to his son Tun Ali (1806–56). The power of the new Bendahara became evident when Tun Ali was allowed to retain control of Pahang as a fief when Sultan Mahmud Shah of Riau–Lingga appointed Temenggong Abdul Rahman to administer Johor and Singapore.

After Sultan Mahmud Shah's death in 1812, a succession dispute erupted because Tengku Abdul Rahman was appointed as sultan prior to the return of the heir apparent, Tengku Hussein, from Pahang. In 1819, Temenggong Abdul Rahman permitted Stamford Raffles to establish a trading post at Singapore (see 'The British entrepôt of Singapore'). However, Raffles recognized Hussein as the sultan of Singapore. The Anglo-Dutch Treaty of 1824 prevented Sultan Abdul Rahman from exercising his control in the Malay Peninsula and also split the Johor–Pahang–Riau–Lingga empire.

Bendahara Ali was one of the earliest rulers to adjust to the new reality of independence. His popularity with his subjects and tactful relationship with his household members enhanced his reputation and position, but this did not last long.

Hugh Clifford, who was appointed the first British Agent to Pahang by his uncle, Governor Sir Frederick Weld, in 1887. Clifford tried unsuccessfully to negotiate a treaty with Sultan Ahmad.

Pahang civil war

After the death of Bendahara Ali in 1856, a civil war between his two sons, Wan Mutahir and Wan Ahmad, divided Pahang into factions. The dissension centred around a will made by Bendahara Ali giving control over the Kuantan and Endau rivers to Wan Ahmad. Wan Mutahir, on ascending the throne in 1857, professed ignorance of this clause. Wan Ahmad

decided to retaliate as he also felt he had a better claim to the throne because his mother was the late Bendahara's legitimate wife, whereas Wan Mutahir's mother was a concubine. He gained the support of the former Sultan Mahmud of Lingga and Sultan Baginda Omar of Terengganu; Wan Mutahir was supported by Temenggong Daeng Ibrahim of Johor.

Wan Ahmad attacked Pahang in November 1857 using Kemaman as his base. The attack was not successful, but Wan Ahmad remained determined to overthrow his brother. Eventually, the tyranny and injustice caused by Wan Mutahir forced the people to switch their loyalty to Wan Ahmad who, with the support of men from the Raub district and also the Pahang chiefs, defeated Wan Mutahir, who fled and died at Kuala Sedili in May 1863.

Bendahara Ahmad

The victorious Wan Ahmad was installed as Bendahara Sewa Raja on 10 June 1863. By 1880, the Bendahara had started to lose his grip over the kingdom. The civil war of 1856–63 had resulted in a rise in dissension among members of the ruling class and the various territorial chiefs, who held the Bendahara responsible for their loss in prestige and autonomy. Bendahara Ahmad's quarrels with his chiefs brought about a power struggle.

A late 19th-century sketch of Pekan, the royal capital of the state of Pahang, which was originally published in *The Graphic*.

Sultan Ahmad of Pahang and his retinue, photographed in traditional dress in front of the royal palace at Pekan in 1885. Wan Ahmad, who ruled Pahang as Bendahara from 1863 until 1884, and as sultan until his death in 1914, was one of the more energetic and aristocratic of the Malay rulers who displayed his military skills during the uprising of the 1890s. According to Hugh Clifford, the British Resident', 'the Pahang Malay thinks chiefly of deeds of arms ... and is, above all things, manly and reckless.... The Pahang boy grows up amid talk of war, which makes him long to be a man that he may use his weapons.'

Wan Ahmad still aspired to become sultan. On his 1881 visit to Singapore, he had seen that the institution of the sultanate signified independence and sovereignty. He was further influenced by Maharaja Abu Bakar of Johor. In December 1884, the Bendahara was formally proclaimed sultan by his chiefs. However, domestic turmoil continued.

The territorial chiefs resented their loss in revenue since it now went to Pekan, the state capital. Members of the royal household also made attempts to gain wider territorial authority and autonomy. The sultan's reign was further complicated by fresh disputes with his half-brother Wan Mansur, who challenged the decision to deny his appointment as heir to the throne and be deprived of his allowances. Wan Mansur turned to Johor for aid; when this was denied, he sought British help to reinstate himself.

The British refused to interfere as they had no treaty rights. Wan Mansur decided to return to Pahang only on Sultan Ahmad's invitation. As the sultan feared British intervention because of the state's internal disputes, he began to welcome foreign investors. This caused his relationship with his subjects to deteriorate further. The establishment of the Pahang Company in 1883, the Penjum Company in 1884 and the Tanum Company in 1886 fuelled greater resentment amongst his chiefs.

British intervention

Sultan Ahmad sought British aid to persuade Wan Mansur to return to Pahang, resulting in an agreement which again recognized Wan Mansur as the heir to the throne, and he returned to Pahang on 18 March 1887 with Hugh Clifford, who unsuccessfully tried to negotiate a treaty with Sultan Ahmad. However, Sultan Abu Bakar of Johor and William Fraser, manager of the Pahang Company, influenced Sultan Ahmad to change his stand. His quarrels with the British over the wording of the agreement delayed the signing until 8 October 1887, when the sultan accepted a British Agent.

The administration was deteriorating: oppression was rife, and murders and pilfering were rampant. The sultan cancelled concessions, forcing holders to seek British aid. This was to the Colonial Office's advantage as under the 1887 treaty the Residential System could be installed if the Agent's position was insecure, or if any British subject was murdered.

After two British subjects, Su Kim and Go Hui, were murdered in early 1888, a letter from the governor, Sir Cecil Clementi Smith, obliged Sultan Ahmad to seek the advice of the Johor sultan and concede to British demands. He finally did this by requesting the services of a Resident on 24 August 1888. This act signified the end of the sultan's supremacy over Pahang; the centre of political power began to move from the sultan to the British government. The arrival of the first Resident, J. P. Rodger, proved to be a sad reminder of the absolute power which Sultan Ahmad had once held.

European mining companies in Pahang in the 1880s

- Gold-mining areas
- Tin-mining areas
- ▲ Pahang Corporation Ltd, Sungai Lembing
- Malay Peninsular (Pahang) Prospecting Co., Selinsing
- ● Penjom and Sungai Dua Semantan Co., Penjom

Sungai Jelai · Sungai Tembeling · Sungai Pahang · Sungai Kuantan · Sungai Lepar · Sungai Semantan · Sungai Pahang

N

0   50 km

Labourers building an embankment at one of the Pahang Company's mines. Both tin and gold were mined by the Company. *INSET*: William Fraser, the founder of the Pahang Company which played an important role in the economic development of the state.

The sultanate of Selangor

The Malay state of Selangor was established in 1766 with the enthronement of Sultan Salehuddin, previously the chief of the local Bugis coastal settlements. In 1782, he was succeeded by Sultan Ibrahim (r. 1782–1826), a strong ruler who repelled external threats. Ibrahim promoted the production of tin as the main export of the state. After his death, however, Selangor slowly subsided into near anarchy, ending with an open civil war (1867–73), which in turn led to British intervention and control in 1874. Selangor was one of the four states which formed the Federated Malay States (FMS) in 1896.

A view of the town of Klang in the 1870s. Klang was the capital of Selangor until 1880 when the capital was moved to Kuala Lumpur.

Sultan Ibrahim

Until 1766, the Bugis settlements on the Selangor coast were an outpost of Bugis leaders at the capital of Riau–Johor. When Ibrahim became sultan in 1782, Selangor was embroiled in the Bugis–Dutch struggle. Near the end of his reign, Ibrahim escaped the threat of a Siamese invasion by his own boldness and British support. Later, he expanded tin mining for export to the Straits Settlements and encouraged Sumatran Malays to settle along the rivers. Ibrahim's efforts to secure a protective alliance with Britain did not succeed, but its measures to stabilize the situation and promote trade were helpful to him. His death in 1826 deprived Selangor of its only strong ruler in the precolonial period.

Sultan Mohamed

Sultan Mohamed (r. 1826–57) was beset by rivalry in the ruling dynasty. At the end of his reign, the power behind the throne was Raja Jumaat, a Bugis from Riau, who made Lukut one of the largest tin-producing districts in the Malay Peninsula. In this period, Chinese arrived to work in the mines, leading to expanded output but also savage quarrels among the Chinese secret societies.

Sultan Abdul Samad

When Mohamed died in 1857, Jumaat prevented his young son from becoming sultan, as had been planned, and secured the throne for Abdul Samad (r. 1857–98), a nephew and son-in-law of the late ruler. Jumaat's death in 1864 left Sultan Abdul Samad in a quandary from which he hoped to escape by delegating to his son-in-law, Tunku Kudin of Kedah, vague powers as a quasi-'viceroy'. In 1867, a struggle for Klang and its export revenues erupted. Tunku Kudin eventually drove out Raja Mahdi, a grandson of Sultan Mohamed, with ambitions to succeed him. Two coalitions of Bugis aristocrats, Sumatran fighting captains and Chinese headmen, with their respective bands of followers, were led by Kudin and Mahdi. In 1872, Mahdi seemed victorious but Kudin, with the aid of levies from Pahang, secured a precarious victory in 1873. Kudin had also benefited from financial aid and official support from the Straits Settlements.

British intervention

In February 1874, Governor Sir Andrew Clarke went to the royal capital of Bandar Langat for the declared purpose of punishing an act of piracy. While there, he had no difficulty in persuading Sultan Abdul Samad to accept a British Resident to advise and act with Tunku Kudin at Klang to maintain order, which was threatened by a possible return from exile of Raja Mahdi.

In the final quarter of the 19th century, British control of Selangor was extended to the interior districts, and in 1880 the capital was moved from Klang to Kuala Lumpur. The sultan gave his full support to the construction of a railway line from Klang to Kuala Lumpur (completed in 1886). He insisted on remaining in his rural retreat at Jugra (Kuala Langat), which he left only very occasionally.

Sultan Abdul Samad's absorbing interest was peasant agriculture, which he sometimes subsidized. Brisk executives such as Frank Swettenham, who was Resident of Selangor in 1882–9, dismissed him as a *roi fainéant* (a do-nothing king). Modern research has shown the importance of a traditional Malay ruler as the ultimate source of authority for government left in the hands of others. A ruler reigned, but he was not expected to govern, though some energetic individuals might choose to do so.

Governor Weld cutting the first sod at Kuala Lumpur in July 1883 to mark the beginning of the construction of the railway line to Klang. This illustration appeared in *The Graphic* on 3 November 1883.

Selangor

N

Strait
of
Melaka

Selangor

South
China
Sea

10   50   100 km

The royal palaces

The *istana* of Sultan Abdul Samad at Bandar Langat, where he lived until 1872, when he moved to Jugra, four miles away.

ABOVE: Sultan Abdul Samad (r. 1857–98) with his retainers outside his *istana* at Jugra in Kuala Langat, c. 1886. Sulaiman, his successor (grandson) is standing at his left.

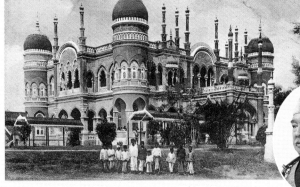

LEFT: Istana Mahkota, a palace of a unique design built in Klang for Sultan Sulaiman, was completed around 1902.

INSET: Sultan Sulaiman (r. 1898–1938).

An account written by J. H. M. Robson, editor of the *Malay Mail*, and published in *The Selangor Journal* in 1892 of the reception at the Jugra *istana* of Sultan Abdul Samad of an important guest: 'on landing [he] is met by the Sultan's two surviving sons, Rajas Kahar and Nosah, ... about half way there he will be met by the Raja Muda, dressed in European fashion but with the sarong added ... with 40 or 50 followers all dressed in their best.... At the Istana gateway stands H. H. the Sultan, dressed in true Malay style, in silk and cloth of gold, and wearing his order of St. Michael and St. George, and surrounded by his chiefs carrying the gold kris, the yellow umbrella and gold sireh-boxes, all part of his insignia, conspicuous amongst which is the sword presented to him by Her Majesty. And together with him are standing perhaps a couple of hundred followers ready to receive the visitor.'

Sultan Sulaiman

When Sultan Abdul Samad died in 1898, at the age of 92, he was succeeded by his grandson Sulaiman, who also had a very long reign (1898–1938). Sultan Sulaiman was a quiet, conscientious figure, whose peace was troubled by financial and family problems. The most acute of these was the dispute during the 1930s over the choice of a designated successor (Raja Muda). The ruler's eldest son was judged to be unsuitable for the position, and the choice between two other sons proved contentious.

Governing bodies

The Selangor State Council, the legislative body of the state which was established in 1877, was the forum for discussion of policy. The ruler or his deputy was the president of the council. However, after Selangor joined the Federated Malay States in 1896, a strong federal bureaucracy soon deprived the state government, and its ruler, of an effective role in policy making, despite dutiful disclaimers to the contrary. The FMS Federal Council, established in 1909, included the rulers of the four member states (until 1927), but they rarely spoke at its meetings. Sultan Sulaiman's occasional interventions expressed his interest in the encouragement of rice cultivation and the safeguarding of Malay landholding.

The state's economy

By the 20th century, Selangor, like the other FMS states, comprised two elements. The Malay community, which included a high proportion of immigrant settlers, had taken to rubber growing as the mainstay of its economy despite official efforts to encourage rice cultivation. The ruler had a voice in the choice of *mukim penghulu* (subdistrict headmen) and kadi and other Islamic officials, who were an important influence in the community.

In parallel with this semi-traditional way of life, which was changing under the impact of education, was a capitalist economy. Rubber plantations and tin mines were the leading feature in this economy. Selangor had about 160 000 hectares of land planted with rubber (see 'The rubber industry and Indian immigration'), and tin mines had been developed at several locations in the state (see 'Chinese immigration and tin mining'). The opening of tin mines at Ampang had led to the establishment of the town of Kuala Lumpur. Commercial firms, large and small, were owned and staffed by Europeans and Chinese (and some Indians) respectively.

In the longer historical perspective, the creation and development of the sultanate of Selangor in the early days were the achievements of the founding Bugis dynasty. It also provided the constitutional framework which kept a Malay community, much divided in its cultural origins, at peace with the intrusive foreign elements, both European and Asian.

Kuala Lumpur in 1909, showing Chinese shophouses, a bullock cart and rickshaws, with the Supreme Court building in the background. Kuala Lumpur had developed rapidly since becoming the capital of Selangor in 1880.

The Negeri Sembilan confederacy

In 1773, Raja Melewar from Sumatra became the paramount ruler, though with very limited powers, of a number of small districts in the Malay Peninsula occupied by Sumatran immigrants. These settlers were from Minangkabau, whose social system (adat perpatih) was based on matrilineal descent. In the mid-19th century, the confederacy disintegrated and the ensuing disorder led to British intervention in 1874. Thereafter, a slow process of reunification led to the restoration of the Yamtuan as paramount ruler of the confederacy in 1898.

The Miningkabau states behind Melaka

The confederacy of Negeri Sembilan, which means 'nine states', is arranged in the shape of a *mandala* (circle). The diagram (inset) shows the organization of the confederacy. In the centre of the circle is Sri Menanti, the seat of the Yamtuan (ruler), whose power radiates across the whole confederacy. Four regions known as *serambi* (verandas) encircle this hub, while another four larger districts headed by the Undang form the outer rim of the circle. The mandala structure of government was created by the Srivijaya empire based on the purely symbolic Indian mandala.

Malay stockades such as this were built along the rivers of Negeri Sembilan by the rulers to control the river traffic in their territory, particularly the growing trade in tin from the mines in Sungai Ujong. The stockades, made of logs arranged several feet thick, were armed with cannons.

TOP: Interior view of a stockade.

A group photograph of Negeri Sembilan nobility, probably taken at the first Malay Durbar, held at Kuala Kangsar in 1897. The seated figures are likely to be have been the four Undang and the Regent of Sungai Ujong (whose Undang was still a youth).

The beginning

The arrival in present-day Negeri Sembilan of Minangkabau settlers from Sumatra began in the 17th century and had spread to most of the state by the end of the 18th century. However, until 1773 the chiefs (Undang) who ruled the separate districts (*luak*) had no political links uniting them. Raja Melewar, who claimed descent from the Minangkabau ruling house, was given the title of Yang di-Pertuan Besar (abbreviated to Yamtuan). His role was to provide a modicum of political and military leadership, as the area was under threat from the coastal Bugis. Some districts on the fringe of the state, notably Naning in Melaka, did not join the new grouping.

The Undang

Raja Melewar appears to have limited himself to regulating the formalities of his dealings with the chiefs. The four most powerful of these chiefs ruled Sungai Ujong, Rembau, Jelebu and Johol, with the title of Undang ('Lawgiver'). They had the right, as an electoral college, to choose a successor to the Yamtuan. Until the 1830s, a sequence of Sumatran princes, ostensibly from Minangkabau, filled these offices. They married wives from the local ruling families, and thus begot heirs who aspired to status and traditional office.

Offshoots of the royal family, whose seat was at Sri Menanti, established themselves in the districts of Rembau and in Jelebu, claiming the title of Yamtuan Muda (heir apparent). Inevitably, there were disputes between rival claimants. Within the local districts, succession to office (on a matrilineal basis) was no less contentious.

Yamtuan Radin was the first local prince to succeed his father, but he was also the last in the precolonial period to enjoy even nominal authority throughout the whole state. Radin's death, in 1861, was followed by a turbulent decade. By 1872, the warlike and quarrelsome Tunku Antah, the son of Radin, had ousted his rivals but had lost the formal recognition, as paramount ruler, of three of the four Undang in the confederacy. Thus, his authority was in effect limited to those small states (*tanah mengandong*) adjacent to Sri Menanti, with grudging acceptance by the Undang of Johol.

In Rembau, there was a dispute over succession to the office of Undang, and the pretender to the office of Yamtuan Muda had been driven out to find an abode in nearby Tampin, which at that time was almost uninhabited. The ruling chiefs of Rembau and Sungai Ujong disputed the collection of taxes on tin passing down the Linggi River, and within Sungai Ujong, the Undang was at logger-heads with the Dato' Shahbandar, who was a mining magnate. In Jelebu, also, the Yamtuan Muda's activities had destabilized the local regime.

British intervention

These episodes on the borders of Melaka were largely responsible for British intervention in Sungai Ujong in 1874. Yamtuan Antah rashly became involved in these troubles, and was driven into a brief exile, from which he returned to the narrow confines of his Sri Menanti fief.

For a decade from the mid-1870s, British intervention ousted the ineffectual Maharaja Abu Bakar of Johor as the local peacekeeper and extended colonial control throughout Negeri Sembilan, but did not reunite it (see 'British mediation and the new sultanate in Johor'). British Residents at Seremban and Kuala Pilah divided Sungai Ujong (and, from 1883, Jelebu) from 'Old Negeri Sembilan' in the interior.

Martin Lister, who became Resident at Kuala Pilah in 1887, showed sympathy and skill in persuading the local magnates to end their mutual hostility and join a state council, which was presided over by the Yamtuan. This was a non-Malay conclave which did not restore to the Yamtuan his lost position as paramount ruler.

Yamtuan Muhammad

The ruler was now Yamtuan Muhammad (r. 1887–1933), who had succeeded his father, Yamtuan Antah, without any formal election to his office. British officials found that he was very intelligent and shrewd, combined with politeness and tact. The Undang, and also the minor chiefs, were slowly and reluctantly persuaded to a restoration of the confederacy, with Yamtuan Muhammad at its head.

This process of adjustment, with various express reservations, was completed in 1898. A few years previously, the administrative structure had been unified, with a single Resident (Lister) stationed at Seremban, with responsibility for the whole state. In making treaties, such as that of 1896 to form the Federated Malay States (FMS), the Yamtuan was joined by the Undang and the Tunku Besar Tampin as joint signatories.

Confederacy government

Although some tin was produced, the basis of the state's economy was agriculture. Hence the collection of the detested quit rent from peasant owners, as the registered owners of their smallholdings, cut across the traditional right to use land, usually vested in the women, which was subject to the authority of tribal chiefs known as *lembaga*.

Lister tried, though with little success, to use the traditional tribal chiefs and heads of families as the intermediaries in these matters. However, on Lister's untimely death (at the age of 40) in 1897, his successor, Ernest Birch, introduced a system which, as in other states, divided a district

ABOVE: Istana Sri Menanti, the four-storey timber palace built in 1902–8 at Sri Menanti, the royal capital of Negeri Sembilan, for Tuanku Muhammad Shah, the Yamtuan of Negeri Sembilan. Designed by two local carpenters, the palace was built in the traditional Malay manner, without the use of nails.

RIGHT: Tuanku Abdul Rahman, a son of Tuanku Muhammad, who succeeded his father as Yamtuan of Negeri Sembilan in 1933. He became the first Yang di-Pertuan Agong of Malaysia in 1957.

Tuanku Muhammad with two of his bodyguards in a photograph taken at the second Malay Durbar, held in Kuala Lumpur in 1903.

into subdistricts (*mukim*) each under a headman (*penghulu*) appointed by the government, assisted by village headmen (*ketua kampung*). This system, and the conflict between Islamic tradition and the matrilineal *adat perpatih*, deprived the lembaga of any real authority, although the inheritance of land continued under the customary rules.

The Yamtuan was not directly affected by these changes, since he had no traditional power to act within the districts of the confederacy. The royal dynasty of Negeri Sembilan followed a patrilineal system of descent, but the Undang still had the right to choose his successor. In 1933, they chose a son of Yamtuan Muhammad, Tuanku Abdul Rahman, to succeed him. With the formation of the Federation of Malaya in 1957, Abdul Rahman was elected as the first Yang di-Pertuan Agong (king).

During the 20th century, the prestige of the Yamtuan tended to grow, but the Undang, with the support of the colonial regime, still insisted that the limits set by the settlement of 1898 be respected. In 1909, Yamtuan Muhammad failed in his attempt to assume the title of sultan, with its connotation of absolute power. However, a triennial ceremony of formal obeisance (*menghadap*) by the Undang to the Yamtuan is a continuing symbol of their respective status.

Martin Lister, the first British Resident of Negeri Sembilan (1895–7).

Guide to traditional structure

The traditional structure of the Negeri Sembilan administration was a hierarchical one, with officials at each level being elected by those in the level below.

Yamtuan (ruler)

↑

Undang (heads of major *luak* (districts)) and *Penghulu* (heads of minor districts); the Undang were the electoral college which chose the Yamtuan

↑

Lembaga (heads of *suku* (clans))

↑

Buapak (chiefs of *perut* (subclans))

↑

Orang besar (officials of the Undang and the Lembaga)

↑

Tua (head of family)

↑

Anak buah (general population)

Some participants of the second Malay Durbar, Kuala Lumpur, 1903. Seated, middle row, from left to right: H. C. Belfield (Resident of Selangor), J. P. Rodger (Resident of Perak), Sir William Treacher (Resident-General of the Federated Malay States), Sultan Sulaiman of Selangor, Sultan Idris of Perak, Sir Frank Swettenham (Governor–High Commissioner), Sultan Ahmad of Pahang, Tuanku Muhammad, Yang di-Pertuan Besar of Negeri Sembilan, and W. Egerton (Resident of Negeri Sembilan).

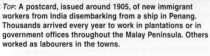

The Hongkong and Shanghai Bank building in Singapore. The bank, which was established in Hong Kong in 1865, opened a branch in Singapore in 1877 and in the same year began to issue banknotes for the Straits Settlements. Branches were later opened in the Malay Peninsula.

TOP: A postcard, issued around 1905, of new immigrant workers from India disembarking from a ship in Penang. Thousands arrived every year to work in plantations or in government offices throughout the Malay Peninsula. Others worked as labourers in the towns.

ABOVE: A 1907 photograph of an opencast tin mine, showing the large numbers of Chinese workers needed to operate such mines. Although there was a continual influx of new workers, there were never enough. Dredges were later introduced by European mine owners to reduce the size of the workforce.

LEFT: Opium addiction had become a widespread problem by the early 20th century, particularly among the Chinese tin miners. It was one of the few comforts which were available to ease their hard life, and could easily be obtained on credit from Chinese revenue farmers (who often also held monopolies on gambling and prostitution).

An early 20th-century postcard showing Weld Quay in Penang lined with substantial buildings housing government offices. The wharves served the busy shipping traffic which brought goods and new immigrants from overseas and sent processed tin and rubber to Europe, as well as pilgrims to Mecca. It was also a busy port for local shipping along the Strait of Melaka.

A portrait by John Singer Sargent of Sir Frank Swettenham, who rose from a civil service cadet to Governor.

Banknotes issued by the Hongkong and Shanghai Banking Corporation. Each banknote was individually dated and signed by the bank's manager. The bank was given the privilege of issuing banknotes as the shortage of foreign coins was hindering trade.

THE BEGINNING OF COLONIAL RULE

In the Malay states, colonial rule began with the rulers of Perak, Selangor and Sungai Ujong (part of Negeri Sembilan) accepting British Residents to advise them in all matters except Islam and Malay custom. Later, a Resident was also appointed in Pahang, and the other districts of Negeri Sembilan were joined with Sungai Ujong into a new confederacy. However, in reality the Residents ruled, while the rulers advised. It was an unequal partnership based on British military might and Malay political survival, on compromise and consultation. The Residential System introduced major administrative changes. To formalize the process of consultation, each state set up a state council composed of Malay officials and representatives of the Chinese community. Although the ruler presided, the Resident set the agenda and directed the proceedings. Nevertheless, revenue increased and the surplus was used for infrastructure such as roads and railways.

The Chinese communities in the various states contributed substantial amounts of capital and taxes to the government, largely through working the tin mines and as tax collectors. Tin mines were initially leased from Malay owners by Chinese entrepreneurs, who later bought them. Malay rulers also benefited from Chinese businessmen to whom they issued revenue farming licences for monopolies on commodity exports or imports—rice, tin, birds' nests, opium—or services, such as ferries and gambling dens. The Residents encouraged the large-scale immigration of Chinese labourers to develop the newly discovered tin fields.

Colonial rule had an adverse effect on Malay economic life. Taxes were imposed on a wide variety of goods, including jungle produce and cash crops such as pepper and coconuts. The new land codes were based on the premise that the ruler owned all the land in his state, effectively giving the government ownership over all land. Land titles were granted to check the Malay practice of moving from place to place. They were encouraged to settle down and plant crops on a piece of land that would become family property. Unlike in precolonial Malaya, land became a commodity which could be mortgaged or sold. This contributed to Malay rural indebtedness and the dispossession of smallholders.

In the late 19th century, Western companies ventured into tin mining and commercial agriculture, gradually breaking Chinese monopolies. They later began shipping, insurance and financial activities. Their growth was facilitated by the formation, in 1896, of the Federated Malay States (FMS), which comprised Negeri Sembilan, Selangor, Perak and Pahang. The federation aimed at making these four states financially self-sustaining so as not to be a burden on Britain. It was hoped that administrative services could be centralized, thus increasing efficiency and saving costs. The federal system became the basis for the present system of government in Malaysia.

Malay vegetable and fruit farmers marketing their produce in a town. The Malays were granted land titles in the hope they would stop moving from place to place.

Sultans and Residents

In 1874, the rulers of Perak, Selangor and Sungai Ujong (part of Negeri Sembilan) each agreed to accept a British Resident, and to seek and act upon his advice in all questions except those touching Malay religion and custom. By 1889, the remainder of Negeri Sembilan (literally, 'nine states') and also Pahang were subject to the same regime. In practice, the advisers ruled, in the executive sense, and the Malay rulers advised them in an unequal partnership which achieved substantial economic progress.

Introduction of Residents

The Malay rulers entered into what became known as the Residential System, partly to strengthen their own position and partly under pressure from the Straits Settlements, where official and commercial opinion was disturbed at the instability of an important economic hinterland. The rulers had

IMPLEMENTATION OF THE RESIDENTIAL SYSTEM			
STATE	YEAR	FIRST RESIDENT	MALAY RULER
Perak	1874	J. W. W. Birch	Sultan Abdullah
Selangor	1874	J. G. Davidson	Sultan Abdul Samad
Sungai Ujong	1874	P. J. Murray	Klana Syed Aman
Negeri Sembilan	1887	Martin Lister	Yamtuan Muhammad
Pahang	1888	J. P. Rodger	Sultan Ahmad

definite expectations—they were looking merely for better management of their state's revenue. The Pangkor Treaty of 1874 (see 'Long Jaafar and the tin miners in Larut'), signed by Sultan Abdullah of Perak, became the model for all four states, providing for the collection and control of all revenue and the general administration of the state to be 'regulated' by the advice of the Resident. It was the British intention that the Residents were to be advisers and no more. No one had a precise idea of the extent of 'Malay customs' in which the Resident might not interfere, but any reform of a traditional monarchy was bound to alter its customs.

The Residents, with the Governor's support, argued that before 1874 royal authority had broken down and they were justified in rebuilding the administrative system to make an 'enlightened' state government. Only they, by executive action in the ruler's name, could achieve this desirable result.

There was some Malay resistance initially, such as the Perak war and other minor conflicts in 1875–6 and the Pahang rising of 1892–4. British reaction was an excessive, show of force which cowed the insurgents, who were mostly Malay chiefs aggrieved at their loss of privilege and power. The attitude of the Malay rulers to the conflict was distinctly ambivalent. In the aftermath, the Residents altered their policy to make changes at a slower pace and to conciliate Malay rulers and the ruling class.

The Residential System

It became normal practice for the Resident to consult the ruler before important decisions were made. To formalize and widen the process of consultation, state councils were set up in Perak and Selangor in 1877, and in other states later. The ruler usually presided at the council meetings, held about six times a year. The Resident sat at his elbow, framed the agenda and opened the discussion on each of the items. The other members of the council were several Malay notables selected by the Resident as likely to be amenable to his proposals, and one or two leaders of the Chinese community, whose advice on mining matters, taxation and authority with their own people was useful.

Regular meetings between the ruler and the Resident in privacy at the *istana* (palace) were much more useful as both men could speak frankly. As in pre-colonial times, the ruler had Malay confidants who gave him information which the Resident might not have. The latter valued royal support in

Reciprocal visits

After British intervention from 1874 and the appointment of Residents to Malay states, the sultans began to reciprocate the visits of the Governor and other British officials from Singapore to their states by travelling to Singapore accompanied by their Resident and a large entourage of followers.

1. A visit to Batak Rabit on the Perak River in 1874 by Sultan Abdullah of Perak and two Straits Settlements officials, J. W. W. Birch and Frank Swettenham (standing), on a semi-official visit to Perak and Selangor. Birch was appointed as first Resident of Perak later in the same year and murdered in 1875. Sultan Abdullah was later exiled to the Seychelles for his role in the plot.

2. Group photograph taken outside Government House, Singapore, on the occasion of a visit of Sultan Idris of Perak (r. 1887–1916) (seated, second from right). On the sultan's right is Hugh Low, Resident of Perak 1877–89, and seated in the centre is Sir Frederick A. Weld, Governor of the Straits Settlements 1880–7.

3. A visit to the opencast tin mine at Kamunting belonging to Ng Boo Bee by Sir Frank Swettenham (centre) on a visit to Perak in his role as Governor–High Commissioner 1900–3.

A model of the Residential System

The first appointment of a British Resident in the Malay states was that of J. W. W. Birch in Perak in 1874. After the brutal murder of Birch in 1875 (see 'Civil wars and British intervention'), J. G. Davidson served for two years, followed by Hugh Low. During Low's 12-year term as Resident (1877–89), he was able to develop an appropriate system of government together with the ruler (Sultan Yusuf and, later, Sultan Idris) and the Malay nobility of the state. His financially prudent management and efficient administrative methods became a model for the Residents of the other Malay states to emulate.

1. Sultan Idris of Perak (r. 1887–1916) (left) pictured with Sir Hugh Low (seated, right) during Low's term as Resident of Perak 1877–89.

2. Sir Hugh Low's Residency in Kuala Kangsar, built in 1876 on the site of Che Mida's house, where British officials pursuing the killers of J. W. W. Birch had stayed. Isabella Bird wrote a vivid account of her visit to this house, including dining with Low's pet apes.

3. Members of the Perak State Council c. 1907, with Sultan Idris in the centre. E. W. Birch, Perak Resident 1904–10 (son of J. W. W. Birch), is at the sultan's left, and at the centre top is Raja Chulan, son of the former ruler, Sultan Abdullah.

4. Istana Negara, Kuala Kangsar, Perak, completed in 1895, was the venue for the first Malay Durbar in 1897. The palace, the inspiration of Sultan Idris, was designed by John Craig Wilson of the Public Works Department. It was demolished in 1930 and replaced by the current Istana Iskandariah.

arguing a case with his superiors in Singapore. Occasionally the Governor visited each state and was received with much ceremony, and toured part of the state. The rulers soon began to make visits to Singapore amid similar pomp and circumstance.

Apart from the Resident, there were a few other European officials in each state, including specialists for police, public works and medical duties. As state revenue grew, so did the number of officials, but up to the mid-1880s much of the local administration was in the hands of Malay aristocrats, with the title of 'Malay magistrate'. Their duties were more vague and more advisory suggested by the title. Large villages were in the charge of *penghulu* (headmen), appointed by the ruler. They were usually prominent members of the community.

By these means the Residential System evolved a rudimentary code of law enforced by local courts, and a small police force working with the penghulu to maintain law and order. A system of recording land ownership was begun and an effective tax collection system devised. Expenditure of state funds was controlled on the basis of annual budgets. Tax collection, including the yield from monopolies, was delegated to local Chinese capitalists as tax farmers (see 'Revenue farming'). With some difficulty Malay peasant cultivators were persuaded to accept a registered title to their land, and paid quit rent (land tax) assessed on their holdings.

After a shaky start in the late 1870s, public revenue increased rapidly in the 1880s, partly because of a sharp rise in the world price of tin. As tax revenue increased above the expenditure on basic government services, the surplus funds were applied in building infrastructure such as roads and railways. While this development provided communications to the tin mines, it also opened much new land for settlement, mainly for Malay immigrants from Sumatra.

Excluded from so much else, the rulers gave more importance to religious affairs. State religious officials were appointed, and were paid from public funds. The rulers also had a special allowance for donations for welfare.

Cecil Wray, Resident of Pahang in the early 20th century.

Centralization

The essence of the Residential System was contact and discussion between sultan and Resident; the latter was deferential and valued what the ruler had to say, even in those infrequent cases where objections were raised. As a result, each state had its own policies, which often differed slightly from those of other states. The formation of the Federated Malay States (FMS) in 1896 was intended to harmonize policy and practice throughout Perak, Selangor, Negeri Sembilan, and Pahang (see 'Formation of the Federated Malay States').

The unfortunate result was too much federal power. That and the increasingly technical aspects of government opened a gap between sultan and Resident. The system continued until World War II, but even in 1895 it was obvious that it was losing much of its hold, and the Malay ruler's influence over his own state was in decline.

The sultans of the Federated Malay States were allocated funds for religious matters, such as donations to funds for the buildings of mosques such as Masjid Jamek in Kuala Lumpur (then the capital of Selangor).

Chinese immigration and tin mining

Opencast tin mining was a very labour-intensive industry in which most of the workers were newly arrived Chinese immigrants. These coolies could be obtained and controlled most easily by the Chinese mining entrepreneurs which gave them, for a time, supremacy over the industry. However, this domination passed to Western companies from the mid-1910s when mechanization of the industry began. Also, stricter control over mining matters by the colonial government, including the banning of Chinese secret societies and the truck system, and the end of revenue farming licences, weakened Chinese control of the industry.

Indentured Chinese coolies

Early Chinese labourers, recruited by brokers who paid for their fares, were sold to Chinese mine owners to whom they were contracted until their debts had been redeemed. Because of the high demand, prices paid for them usually far exceeded the cost of their fares. Due to this system, which prevailed in the Larut and Selangor mines during the mid-19th century, and the widespread habit of opium smoking—opium was often provided in lieu of wages—many workers were tied to their employers for extended periods. By the time the Kinta mines were opened in the 1880s, however, this system was dying out.

Phases of tin mining

PHASE ONE

YEAR	LOCATION
1815	Lukut, Negeri Sembilan
1827	Pahang
1828	Sungai Ujong, Negeri Sembilan Terengganu
1830s	Batang Padang, Perak Petaling and Serdang, Selangor

PHASE TWO

YEAR	LOCATION
1840s	Ampang, Ulu Langat, Ulu Selangor and Klang, Selangor Larut, Perak

PHASE THREE

YEAR	LOCATION
1880s	Kinta, Perak

The headquarters of the Negeri Sembilan Miners' Association, which was established in 1904 to protect the interests of miners in that state.

Early beginnings

The Chinese were first reported to be involved in tin mining in Lukut, Negeri Sembilan, in 1815. In the first phase (until the 1830s), mines were also opened in Sungai Ujong, Pahang, Terengganu, Perak and Selangor (see 'Early Malay tin mining'). Only small numbers of Chinese worked in these mines. Chinese financiers usually advanced the necessary capital to Malay chiefs, who worked the mines with Chinese labour. All the ore was consigned to the financiers, while the chiefs collected levies.

A second phase of more direct but contentious Chinese involvement began in the 1840s with the discovery of rich tin fields in Ampang, Selangor and Larut, Perak (see 'Long Jaafar and the Chinese tin miners in Larut'). Much money was invested and many coolies were brought in from China. Due to growing demand for Malayan alluvial tin by the fast expanding European canning industry, tin prices began to rise rapidly. The attractive profits spurred competition, but also disputes over mine ownership. The Chinese mine owners pitted their workers, who belonged to different secret societies, against one another. When the Malay chiefs were drawn into these disputes, civil wars engulfed Selangor, Perak, Sungai Ujong and Melaka, only ending with British intervention in 1874.

With order restored and the European demand for Malayan tin continuing unabated, the industry grew spectacularly. The third phase of Chinese tin mining coincided with the discovery of the richest tin deposits, in Kinta, Perak, in the early 1870s. Chinese entrepreneurs exerted control over the industry for the next 35–40 years because they controlled the labour force, the most critical factor of production at a time when labour was scarce and the method of extraction highly labour-intensive.

Financing mine operations

Little capital expenditure was necessary to start an opencast mine. The most expensive item was wages which, according to a 1906 estimate, accounted for 80 per cent of total production costs. Coolies were not paid until the ore had been smelted and sold.

This occurred every six months. In the interim, the mine owner provided the workers with provisions, deducting the cost from their wages. In turn, the owner entered into an agreement with an 'advancer' who provided provisions and even mining tools on credit in exchange for guaranteed sale of all the ore

One of the many opencast tin mines which used the very labour-intensive method of employing large numbers of Chinese coolies to remove the ore-bearing soil in baskets.

at fixed prices. This was the 'truck system' (see 'Long Jaafar and the Chinese tin miners in Larut'). The price of ore was fixed below its market value, but the items provided by the advancer were charged well above market rates. However, the system endured as a mine could be opened with little capital. In 1903, a British official noted that after raising an initial loan of $5,000 (to acquire a mining lease, construct coolies' quarters and buy a *chin-chia* (chain pump)), the miner could depend on credit to extend the operations to a total cost of $25,000.

Labour shortage

The constraint to further growth was an inadequate supply of labour. In 1898, when there were already 45,468 labourers in the Kinta mines, W. H. Treacher, the British Resident of Perak, estimated that at least 20,000 more coolies were needed to work the land already alienated for mining. In 1907, E. W. Birch, then Perak Resident, also noted that the labour supply lagged behind demand. Because most mines were labour-intensive, the problem was acute even though 1.5 million Chinese immigrants arrived in Perak and Selangor in 1881–1900. Only 20 per cent of Perak's Chinese population were females and 11.2 per cent were children. In the absence of families, secret societies emerged as one of the most important social institutions. Opium smoking, gambling, prostitution, drinking and fighting further characterized the Chinese mining society.

The passing of an era

Chinese mining entered a new phase about 1915 as the industry became increasingly mechanized. With the introduction of boilers and steam engines, hydraulic monitors and gravel pumps and,

POPULATION OF KINTA	
YEAR	POPULATION
1880s	4,000
1891	58,587
1901	122,737
1911	184,693

ultimately, the dredge, domination of the industry shifted to European entrepreneurs. The colonial government also began rationalizing its operations by taking responsibility for revenue collection, establishing law and order, and asserting control over mining matters generally. The result was the outlawing of secret societies, the end of the truck system, and direct control over opium sales and its use, which had facilitated the Chinese owners' domination of the industry. With the depletion of rich areas with easily accessible deposits, focus shifted to deeply buried deposits which could only be mined with the new technology.

Mining methods

ABOVE: Hydraulic elevators and a series of pipes (monitors) were used in opencast mines to transport water, forcefully, from the rivers.

LEFT: Coolies removing ore from load-bearing veins for transport to the *palong*.

Although the traditional Malay methods of ground sluicing and sinking pits were initially utilized (see 'Early Malay tin mining'), the Chinese mine owners soon switched to *lombong* (opencast) mining, employing 50–70 coolies per mine. By the additional use of a *chin-chia* (a chain pump driven by a water wheel), water could be removed from a 10-metre deep mine pit, surpassing other existing methods.

The *karang* (tin-bearing earth) was carried to the *palong* (sluice box), a Malay mining contraption which the Chinese adapted by extending its length and by mounting it on a wooden scaffolding. A stream, usually having been diverted to flow down the sloping sluice box, washed the earth as a group of labourers stirred it, resulting in the heavier tin ore being collected in the ruffles placed at intervals along the box. The waste, often called 'tailings', was washed away. A final washing was done in a *lanchut* (wash box), a coffin-shaped trough which worked on the same principles as the sluice. The crude concentrate was then dried and smelted to produce the ore.

These labour-intensive methods were phased out with the introduction of machinery which could do the same job more efficiently and with fewer labourers. The mechanization process culminated with the introduction of the dredge. With these changes in technology came changes in mine ownership as it was only the large Western enterprises which had both the technical knowledge and the financial backing needed to operate such large-scale tin-mining operations

The Chinese miners introduced the *chin-chia* (chain pump and water wheel), a much more efficient method of removing water from a deep mine.

Dredges introduced by European mining companies in the early 20th century increased productivity and made the use of large numbers of coolies unnecessary.

Malay peasants and land laws

By introducing the recording of land ownership, the British authorities hoped to encourage Malay farmers to settle; they also wanted to identify unclaimed land available for commercial crops. As a result, the Malays faced difficulty in collecting forest products, an important traditional source of income, from land they did not own. The Malay Reservation Enactment of 1913, which was aimed at reserving land for Malays, also did not have the desired effect and kept the land price low.

Rice cultivation formed the basis of Malay village economy as it was the staple food. Buffaloes were used to plough the fields before planting.

Rattan was one of the forest products traditionally collected for both local use and for the export trade. The canes are being sorted, straightened, stripped and prepared for delivery.

Malay peasants

During the 19th century, the Malay population of the Malay Peninsula could be divided into two categories. The maritime population lived along the coast and engaged in fishing and trade, which sometimes shaded into piracy. The non-maritime population lived in the interior, often along rivers, which were their primary means of transport. The Malays planted rice and other crops, and also gathered jungle produce, did craft work, made palm sugar, caught freshwater fish, and in some places also mined for tin or gold. Goods grown or collected in the interior were traded with the coastal dwellers, who in turn sent fish, salt and manufactured products to the interior.

Malay farmers did very little to improve the land they cultivated, and depended on rainfall or simple dams to flood the rice fields. The fertility of land diminished under continuous cultivation, and houses, constructed from bamboo and nipah palm leaves, needed to be replaced every few years. For these reasons, and because there was ample free land, farmers relocated at frequent intervals, though they would not necessarily move great distances.

The large number of commodities collected from the forest included various kinds of rattan, wax, resins, timber and aromatic woods. Some of these products were for domestic use, but others were sold and exported to European countries.

These activities provided for most of the needs of peasant families, and supplied enough income to purchase goods which were not produced locally.

The most striking feature of descriptions of the Malay states before and during the 19th century is the abundance and variety of goods the Malays produced and possessed. The period of colonial rule had an adverse effect on Malay economic life. Legal restrictions made it difficult for Malays to carry on traditional activities. Access to the forest was restricted, and there were obstacles in the way of farmers who wanted to open up new rice fields.

Malay customary laws protected cultivated crops by providing that a person had rights to any land he had cleared as long as it remained under cultivation, and also to trees he had planted while they continued to bear fruit. Although these provisions seemingly deal with land, they guaranteed a man the product of his labour. They were also precisely suited to the traditional economic pattern.

Change due to land legislation

Some of the great changes brought to peasant life by British land legislation were intentional, but others were inadvertent. British officials objected to the Malay practice of moving from place to place as this habit was an administrative inconvenience, making it difficult to collect rents and maintain land records. The British assumed that with a colonial administration which did not make excessive demands, people would settle down and plant their crops year after year on a piece of land that would become their family property and would be handed down from generation to generation as a cherished possession. To encourage this, colonial officials tried to make it difficult for farmers who already had title to land in one location to apply for land elsewhere.

Maritime activities

Fishing activities were carried out from both the shore and the sea.

1. Fishing boats in which many villagers set out to sea.

2. A 1920s photograph of Malay fishermen selling their catch.

3. Boat building was a vital part of the Malay economy, especially in the east coast states of Terengganu and Kelantan.

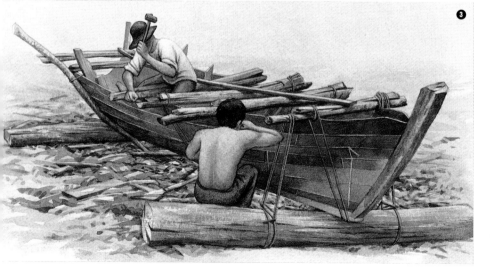

British land codes were also designed to establish that certain areas were not owned by peasants, and could therefore be allocated for the planting of commercial crops. The land codes began with the assumption that the ruler owned all the land in his state, a provision which translated into state ownership of all land and allowed vast areas to be declared state property. Determining ownership of land was important for attracting investors, who wanted unhindered access and security of tenure for a period long enough to recover their capital and realize a profit. So-called 'waste' land could be 'alienated' to investors for the cultivation of commercial crops, or reserved for the exploitation of forest resources or future mining activities. A farmer who intruded into state property without a permit, whether to collect jungle produce or to clear the land for cultivation, committed an offence.

Land codes

The unintentional consequences of colonial land codes proved difficult to remedy. The land code promised security of tenure to peasants, but in practice it made land a commodity which could be mortgaged or sold. It thus contributed to rural indebtedness and the dispossession of Malay peasant smallholders. Also, restrictions on mobility and on access to the forest made it very difficult for Malays to collect forest products as they had previously done. The Malay population emerged from the process of transition with a very limited range of economic options, and in a disadvantaged position.

A worldwide rubber boom early in the 20th century resulted in land being in great demand. The land code made it possible for the government to lease state land to rubber companies, and many areas were developed on this basis. However, riverside sites that offered ready access to transport were often occupied by Malay kampongs, and rubber planters began purchasing such land from the owners. To protect Malay interests, in 1913 the British administration introduced the Malay Reservations Enactment which allowed certain lands to be designated for Malay ownership exclusively.

Prosperous Malays

James Low described the possessions of a prosperous Malay peasant in the early 19th century: 'It will be found that those Malayan householders "who have been several years settled", and who occupy from two to five acres of land ... are possessed of personal property, to an amount varying from ten up to a hundred dollars. This consists of ... a koran, brass kitchen utensils, cuspidors of brass, about a dozen China cups and plates, bedding and mosquito curtains and mats, water jars ..., a chest, rice mortars and sieves, betel-box, fishing apparatus, grain and oil measures; a spear and kris, and knife or parang, baskets of rattan work, a boat when close to the sea or

This group of Sarawak Malays photographed in the 1890s would have belonged to the prosperous category of Malays described here by James Low.

the bank of a river; massive gold earrings, for the women of the family, also gold and silver buttons and silver bracelets, chains and other ornaments; silk and cotton dresses.'

Originally designed to protect existing holdings, the law was later used to preserve large areas for future use by Malays. Although the law kept land in Malay hands, restrictions on the use and disposition of reservation land held its value at low levels compared to non-reserved land.

As the 20th century progressed, Malay farmers abandoned shifting cultivation. There was less land available, and the procedures for acquiring land became increasingly cumbersome. Also, the population was growing rapidly, through both natural increase and immigration. However, the rural Malay population did not emerge as the prosperous farmers envisioned by British officials. Many villagers fell into debt as they tried to cope with a new lifestyle in which their traditional values and practices were no longer viable.

Rubber cultivation on smallholdings offered a brief respite, but rubber proved vulnerable to market conditions outside Malaya, and demand fell sharply after World War I. The Malay Reservations Enactment and British policies limiting rates of interest and offering alternative sources of loans provided some relief, but the combination of colonial land policies and the capitalist economy of the early 20th century produced a peasantry which was economically weak and poorly equipped to compete with non-Malays operating outside the protected sphere of the Malay reservations.

A land title signed by the Assistant Resident Superintendent of Land Revenue Department ensured the security of ownership to the Malay farmer who had tilled and cultivated the piece of land.

During the 19th century, many Malay fishermen lived in coastal or water villages (*kampung air*) with houses built on tall supports in the water, allowing them easy access to their boats.

A postcard of a Malay village of houses made of woven bamboo walls with thatched roofs, shaded by tall coconut palms which the villagers used as a source of both food and fuel.

Revenue farming

Revenue farming was a widespread institution in pre-modern states and empires. Its basic modus operandi was the payment of a fixed price in exchange for the right to collect revenue due to the state. In the Malay Peninsula in the 18th century, and especially, the 19th century, revenue farming meant not only the award of licences to collect revenue but also grants of monopolies to conduct various activities. By the early years of the 20th century, the system had been replaced by government revenue collection, first in the Straits Settlements and later in the Malay states.

Before the development of tin mining, agriculture was the most important source of income for revenue farmers. Commercial crops included: 1. spices; 2. pineapples; 3. gambier; 4 coffee; and 5. pepper.

Tin mining developed very rapidly during the 19th century, particularly in Perak. Licences for the collection of duty on all tin produced were issued to revenue farmers.

INSET: Tin ingots ready for export overseas.

The estate manager and workers in the factory on the Sungai Kapar Rubber Estate at Klang. Revenue farmers collected the export duties on processed latex.

INSET: Tapping rubber under careful supervision by a planter.

The revenue farming system

Revenue farms covered not only the licence to collect revenue on the export of commodities such as tin, but also the grant of a monopoly to import and sell opium or to run a gambling den or to operate a ferry service across a particular river. In one well-known instance, that of the *kangchu* (river lord) system in Johor (see 'The Temenggongs of Johor'), the grant was a virtual monopoly on all activities, crucially gambier planting, in a river system. The system was not confined to the Malay states, but also operated in British-controlled territories such as Penang and Singapore. Possibly the system was brought to the region by the British.

Revenue farming was a transitional institution which lasted for about a century. Preceding it was a system of royal trading monopolies conducted through the ruler or ruler's agent; the bestowal of appropriate gifts upon the ruler and select officials was essential. The successor to revenue farming was a system of directly administered taxation or government monopolies.

Revenue farming thus marked the transition of the state to a modern, more centralized form, and registered the beginning of the distinction between the privy purse and state revenue. In some instances, it was probably the only realistic means for the development of the state and, when well controlled, probably the cheapest means of obtaining revenue.

Ferry services across rivers were among the many licences issued to revenue farmers. This watercolour shows boatmen on the Pahang River in about 1885.

However. if improperly managed, revenue farmers could siphon off sufficient revenue to cause the state financial difficulties.

In the Malay states, revenue farming was not just a story of state-building. It was also about the early capital accumulation by businessmen (mostly Chinese) in close association with the rulers and aristocracy. While it was often true that only the Chinese businessmen could raise sufficient capital to bid for the revenue farms, it was often equally true that it was in the interest and to the advantage of the Malay rulers to operate the farms through foreign businessmen. They could use the system to deprive potential rivals of a source of wealth and economic leverage, and hence the means to mount a political challenge. However, this could also give economic leverage to the businessmen, who could use it to their own advantage. Attempts to protect monopolies sometimes resulted in wars. The best known were the Larut wars in Perak between rival factions of Chinese, each with its Malay aristocratic patrons (see 'Long Jaafar and the Chinese tin miners in Larut').

At their best, revenue farms were a means by which revenue sources could be tapped, relatively cheap credit obtained and commercial development encouraged. The farming of revenue on rice exports, for example, encouraged the revenue farmer to stimulate the commercial development of rice cultivation as his profits were dependent upon increasing rice exports.

As the price of the revenue farm depended upon the state's economic condition, the rulers also had an interest in the economy. During a bad crisis in Kedah, the ruler proposed that the revenue farmer provide irrigation pumps, citing their mutual economic interests as well as the cultivators' welfare.

Johor, under the kangchu system, was an even clearer example of the use of revenue farming. The system provided great incentives for the kangchu to encourage enterprise in his river system, while the ruler obtained revenue with minimum outlay.

The costs and benefits of the system

Even at its best, revenue farming had its trade-offs. An obvious instance was the opium, liquor and gambling farms. Another was the award of farms on a district rather than state-wide basis—such as for the collection of duty on the transport of fruit in Kedah—which was an obstacle to the development of internal trade and a burden on the people.

Generally, revenue farming made it harder for people to avoid the payment of duties and increased their economic burden in return for little in the way of public works. In Kedah, for example, the system indirectly encouraged farmers to get into debt, as indebtedness forced cultivators to increase the amount of rice for sale, and hence for export. Apparently, the farmers operated through agents who gave cultivators loans and obtained repayment through purchases of rice, probably at a discount.

For the state rulers, an obvious negative aspect was the tremendous potential for leakage from the state coffers and for abuse by licensees/farmers. The farms were formally auctioned, but it was impossible to prevent collusion between potential bidders. Also, there was no means of ensuring certain licensees would not be selected in return for favours rendered to powerful figures in the state administration. Poor information on the state of an economy also meant poor information on the actual worth of a revenue farm, although the value could increase over time.

At its worst, a revenue farming system could be used by extravagant rulers to raise loans in return for the grant of future licences at current prices, thus not only depriving the state of the benefits of economic growth but also mortgaging future revenue. Such a situation, however, was more a function of the nature of the political system than of the system of revenue farming per se.

Few options were available when a state administrative apparatus was rudimentary, when the cost of establishing the necessary apparatus for revenue collection was prohibitive, and when there was great uncertainty on the amount of available revenue. Perhaps the ultimate benefit of the revenue farming system was the provision of information on the potential amount of revenue.

The demise of revenue farming

In the early years of the 20th century, revenue farming came to be regarded as an unmitigated evil and it was rapidly phased out in all the Malay states, after being eliminated in the Straits Settlements as the government began direct revenue collection.

This perspective of the evils of revenue farming has since come to dominate thinking about the system. However, the realization of the unfortunate effects of the system was closely linked with the development of the state's administrative and tax system to the requisite stage for assuming direct control over taxation and revenue collection. It was this development, rather than any actual inherent evils of the system, which caused its elimination.

Well-known revenue farmers

Loke Yew

Loke Yew (1847–1917) was perhaps the most famous of all revenue farmers, though he also became involved in many other ventures. His was a classic rags-to-riches story. Arriving in Singapore as a penniless child, he worked in a shop and saved $99 in four years. On moving to Perak, he made, and lost, money in tin mining; he then supplied the British troops during the Perak war. Settling in Selangor, he leased revenue farms in gambling, pawnbroking and spirits. Among his many ventures were tin mines in Sungai Besi and Bentong, rubber estates (he was one of the earliest planters), cement works and a coconut oil mill. He invested heavily in real estate and hired J. H. M. Robson (who established the *Selangor Journal* and the *Malay Mail*), to manage these. He was also a member of the Selangor State Council. A generous philanthropist, Loke Yew donated a great deal to the Hong Kong University.

Loke Mansion, which Loke Yew bought from his patron, Loke Chow Kit. It was one of the first houses in Kuala Lumpur to be supplied with electricity.

Loke Chow Kit

Loke Chow Kit was born and educated in Penang. He worked for Messrs Katz Bros before joining Messrs Huttenbach & Co., who sent him to Kuala Lumpur as the assistant manager of their branch there. He was later appointed by Loke Yew and Chow Ah Yok, who held the lease of the railway lines in Selangor, as the railway traffic manager. After the expiry of the railway lease he was employed by Loke Yew as general manager of his revenue farms in Selangor, Pahang and Negeri Sembilan.

Chow Kit established himself in business by later leasing these farms himself. He was also the owner of the retailing firm Chow Kit & Co., which was one of the largest companies in Kuala Lumpur at the beginning of the 20th century. He was also a shareholder or director of several companies, particularly in mining, and was an agent for shipping and insurance companies.

In addition to his business activities, Chow Kit was also president of the Straits Chinese Association and was involved in a number of other welfare organizations.

1. Loke Chow Kit. 2. Spirit distillery. 3. Selangor opium farm. These were only two of Loke's revenue farms.

The role of large-scale Western enterprise

During the 19th century, Western nations competed to expand sources of supply of industrial raw materials as well as markets for their manufactures. Britain was the leading capital exporting country in the world. In the Malay Peninsula, it was both the largest foreign investor and a significant trading partner as Britain was both a supplier of imports and a market for tropical primary commodities. However, the Western nations had to compete with Asian mercantile communities (Indian, Arab, Chinese) who had long been established in the region.

With the growing prosperity in Penang from the increasing participation of large-scale Western enterprises, the method of transportation changed from bullock carts and trishaws to motorized vehicles.

Malayan documents and currencies
CLOCKWISE, FROM TOP LEFT: policy of Commercial Union; 1893 advertisement of Netherlands Trading Society which appeared in the *Pinang Gazette*; 19th-century currency notes from Hongkong Bank; firemark of Commercial Union, still seen on shophouses in Ipoh.

Phases of economic activity

There were three distinct phases of economic activity in the 19th century. The first was in the early part of the century when lively commerce in the British ports of Singapore and Penang set the stage for a change in the pace of development. While Western merchants were chiefly concerned with trading activities, a few ventured into the planting of gambier and spices, particularly pepper. Initially these ventures, which were usually cooperative projects with European capital and Chinese management and labour, were located in Penang and Singapore. However, they later expanded to Province Wellesley and also Johor. Sugar was introduced in the 1830s.

The second phase began in the middle of the century when tin-mining activity in Larut and Kuala Lumpur surged following the discovery of rich new fields. Straits Settlements Chinese merchants provided the investment capital while an influx of Chinese immigrants supplied the labour for the mines.

The third phase commenced after British intervention in Perak and Selangor in 1874, and later in Negeri Sembilan and Pahang. Western companies ventured into tin mining and also into commercial agriculture. With the improved political conditions in the 1880s, the development of the Malay Peninsula accelerated markedly. Commodity production rose sharply, reaching new heights with rubber at the beginning of the 20th century.

The agency houses

The merchant firms of the Straits Settlements dominated Western business throughout the 19th century (see 'European agency houses and the Malay states'). As their involvement extended beyond import–export, they evolved into large 'mixed' business houses, earning the name 'agency houses'. As such, they served as agents for related commercial activities such as shipping, insurance and finance. At the end of the century, a number of these agency houses assumed another function, that of management of firms which were registered in Europe, primarily in London. Among the merchant companies which acquired agencies in the principal ancillary services required for trade were Guthrie, Boustead, Sandilands, Buttery & Co., Harrisons & Crosfield and McAlister.

Later, other European and even American and Japanese companies selected established enterprises in the region to market their services. United American Lines, Banque de l'Indo Chine, National Bank of China, Norddeutscher Lloyd and Hamburg Underwriters were among the non-British enterprises available in the Malay Peninsula. Dutch and German companies were among the more active of the various non-British enterprises. Behn Meyer & Co., one of those companies, is still operating in Malaysia.

The managing agency system, which had emerged in India, blossomed in the Malay Peninsula in response to the demands of the new rubber industry. To raise the large amounts of capital required for estate development, Western enterprises sought to float new companies in Europe. Investors

Staff of Sandilands, Buttery & Co., which was established in Penang in 1854 by John Buttery and G. M. Sandilands. It was one of the many agencies employed to represent the business interests of European companies.

Major activities of Western enterprise

Weld Quay, Penang, c. 1907, a busy import–export centre.

Tin mining
Chinese capital and labour had dominated the sector at the time of the early discoveries in the mid-19th century. Political stability with the appointment of British Residents, as well as major finds of tin in the 1870s, encouraged Western companies to begin large-scale activities in tin mining in the early 20th century and to introduce modern machinery.

Hydraulic machinery such as this was introduced by the large Western enterprises in the early 20th century.

The Penang branch of Mercantile Bank.

Banks
British banks were the earliest to appoint agents in the Straits Settlements. They were followed by Asian banks which provided services to the citizens of their home countries. Later, domestic banking services were introduced. While some banks closed, others expanded.

Trade
In the early 19th century, Singapore and Penang were the hub of trading activities in the Malay Peninsula. Western merchants expanded their business from commerce to planting. Using Chinese management and labour, they also began planting export crops such as pepper, gambier and sugar. In the early 20th century, large rubber estates were opened by the European plantation companies.

were persuaded to subscribe to companies which would be managed by merchant houses with vast business experience in the East, the reputation of the company being the hedge against the risks of overseas investment. Some of the well-known merchant companies were the efforts of individual entrepreneurs, such as A. C. Harper. Such men started either as a merchant or a planter and went on to build up successful agency houses.

Banks
A third type of enterprise in the mid-19th century was the overseas bank, which began by financing trade and later conducted domestic banking. Some banks appointed agents to represent them before setting up their own branches. Long-established British banks, such as Coutts, Bankers of London and Baring Brothers, appointed agents in the Straits Settlements ports earlier than the more well-known overseas banks, such as Chartered Bank of India, Australia and China, the Chartered Mercantile Bank of India, London and China and the Hongkong and Shanghai Bank. The Oriental Bank Corporation was prominent in the 19th century, but closed in 1892. Some major banks founded in the 19th century are still operating today.

The role of Western enterprise
The British businessmen were the acknowledged notables of colonial society. Their chambers of commerce had the privilege of

electing municipal councillors and, from 1886, unofficial members of the Straits Settlements' Legislative Council. Their nominees represented not only the business community, but also the larger society. The standing of the European community was also indicated by the administration's consultation on vital matters.

The 19th-century merchant–agency firms and the plantation companies were well placed in the early 20th century to embark on large-scale tin mining and rubber planting ventures. These two industries became the mainstay of the economy, contributing substantially to the rapid growth and prosperity of the Malay Peninsula in the period prior to the outbreak of World War II.

One of the multiple roles of the agency houses was to represent British insurance companies, and issue policies on their behalf.

Hongkong and Shanghai Banking Corporation in Penang, c. 1900. Originally established to cater to the needs of foreigners in the Malay Peninsula, it now has a strong presence in domestic banking.

SELECTED BANKS AND INSURANCE COMPANIES IN THE MALAY PENINSULA

BANK/INSURANCE CO.	AGENT	ESTABLISHED	BRANCHES
Oriental Bank	none	1842 Bombay	1846 Singapore
Chartered Mercantile Bank of India, London and China (Mercantile Bank)	none	1858 Bombay	1855 Singapore; 1859 Penang; 1911 Kota Bharu; 1926 Kuantan; 1936 Kuala Terengganu
Chartered Bank of India, Australia & China (Chartered Bank)	Fraser & Co.	1853 London	1859 Singapore; 1875 Penang; 1888 Kuala Lumpur, Taiping; 1909 Klang; 1910 Seremban; 1911 Melaka; 1912 Ipoh
Hongkong & Shanghai Banking Corporation	Boustead	1865 Hong Kong	1877 Singapore; 1884 Penang; 1909 Ipoh; 1888 Kuala Lumpur, Johor Bahru, Melaka
Netherlands Trading Society	none	1824 Amsterdam	1883 Singapore; 1888 Penang
Khean Guan Insurance Co. Ltd	none	1885 Penang	none
Union Insurance Society of Canton Ltd	Boustead A.A. Anthony	1835 Hong Kong	1874 London
Royal Insurance Co. Ltd	Boustead	London	none
Commercial Union Assurance Co. Ltd	A.A. Anthony	1861 London	1919 Ipoh
New Zealand Insurance Co.	Gilfillan, Wood	1859 Auckland	none
South British Insurance Co. Ltd	Boustead Hampshire Lee Kee Hin	1872 Auckland	1909 Singapore

The formation of the Federated Malay States

The official establishment on 1 July 1896 of the Federated Malay States (FMS), comprising the four states of Selangor, Perak, Negeri Sembilan and Pahang, was the first step towards the present federal government system of Malaysia. The formation of the FMS was the direct result of the problems which the British faced after intervening in the administration of Pahang. Heading the federation was a Resident-General based at Kuala Lumpur, the capital of Selangor, which became the federal capital because of its central position.

'Carcosa' in Kuala Lumpur was completed in 1898 as the official residence for the Resident-General of the Federated Malay States. After Independence it became the official residence of the British High Commissioner, and is now a luxury hotel set in extensive, landscaped grounds.

REVENUE AND EXPENDITURE IN PAHANG, 1889–1895 (STRAITS $)		
YEAR	REVENUE	EXPENDITURE
1889 (half year)	30,390.05	141,683.38
1890	62,077.01	284,647.07
1891	77,386.50	238,174.22
1892	50,044.34	206,735.79
1893	83,688.47	246,606.67
1894	100,220.43	207,514.27
1895	106,743.80	206,317.48

The main shaft of a gold mine in Raub, Pahang. Exports of gold from Pahang had begun in very early times. However, profits were eroded by expenditure on civil disturbances.

British intervention in Pahang

In 1888, J. P. Rodger was appointed as the first Resident of Pahang (see 'The new sultanate of Pahang'). The Colonial Office sanctioned the appointment of a Resident because of the persuasive arguments of local British officials that Pahang was potentially the richest of the Malay states. Gold had been exported since very early times, and tin mining had already begun. The officials considered it even more important that Pahang was the largest of the Malay states and had ample undeveloped land available for agriculture. By the 1880s, British policy towards the Malay states was to promote commercial agriculture, rather than tin mining, because agriculture could be sustained indefinitely whereas the supply of tin would eventually be exhausted.

British imperial policy required colonies or protected states to be self-sustaining and not be a burden on Britain. In Pahang, the administration began with loans obtained from the Straits Settlements, but before the British could consolidate their position an uprising occurred in 1891. This disturbance, which the British failed to quell until 1895, incurred heavy expenditure. By the end of 1892, Pahang owed the Straits Settlements administration $800,000, not including the expenditure incurred because of the disturbances. It was estimated in 1892 that Pahang would need to borrow $175 000 a year for the next three years at least, but the Straits Settlements was not in a position to provide further loans to Pahang.

The position of the British

By mid-1892, Sir Cecil Clementi Smith, governor of the Straits Settlements, was asked by Edward Fairfield, Assistant Under-Secretary in the Colonial Office if it was wise to continue the Residential System in Pahang as economic development of the state appeared impossible. Smith challenged Fairfield's judgment, reiterating the belief that gold and tin mining, as well as agriculture, had a bright future in Pahang. Time, however, was needed. To overcome the state's inaccessibility, he suggested that a railway line be constructed joining Pahang with at least one of the west coast states.

Smith also suggested that Britain give aid to the Straits Settlements (as it had financial problems) to enable assistance to Pahang to continue. Smith was considering the possibility of Pahang merging with Selangor, which had surplus revenue.

C. P. Lucas, who was in charge of the Eastern desk, supported Smith as he too believed that Pahang was a profitable investment. Continuing with the Residential System would, he argued, benefit Pahang directly. Revenue would be greater under even the existing imperfect Residential System compared to the old indigenous regime.

Lucas argued that there were other reasons other than financial to maintain the system. British intervention could be morally justified because it would wipe out cruelty and oppression, which were rife at that time. The decision could also be defended on imperial grounds that the Malay

The Pahang War, 1891–1895

To the people of Pahang, the British were seen as a political menace against whom resistance was the only solution. It was primarily the political reforms of the 19th century, aimed at achieving greater administrative efficiency, which resulted in the rise and development of a native anti-colonial movement.

The uprising, which lasted from 1891 until 1895, incurred heavy expenditure by the British, raising doubts about the wisdom of interfering in the state's affairs.

The Gopeng contingent which fought in the Pahang War, May 1892.

Peninsula had been divided between Britain and Siam, and that Pahang was located in the British sphere of influence. It should be kept in that sphere to allow the whole southern part of the Peninsula to remain within undisputed British control.

J. P. Rodger, the Resident, had earlier suggested that if Britain was no longer willing to spend money on Pahang, one of two measures ought to be adopted: Pahang should be annexed to one of the protected states (Perak, Selangor or Negeri Sembilan), or all European officers should be withdrawn from Pahang, with the only the Resident remaining, purely as an adviser.

Lucas did not favour either the withdrawal of the British administration or placing Pahang under one of the protected states. He suggested instead that Raub, a gold mining district situated close to Selangor, should be administratively absorbed by Selangor. In addition, he made three other proposals. First, the military contribution of the Straits Settlements, which was the highest paid by any colony, should be reduced by 25 per cent so that the colony could continue to assist Pahang. Second, to assist the development of Pahang capital should be expended to improve communications infrastructure. Though it was not the right time to contemplate railway construction, a road could be built from the west coast to Pahang. Third, since a number of concessions granted earlier by the ruler would lapse after 1894, land would then become available for sale or lease to the Chinese (rather than Europeans), who would quickly take it up, thus producing a new source of revenue for the state.

Fairfield continued to stand his ground, though neither Robert Meade, the Permanent Under-Secretary nor Sydney Buxton, the Parliamentary Under-Secretary, supported Britain's withdrawal from Pahang. However, they did acknowledge that the intervention in Pahang had been taken somewhat hastily.

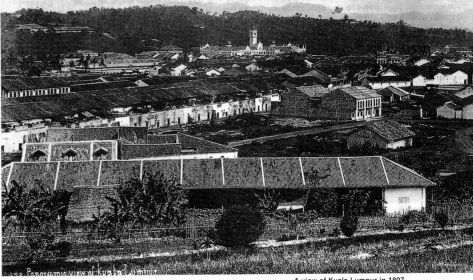

A view of Kuala Lumpur in 1897, including the rear view of the Sultan Abdul Samad Building. Kuala Lumpur became the capital of the Federated Malay States in 1896 and, following Independence, the capital of Malaysia.

Federation proposal and implementation

On 28 April 1893, Buxton proposed to Meade and Fairfield that a federation be formed as a possible solution to the Pahang problem. A confidential dispatch, dated 19 May 1893, was sent to the governor, Sir Cecil Clementi Smith, asking him to consider making modifications to the existing situation by drawing the protected states closer together so that Selangor and Perak, which both had surplus revenue, could assist the development of Pahang. The annexation of Pahang by one of the other protected states, he thought, would offend the Pahang ruler, while joining a federation would not.

Because Frank Swettenham, who at that time was the Resident of Perak, had considerable influence over the Malay rulers, he was instructed on 5 June 1895 to secure the consent of the four rulers to the formation of a federation. By the middle of 1896, agreements had been signed between Britain and the rulers of Perak, Selangor, Pahang and Negeri Sembilan (including separate agreements with the chiefs of Johol, Rembau and Tampin as the reunification of Negeri Sembilan was in the process of being effected).

On 1 July 1896, the Federated Malay States was established with Kuala Lumpur (the capital of Selangor), because it occupied a central geographical position, as the capital of the federation. Frank Swettenham was appointed as the first Resident-General (1896–1900), placing him above the Residents of the four states. The first High Commissioner was Sir Charles Mitchell (1896–9), who simultaneously held the position of governor of the Straits Settlements, as did all subsequent High Commissioners until 1941. The Resident-General was based in Kuala Lumpur, while the High Commissioner resided in Singapore.

Sir Cecil Clementi Smith, governor of the Straits Settlements (1887–93), suggested that the British government should relieve the Straits Settlements of part of its military contribution or provide pecuniary assistance so that it could continue to help develop Pahang.

Two early 20th-century guidebooks to the Federated Malay States.

A *Straits Produce* cartoon reads: 'Raffles: I founded Singapore. Clark: I pacified the Malay States. Swettenham: I federated them. Anderson: I created Greater Malaya. The Dreamer: There must be a next step somewhere.'

Rulers at the time of formation of the Federated Malay States in 1896

Sultan Idris (r. 1887–1916)

Sultan Ahmad (r. 1863–1914)

Perak

Pahang

Selangor

Negeri Sembilan

Sultan Abdul Samad (r. 1857–98)

Tuanku Muhammad, Yamtuan (r. 1887–1933)

1. Modern facilities were developed at Penang port to provide services for the numerous ships which called there every year.

2. The Seremban railway station, from which passengers could travel north to Kuala Lumpur or Penang, or south to Singapore.

3. Tree-lined Station Road, Ipoh, in 1907. Rickshaws were still common, although the buildings are modern.

4. Electric trams provided an efficient transport system for Penang prior to their elimination in 1936.

RIGHT: King Chulalongkorn of Siam (r. 1868–1910) (centre) photographed in 1870 with his two brothers, Prince Chaturanta Rasmi and Prince Bhanuraigsi Savangwongse.

THE MALAY STATES

The present federal system of Malaysia began with the administrative structure of the Federated Malay States (FMS) which united four states—Perak, Selangor, Negeri Sembilan and Pahang—in 1896. These states gradually lost their powers to the federal government, but later sought to recover them through decentralization.

The process of centralization began with Frank Swettenham, the first Resident-General of the FMS (1896–1900), who consolidated power into his own hands. His successor, William Taylor, did the same. In 1911, the title of Resident-General was replaced with Chief Secretary. Thereafter, the Governor-High Commissioner in Singapore used the Chief Secretary to consolidate his own powers and enhance centralization in the FMS. To mollify the rulers and the Residents, they were invited to become members of the Federal Council which was set up in 1909. The Federal Council constitution effected a division of powers between the federal and state councils. While the Federal Council had almost unlimited powers, the rulers were left sovereign in their own states, which were administered on the advice of their Residents. However, the Residential System lost much of its vitality during this period as each state's power continued to be curtailed until the 1920s when new policies devolved various federal responsibilities back to the rulers and Residents.

Before World War II, the states had won back some of their powers, including the allocation of specific budgets to the states, which were also allowed to collect certain taxes to avoid over-dependence on federal budgets. The Federal Council, however, was empowered to approve the annual federal and state budgets.

The decentralization policy was devised as a conciliatory measure to return several powers to the rulers and the Residents. In 1925, major reforms included the abolition of the post of Chief Secretary and the devolution of powers of the federal secretariat to the Residents, state councils and federal heads. The process was expedited by Governor Sir Cecil Clementi (1930–4), who used the sultans to play a more active role in public affairs and to help the Malays compete more effectively with the non-Malays. He also enlarged the Durbars by inviting the sultans from the Unfederated Malay States.

The Unfederated Malay States (Kelantan, Terengganu, Perlis, Kedah and Johor) did not all come under British control until 1919. British Advisers were appointed to Perlis, Kedah and Kelantan in 1909, and Terengganu in 1918. Prior to the 1909 Anglo-Siamese Treaty, Siam had held suzerainty over these four states. Under Sultan Abu Bakar, Johor had a special relationship with Britain, spelt out in the 1885 Anglo-Johor Treaty. However, this ceased with his death, and a General Adviser was appointed in 1914.

Despite the loss of state powers, the federal system left intact the sovereignty of the Malay rulers and their respective states. After the war, following the debacle of the Malayan Union scheme, it was this consideration which persuaded all the Malay rulers to accept the federal system further when they signed the Federation of Malaya Agreement in 1948.

A group photograph taken at the first Malay Durbar held at Kuala Kangsar in 1897. Seated, from left to right, are: Hugh Clifford (Resident of Pahang), J. P. Rodger (Resident of Selangor), Sir Frank Swettenham (Resident-General), Sultan Ahmad of Pahang, Sultan Abdul Samad of Selangor, Sir Charles Mitchell (High Commissioner of the Federated Malay States), Sultan Idris of Perak, Tuanku Muhammad of Negeri Sembilan, and W. H. Treacher (Resident of Perak).

Sir John Anderson, Governor–High Commissioner 1904–10, established the Federal Council.

The Malayan Durbars

During the period from 1897 to 1939, 12 Durbars—meetings of the Malay rulers of the Federated Malay States (and also the Unfederated Malay States in the 1930 and 1934 All-Malaya Durbars) and British officials—were held to discuss matters of mutual concern. The early Durbars were largely ceremonial events, but the later meetings were much more serious affairs. On the whole, the Durbars increased goodwill and influenced colonial policy and practice.

		THE DURBARS	
NO.	DATE	LOCATION	TYPE
1	July 1897	Kuala Kangsar, Perak	FMS Durbar
2	July 1903	Kuala Lumpur	FMS Durbar
3	Aug. 1927	Kuala Kangsar, Perak	FMS Durbar
4	Sept. 1930	Klang, Selangor	FMS Durbar
5	Oct. 1930	Singapore	All-Malaya Durbar
6	Aug. 1931	Sri Menanti, Negeri Sembilan	FMS Durbar
7	April 1932	Pekan, Pahang	FMS Durbar
8	Sept. 1933	Kuala Kangsar, Perak	FMS Durbar
9	Feb. 1934	Singapore	All-Malaya Durbar.
10	Nov. 1935	Kuala Lumpur	FMS Durbar
11	Nov. 1937	Klang, Selangor	FMS Durbar
12	Nov. 1939	Sri Menanti, Negeri Sembilan	FMS Durbar

To commemorate a century of the Conference of Rulers (1897–1997), Pos Malaysia issued a set of three stamps in 1997. The 30-sen stamp shows the participants at the first Conference of Rulers (Durbar) held at Kuala Kangsar, Perak, in 1897. The 50-sen stamp shows the crests of all 13 states of Malaysia, and the RM1.00 stamp depicts the official seal of the Conference of Rulers.

The origins of the Durbars

The Durbars originated from the suggestion by Sir Charles Mitchell (Governor–High Commissioner 1894–9) of a consultative and advisory Federal Council in the administrative scheme for the Federated Malay States (FMS). Frank Swettenham, the first Resident-General of the FMS (1896–1900), chose instead to hold an annual Durbar, with the aim of enhancing the dignity and prestige of the FMS rulers and using the meetings to demonstrate the rulers' support for the federation.

The early Durbars

The six-year gap between the first Durbar, held at Kuala Kangsar, Perak, in July 1897, and the second, held at Kuala Lumpur in July 1903, was chiefly due to Swettenham's desire to retain a free hand in governing the states. Until 1920, the British were not sufficiently sensitive to the feelings of the rulers or to the relative backwardness of the Malays. Perhaps more importantly, the British assumed the Durbars were no longer needed as the FMS rulers became members of the Federal Council in 1909.

The early Durbars were largely ceremonial events attended by the High Commissioner, the Resident-General, the Residents and the FMS rulers. At the Durbars, the Malay rulers spoke on Islam and Malay customs and welfare, while administrative issues were left to British officials. The Durbars generally made the rulers more aware of the reality of federation. However, at the 1903 Durbar, Sultan Idris of Perak (r. 1887–1916) spoke out against the centralization of power in the FMS.

The later Durbars

Under Governor–High Commissioner Sir Laurence Guillemard's (1920–7) reforms in 1927, the FMS rulers withdrew from the Federal Council and were offered an annual Durbar. The third Durbar was convened by Sir Hugh Clifford (Governor–High Commissioner 1927–9) at Kuala Kangsar in 1927. Durbars became regular events and underwent important changes. They were smaller in scale and, except for the all-Malaya Durbars of 1930 and 1934, attended by only the High Commissioner, the Chief Secretary (Federal Secretary after 1935), the Residents and the FMS rulers. Non-Malays were no longer able to attend. The meetings became strictly Anglo-Malay affairs, reflecting the assumption that the FMS were independent sovereign Malay states under British protection. With much less pomp and ceremony than the early meetings, the Durbars became serious and business-like Anglo-Malay discussions utilized by both the British and the rulers to promote their respective interests.

The changes stemmed partly from a new British Malay policy after 1920 as they sought to enhance indirect rule, and also from the desire to overcome the FMS rulers' grievances arising from their loss of power and from Malay poverty. The rulers were

encouraged to play a more active role in public affairs and to help Malays compete more effectively with non-Malays. This policy contributed to the rulers' assertiveness in the Durbars.

Sir Cecil Clementi, who was Governor–High Commissioner 1930–4, made further changes in the Durbars, including the use of English as well as Malay. He also enlarged the Durbar twice (in 1930 and 1934) to include the rulers of the Unfederated Malay States (UMS) in connection with his decentralization policy in the FMS (see 'The decentralization policy') which aimed at devoluting power from the federal centre to the state administrations and persuading the UMS to join the FMS in forming a Malayan federation.

A telegram to Queen Victoria

At the opening ceremony of the first Durbar, the Resident-General, on behalf of the Malay rulers, requested the High Commissioner to forward a telegram to Queen Victoria. It read:
We, the Sultans of the Malay States of Selangor, Perak, Pahang and Negeri Sembilan, by the invitation of Your Majesty's High Commissioner, are met together, for the first time in History, to discuss the affairs of our States confederated under Your Majesty's gracious protection. We desire to offer to Your Majesty our respectful and cordial congratulations on a reign of unexampled length and unequalled progress, and we pray for Your Majesty's long life and the continuance of that protection which has already brought such prosperity to Malaya.

The promotion of British policy

Clementi utilized the Durbars to promote British policy and to secure the rulers' support, enabling him to win over the Colonial Office and to counter opposition to the decentralization policy from the non-Malays and European capitalist interests. While he received strong support from the FMS rulers, he met resistance from the UMS rulers, who feared their states would lose autonomy in a federation. His successor, Sir Shenton Thomas (1934–42), held only two official FMS Durbars, and also an unofficial one with the FMS rulers in 1935.

Entertainment at the Malay Durbars

The Prince of Wales theatre group, which was known for its 'modern' productions, performed for the guests at the first Durbar on 15 July 1897, held at Kuala Kangsar.

In a football match at the Padang in Kuala Lumpur on 20 July 1903, watched by 4,000 spectators, Victoria Institution beat the town team.

A garden party at the Residency, Kuala Kangsar, in 1897. Governor Sir Charles Mitchell (left) is seated next to Sultan Ahmad of Pahang. Tuanku Muhammad of Negeri Sembilan (second from right) is seen talking to Lady Mitchell. Frank Swettenham is standing to the right of the central group, while Hugh Clifford and Ernest Birch are on the elephants.

The FMS rulers welcomed the revival of the Durbars as they felt the Federal Council offered them less say than the Durbars. They were more assertive in promoting Malay interests in the 1930s Durbars as the growing non-Malay challenge made them concerned about Malay survival.

The impact of the Durbars

The Durbars enhanced British indirect rule in the FMS and heightened British awareness of Malay views on national problems. Whether the rulers' views became official action depended largely on the degree of confluence of British and Malay interests. After 1920, the British officials tried to accommodate the rulers' views as long as they were not contradictory to British interests, being most responsive when British and Malay interests coincided. Ultimately, however, British interests prevailed in the outcome of Durbar deliberations.

A photograph taken by Alexander Koch on the occasion of the second Durbar, held in Kuala Lumpur in 1903. Some of the important participants are in the centre row. Starting from the European seated sixth from the left, they are: Henry Conway Belfield (Resident of Selangor), John Pickersgill Rodger (Resident of Perak), William Hood Treacher (Resident-General of the FMS), Sultan Sulaiman of Selangor, Sultan Idris of Perak, Sir Frank Swettenham (Governor of the Straits Settlements and High Commissioner for the FMS), Sultan Ahmad of Pahang, Tuanku Muhammad, Yang di-Pertuan Besar of Negeri Sembilan, Walter Egerton (Resident of Negeri Sembilan), and Douglas Graham Campbell (acting Resident of Pahang).

The Resident-General and the Federal Council

From the establishment of the Federated Malay States (FMS) in 1896, its head in Kuala Lumpur, the Resident-General, was inclined to act in a quasi-independent manner. In 1909, the High Commissioner—the superior of the Resident-General (based in Singapore)—established a legislative body, the Federal Council, to give himself direct access to the FMS administration. In this way, the High Commissioner hoped to enhance efficiency in the federation, placate the rulers of the FMS, and offer European commercial interests a say in government.

Frank Swettenham

Frank Swettenham, the first Resident-General of the Federated Malay States (1896–1900), and later Governor–High Commissioner (1901–3).

After establishing himself as the quasi-independent head of the Federated Malay States (FMS), Swettenham began to build a centralized federal administration, conducive to both efficiency and economic development, in the FMS. He substantially deprived the Residents and the rulers of their powers and prerogatives in the states. To maintain freedom of action, Swettenham refused to set up a Federal Council as provided for in the FMS administrative scheme. Sultan Idris of Perak was antagonized by the decision of Swettenham to replace the Rulers-in-Council with the FMS Judicial Commissioner as the judge of appeals from the state courts. Indeed, in private Sultan Idris accused Frank Swettenham of violating a personal undertaking that the federation would not diminish the rulers' powers and prerogatives. Supported by the other rulers, Sultan Idris utilized the 1903 Durbar as a forum of protest and, much to Swettenham's embarrassment, openly attacked administrative centralization in the FMS.

Senior British officials who attended the second Durbar held in Kuala Lumpur in 1903. *LEFT TO RIGHT*: H. C. Belfield (Resident of Selangor), W. H. Treacher (Resident-General of the FMS), Sir Frank Swettenham (High Commissioner of the FMS), J. P. Rodger (Resident of Perak), W. Egerton (Resident of Negeri Sembilan), and D. G. Campbell (Resident of Pahang).

The Resident-General and the states

From 1896 to 1911, the FMS was headed by a Resident-General, based in Kuala Lumpur, whose advice was binding on the rulers except in religious matters. His role was to assist his superior, the High Commissioner in Singapore, to secure administrative efficiency and uniformity and promote development in the FMS. However, his position vis-à-vis the High Commissioner as well as the Residents and the rulers was not clearly defined. This factor, together with the personality of the incumbent, eventually determined the role played by the Resident-General during his tenure.

Frank Swettenham, the first Resident-General (1896–1900), set the tone for his successors by acting as a powerful head of the FMS. He developed a centralized federal administration conducive to both administrative efficiency and economic development and which substantially deprived the rulers and the Residents of their powers and prerogatives in the states. To maintain freedom of action for himself, Swettenham declined to set up a Federal Council as provided for in the FMS administrative scheme.

Sir John Anderson

Sir John Anderson, Governor–High Commissioner 1904–11, with his daughter, who assisted her father in his social duties.

RIGHT: A newspaper advertisement of 27 February 1905 by Raffles Hotel, Singapore, announced the patronage of Sir John Anderson among the 'elite ... and first-class visitors only'.

Sir John Anderson (seated, centre) in a group photograph of British and Kelantan officials on his visit to Kota Bharu in 1909, the year in which the Anglo-Siamese Treaty gave Britain control over Kelantan as well as Terengganu, Kedah and Perlis.

Sir John Anderson, who was Governor–High Commissioner from 1904 until 1911, was responsible for the introduction of the Federal Council as the central legislature for the Federated Malay States of Perak, Selangor, Pahang and Negeri Sembilan. As the president of the council, Anderson was able to exercise stronger control over the federation. He also sought to consolidate his position by changing the title of Resident-General to Chief Secretary.

These developments engendered strong resentment and dissatisfaction among the Residents and the FMS rulers. As centralization increased substantially with the creation of more and more federal departments and the appointment of executive heads for these departments in 1902, the rulers' disenchantment with Swettenham deepened. Supported by the other rulers, Sultan Idris of Perak (r. 1887–1916) utilized the 1903 Durbar as a forum of protest and openly attacked administrative centralization in the FMS (see 'The Malayan Durbars'). The rulers' growing disillusionment with Swettenham's actions possibly contributed to the latter's decision to retire prematurely in 1903.

Sir John Anderson, Swettenham's successor as High Commissioner (1904–11), selected William Taylor, an ex-Ceylon official, as Resident-General (1905–10). Both Anderson and Taylor were new to Malaya and they could not speak Malay, which hindered their relations with the FMS rulers. Under Taylor, major advances in administrative centralization in the FMS—in line with Anderson's policy of developing the FMS into a political union—led to conflicts between Taylor and Sultan Idris and Ernest Birch, his Resident (1904–10).

The Federal Council

The members of the Federal Council, which had its first meeting on 11 December 1909, were the High Commissioner, the Resident-General, the FMS rulers and their Residents, and three European and one Chinese nominated unofficials. The Council was set up by High Commissioner Sir John Anderson, partly to enable him to enter directly into the FMS administration as the Council's president. Commercial interests and the Residents welcomed the Council, as did the rulers, who hoped the Council would be favourable to them. For the first time, the division of power between the federal and state councils was set out, but it was vague. Only state matters—Malay religion, political pensions, the appointment of *penghulu* (headmen) and the conversion of agricultural and mining lands—were clearly set out. The explicit powers of the Federal Council were not defined. The Council took charge of legislation, finance, and matters affecting more than one state in the FMS, assuring the rulers that their powers were in no way curtailed.

The Malay rulers and British officials who attended a meeting for the signing of an agreement to reconstruct the Federal Council in 1927. The four rulers of the Federated Malay States withdrew from the council, and three Malays and five federal heads were admitted as new members.

The Resident-General and the High Commissioner

As High Commissioner, Swettenham (1901–3) dominated Resident-General William Treacher (1902–4). William Taylor, the next Resident-General (1905–10) was more independent, refusing to follow Treacher's practice of submitting every working paper to the High Commissioner. He disagreed with Anderson's (High Commissioner 1904–11) policy of using the financial surplus from the FMS for British expansion to the northern Malay states and Borneo and projects in the Straits Settlements.

Anderson was equally determined to act as the real head of both the Straits Settlements and the FMS. He thought this was necessary to ensure there was no divergence in policy and practice between the two administrations and to reap the many advantages of closer colony–FMS relations.

Anderson's reforms

The Colonial Office entrusted the planning of the future of Malaya to Anderson, who was dissatisfied with the FMS administration left by Swettenham. He believed the FMS should have a central legislature instead of four state councils.

Anderson had also to accommodate the interests of the growing European community (which had increased from 791 in 1891 to 3,284 in 1911; two-thirds were in the private sector). Through the Planters Association of Malaya and English language newspapers such as the *Malay Mail*, Europeans increasingly demanded a say in government. Anderson sympathized with this demand for representation and believed the FMS administration could, through a Federal Council, benefit from European expertise and advice, especially in the areas of finance and economic development.

In 1909, Anderson persuaded the Colonial Office to introduce a Federal Council, partly to enable him to enter directly into the FMS administration as the Council's president. The Council was warmly welcomed by commercial interests and was supported by the Residents. The rulers were also on Anderson's side, although for different reasons. Sultan Idris hoped that the Federal Council would offer more consideration to the state

councils' views, whereas Anderson regarded its establishment as a further stage in administrative centralization of the FMS.

Anderson's proposal for an administrative council comprising the High Commissioner, Resident-General, Residents and the FMS rulers was rejected by the Colonial Office. Instead, it allowed Anderson to chair the conference of the Resident-General and the Residents and thus enter further into the FMS administration.

Anderson also lobbied the Colonial Office to change the title of Resident-General to Chief Secretary after Taylor retired in 1911 to establish beyond any doubt that the High Commissioner was the real head of the FMS, and that the Chief Secretary was his subordinate.

For some time, Anderson had felt that his role in the FMS had been hampered by an uncooperative Resident-General. To undermine Taylor, he had begun to work more closely with the Residents and the rulers. The rulers hoped the change would be a check on centralization, while the Residents felt they would work more congenially with the High Commissioner. The support far outweighed the vigorous opposition of FMS commercial interests. The Chief Secretary Enactment, which changed the title of the head of the FMS, was passed in 1910 and came into effect early in 1911.

A satirical look at an average, 'very busy' and eventful day in the life of the Governor–High Commissioner, was published in the *Straits Produce* on 15 December 1927.

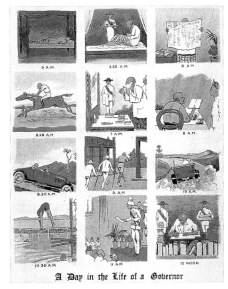

A Day in the Life of a Governor

Sharing revenue and economic development

Separate British Residential Systems in Perak, Selangor, Pahang and Negeri Sembilan caused unequal growth of the economy and population in those states, depending upon the natural resources of each state and the capability of the individual Residents. With the formation of the Federated Malay States (FMS) in 1896, federal regulations enabled the central government to coordinate economic developments throughout the federation. The period between 1896 and 1941 saw the growth of export crops and the development of infrastructure.

A 1927 *Straits Produce* cartoon which took a satirical look at the highly capital-intensive European mining methods. The bucket dredge could shift large volumes of soil in a day and made the exploitation of less rich deposits feasible.

TRADE OF THE FEDERATED MALAY STATES, 1895–1938 (STRAITS $)			
YEAR	IMPORTS	EXPORTS	TOTAL TRADE
1895	22,653,271	31,622,805	54,276,076
1900	38,402,581	60,361,805	98,764,386
1905	50,575,455	80,057,654	130,633,109
1910	53,255,151	102,851,990	156,107,141
1915	60,015,935	181,838,118	241,854,053
1920	170,522,123	288,715,698	459,237,821
1925	137,116,207	411,878,610	548,994,817
1930	168,020,418	213,652,044	381,672,976
1935	87,102,149	186,770,827	273,872,462
1938	123,380,927	174,804,222	298,185,149

The economic structure of the FMS

With the formation of the FMS in 1896, two prime export items, tin and rubber, extended across state boundaries. Thus, it became essential to develop communications systems and new administrative forms. The setting up of a Federal Treasury was followed by the introduction, in 1909, of a Federal Council, presided over by the High Commissioner (also the governor of the Straits Settlements) (see 'The Resident-General and the Federal Council'). The Council, whose membership included the four Residents and other official and unofficial members, had the power to consider and approve the annual federal as well as state budgets.

As the economy grew and political as well as administrative power became more centralized in the hands of federal officials, there were moves to reduce some of these powers and to return the confidence of some of the disgruntled sultans. In 1925, Governor Laurence Guillemard was able to secure financial arrangements for all federal services to be budgeted under the Federal Assessment and state services to be budgeted by the states. However, the Federal Council approved and determined both the federal as well as state expenditure.

The decentralization process was expanded under Governor Sir Cecil Clementi (1930–4), who suggested that the states take responsibility for all sectors except finance (see 'The decentralization policy'). Specific budgets were allotted to the states which could collect certain taxes, so as not to be dependent upon the federal budget. Second, federal officers were appointed to head state departments to oversee expenditure. Third, surplus funds from the states reverted to the federal government. These arrangements continued until 1941.

The total revenue of the FMS increased from $8,434,084 in 1896 to $105,404,458 in 1927. Exports increased from $28,395,855 in 1896 to $445,600,203 in 1926, with rubber and tin being the major contributors. In the years before World War II, these two commodities contributed 65–75 per cent of the total export revenue. This figure was economically unstable because prices were subject to the fluctuations of the world economy. It was the implementation of the international rubber and tin restriction schemes in the 1930s, introduced by the federal administration, that enabled the economy to revive just before World War II. The FMS were economically more progressive than the Unfederated Malay States (UMS)—Kedah, Perlis, Kelantan, Terengganu and Johor—and the Straits Settlements of Singapore, Penang and Melaka.

The backbone of economic development

Roll-call was held every morning on rubber estates before the labourers began the day's work.

INSET: A coupon permitting the export of 1 picul of rubber. Coupons were introduced during the depression in an attempt to limit rubber production.

In the late 19th and early 20th centuries, the economy of the Malay Peninsula depended very heavily on just two commodities, tin and rubber, which were needed in increasing quantities by the factories and motor vehicle industries of Europe and America. Revenue from exports of these products enabled rapid developments in infrastructure. The size and composition of the population also changed radically as thousands of new immigrants arrived to work in the mines and estates. Though many later returned to their home countries, many others settled permanently.

TIN PRODUCTION FROM EUROPEAN- AND CHINESE-OWNED MINES, 1910–1937 (%)		
YEAR	EUROPEAN MINES	CHINESE MINES
1910	22	78
1920	36	64
1930	63	37
1937	68	32

A mineral train on its way to Singapore from the Malay Peninsula. Direct rail transport of goods to Singapore for export became possible after the completion of the railway to Singapore in 1909.

The development of an export economy

The British exercised an open economic policy in the FMS, encouraging investments in tin and rubber as these products were in great demand by European industries. The formation of the federation enabled liberal policies on land, immigration, customs and other taxes favourable to investors. Good systems of communications were also developed, especially in the areas dominated by these products. Between 1896 and 1941, the Malay states became the world's biggest tin and rubber producers.

Infrastructure development at the centre

This structure (erected in 1890) replaced the original building of the Selangor Club (founded in 1884 for British members) beside the Padang, used for cricket matches and other team games.

Kuala Lumpur, which began as a small mining settlement with temporary dwellings often razed by fires, became the capital of Selangor in 1880 and the capital of the newly formed Federated Malay States in 1896. With the increased British presence came a period of rapid development. Many large government buildings were constructed as well as many new commercial premises by banks and retailers. The railway, new roads and bridges enabled easier travel both within the city and to other towns.

Old Market Square (now Medan Pasar) in 1925, with the Hongkong and Shanghai Bank at the end of the square. By that time, cars were already in common use by the wealthier businessmen.

First home of the Selangor Club

Parade Ground (now Merdeka Square)

Gombak Road

Thatch-roofed buildings later replaced by the Secretariat (Sultan Abdul Samad) Building.

Market Street (now Lebuh Pasar Besar)

A view of Kuala Lumpur in 1884, showing the buildings of the early town, together with insets of the modern buildings which quickly replaced the old structures after Kuala Lumpur became the capital of the Federated Malay States in 1896.

LEFT: The Sultan Abdul Samad Building (known originally as the New Offices), which was built in 1897, was the centre of administration.

RIGHT: Railway yards and workshops were set up in Kuala Lumpur for the maintenance of the new railway system.

INSET: The third Kuala Lumpur railway station building, opened in 1911.

More than 90 per cent of the tin and rubber produced in the FMS was exported. Favourable policies encouraged large investments, especially from European and Chinese capitalists. The Chinese initially dominated the tin industry, but it was gradually taken over by the Europeans in the 1930s.

The export trade of tin and rubber, as well as the import of rice and other goods directly or indirectly related to their production, became the backbone of economic development in the FMS.

The growth of tin and rubber brought in thousands of people from China, India and Indonesia; some became entrepreneurs, but the majority worked as labourers. British policies, and perhaps cultural differences, grouped these labourers according to their economic activities. Hence, the majority of Chinese were found in mining, while the Indians and, to a certain extent, Indonesians, worked in rubber plantations. The majority of the local Malays remained in the production of the locally consumed rice crop.

The general population opened smallholdings for rubber cultivation. Large estates were still owned by Europeans and a small number of Chinese. From 1929 to 1939, estates contributed about 63 per cent, and the smallholders 35 per cent, of the total production from the federation. Besides rubber and tin, very small quantities of copra (dried coconut kernel) and coffee were also exported.

Rice was also imported as local production was insufficient to support the fast-growing immigrant population. In 1938, rice imports formed 10 per cent of the total value of imports. Until 1912, opium imports were second in importance to rice. Then opium became a controversial issue and its position was taken over by other products.

The annual increase in revenue and surplus enabled the FMS to develop good roads, railways and other forms of communication. These were later extended to the UMS to further enhance and facilitate economic development, especially in areas dominated by revenue-generating crops.

This cartoon, which was published in the *Straits Produce* issue of 15 December 1927, bore the caption 'An A1 colony with a B2 budget'.

The decentralization policy

The decentralization policy of the colonial government sought to overcome the rulers' discontent with administrative centralization and general Malay neglect. It also aimed to loosen the hold of the Federated Malay States (FMS) administration in Perak, Pahang, Selangor and Negeri Sembilan sufficiently to enable the British to persuade the Unfederated Malay States (UMS) of Perlis, Kedah, Kelantan, Terengganu and Johor to join the FMS in a Malayan federation. During the 1920s, the British vision of this federation excluded the Straits Settlements, though they were included in later plans.

Sultan Sulaiman of Selangor (r. 1898–1938) and Sir George Maxwell, Chief Secretary 1920–6. The photograph was probably taken during that period.

The Maxwell initiative

The idea of decentralization was suggested by Sir John Anderson (Governor–High Commissioner 1904–11) in 1908, but the decentralization policy was formulated in 1920 by George Maxwell (Chief Secretary of the Federated Malay States 1920–6). Maxwell's key achievement was the implementation of the Hose scheme, which offered the first stage of a power transfer from the federal (department) heads to the Residents of the FMS.

Maxwell's long-term aim for the policy of decentralization was to transform the federal heads from executive officers to advisory and inspecting officers as in the FMS prior to 1902, when the Residents had substantially more power. However, it was clear by the end of 1924 that Maxwell had centralized power in his own hands.

The Guillemard scheme

On a visit to the Colonial Office in 1924, Sultan Iskandar of Perak requested drastic decentralization to change the Chief Secretary's role into that of a coordinating officer. The Colonial Office instructed High Commissioner Sir Laurence Guillemard (1920–7) to develop a new policy. His scheme had the same motivation as Maxwell's policy, but was influenced by his desire to abolish the position of Chief Secretary and remove George Maxwell so he could gain more control over the FMS.

Guillemard wanted to devolve the immense power of the Chief Secretary to the Residents, the state councils and the federal heads, with any remaining power to be absorbed by the High Commissioner. Guillemard enjoyed the support of the Colonial Office, a minority of British officials who were pro-decentralization, and the FMS Malay rulers. However, there was powerful opposition from the European business community, the English newspapers, most British officials and George Maxwell. His

A cartoon showing the 'Handing Over' when Sir Hugh Clifford succeeded Sir Laurence Guillemard in 1927. The caption reads: The retiring charlady: 'It's a nice little 'ouse, dearie, but it do take a lot of work to keep it clean and tidy!'

GOVERNMENT OF SINGAPORE

opponents believed the Guillemard scheme would reduce administrative efficiency and adversely affect economic development. By June 1926, Guillemard conceded defeat. In 1927, he was succeeded by Sir Hugh Clifford. Meanwhile, the Chief Secretary continued to head the FMS.

However, Guillemard had made two important changes. He strengthened the Federal Council by appointing three Malays and five federal heads as new members. The FMS rulers, however, withdrew from the council and attended an annual Durbar instead. He also transferred 12 services to the states, to be financed by funds agreed upon by the Federal Council, but allocated by state councils.

The Clementi scheme

In 1931, High Commissioner Sir Cecil Clementi (1930–4) enlarged the decentralization policy on the personal appeal of the FMS rulers. Clementi also intended to use these sultanates to exclude the Chinese from a share of political power. His ultimate objective was a Malayan federation of the Malay states and the Straits Settlements, headed by the Governor-High Commissioner in Singapore. By vesting more power in the FMS government, he hoped the UMS would join the FMS. After its formation, he wanted to recentralize the federation.

With provisional support from Lord Passfield, Secretary of State for the Colonies, Clementi presented his scheme during the Durbar at Sri Menanti in August 1931. He proposed the abolition of the position of Chief Secretary and the devolution of his power to the states. Clementi also proposed the transfer of 11 federal departments to state control and of a large degree of financial and legislative power to the state councils. This created an uproar. On one side, the determined Clementi and his minority of pro-Malay officials pressed his scheme forward in a hasty and autocratic manner, backed by the FMS rulers, the Malay élite and the Malay newspapers. Against the scheme were most Malayan British officials, European commercial houses, the UMS rulers and non-Malay Asians. The latter felt they were being discriminated against and their contributions to the country's development were not recognized. The UMS rulers feared their states being dragged into the federation as they would be deprived of their autonomy and rights.

Sir Philip Cunliffe-Lister, Passfield's successor, condemned the scheme outright. He agreed with European commercial interests that the Clementi scheme would damage administrative efficiency and harm economic development. In 1932, he sent his top official, Sir Samuel Wilson, a tactful man with balanced views on Malaya, to solve the problem.

Wilson endorsed the abolition of the Chief Secretary, but not the proposal that most of the office's coordinating functions be placed under the Secretary to the High Commissioner in Singapore. He proposed, instead, that a relatively junior FMS head coordinate federal affairs from Kuala Lumpur. However, Wilson agreed with Clementi that the FMS should be developed into a genuine federation with a rigid division of power between the centre and the states, as a prelude to the larger Malayan federation. The Wilson plan intended this federation be established in three stages.

Within four years, 11 federal services were to be transferred to the states, where the federal heads were to retain much of their executive authority but be more accountable to the Residents. Another aim was to progressively vest the state councils with financial power until they were self-supporting. During this period, the state councils would allocate money voted by the Federal Council to fund these services; this would increase from 11 per cent to 50 per cent of FMS budgets. The state councils were also authorized to legislate on purely state matters and certain federal issues where uniformity was not essential. Along with this, European and non-Malay members were appointed to the councils.

Thomas and decentralization

Clementi was succeeded by Sir Shenton Thomas (1934–42), a firm believer in both strong central government and economic development. Thomas implemented the first stage of Wilson's plan, and in 1935 appointed a Federal Secretary to coordinate federal affairs and serve as the mediator between the High Commissioner and the Residents. Although junior to the Residents, the Secretary was a strong FMS head with considerable 'borrowed power'.

Thomas also set limits on devolution to the states, fearing Wilson's open-ended approach might weaken the Federal Council and cause legislative chaos in the FMS. The policy disappointed the

FMS rulers. In 1937, the sultan of Pahang called for accelerated decentralization in order to place the Pahang State Council on a par with that in Johor.

Thomas hindered the development of the state councils in another direction. He abandoned the proposal to train the rulers-in-council to exercise executive power in the state administrations, as was the case in the UMS. This made it even harder to persuade the UMS to join the FMS.

The impact of decentralization

The decentralization policy affected the Malay states in two major ways. First, it decentralized the FMS administration to a significant extent, but failed to bring the goal of a Malayan federation any closer. In 1939, a government committee was formed to study the implementation of the second stage of Wilson's programme. However, this was soon disbanded with the outbreak of World War II.

Second, decentralization injected racial considerations into political and economic life. In response to Clementi's policy, the Chinese became openly involved in Malayan politics, and fought more vigorously for equal rights with the Malays.

Decentralization also helped Malay nationalism turn overtly political and anti-non-Malay during the 1930s. The Malay rulers and the élite were disillusioned by Thomas's lack of support for decentralization. Combined with Chinese political assertiveness, politically conscious Malays became convinced that their community would lose out unless they were organized politically. Decentralization therefore contributed substantially to the emergence of nationalistic Malay state associations after 1937.

A photograph taken on the occasion of a lunch hosted by Tun Tan Cheng Lock (seated, fourth from left), the first Chinese non-executive director of the agency house Sime Darby, for Sir Cecil Clementi, Governor of the Straits Settlements and High Commissioner of the Malay States (third from left).

From the late 1860s, stamps minted in Britain for use in the Straits Settlements carried a portrait of Britain's reigning monarch, such as King Edward VII from 1899 to 1911 (1). After the formation of the Federated Malay States in 1896, stamps usually featured local themes: a Malayan tiger (2), a group of elephants, or the Kuala Lumpur railway station. Starting around 1910, the Malay states, one by one, began to issue postage stamps bearing the face of their ruler.

The Unfederated Malay States

Prior to the Anglo-Siamese Treaty in 1909, Siam had suzerainty over the northern Malay states. The British takeover of the northern states, which began with the 1902 Anglo-Siamese Agreement, was completed by the 1909 treaty. British Advisers were appointed to Perlis, Kedah and Kelantan in 1909, and Terengganu in 1918. Johor, at the southern tip of the Malay Peninsula, enjoyed a special relationship with Britain— friendship rather than dependency—during the reign of Sultan Abu Bakar. However, under his successor, Sultan Ibrahim, relations were not so cordial and a General Adviser was appointed to the state in 1910.

A replica of the *bunga mas* (golden flowers) presented to Siam as tribute by Kedah during the period of Siamese suzerainty over the state.

The northern states

The payment to Siam of *bunga mas* (golden flowers) every five years or *bunga perak* (silver flowers) every three years by the four northern Malay states— Perlis, Kedah, Kelantan and Terengganu—was interpreted differently by the two sides (see 'The Burney Treaty, Siam and the northern Malay states'). The Siamese considered the presentation as tribute, a sign of submission, while the Malay states regarded it as a sign of friendship or token of gratitude for Siamese non-aggression. Certainly, if the tribute was not sent, the states were inviting attack. For most of the 19th century, the northern Malay states were under the direct threat of Siam and therefore attempted to play Britain against Siam. Britain was still courted by the Malay states as a friendly power as its policy at the time was not to interfere in the Malay–Siamese disputes, but to recognize the northern states as Siamese tributary states. Therefore, it ignored the pleas for help from these states.

Kedah had suffered grievously from British indifference or vacillation over the Siamese threat. Despite Kedah's agreements allowing British settlement in Penang in 1791 and Province Wellesley (Seberang Perai) in 1800 as a means of protection, Britain stood idly by as Siamese forces ruthlessly attacked Kedah in 1821 and occupied the state for the next 20 years. The only help offered by the British was in allowing Sultan Ahmad Tajuddin to seek refuge in Penang (he later moved to Melaka). The 1824 Anglo-Dutch Treaty established Britain as the sole European power in the Malay Peninsula. It thus gave the Malay rulers in Selangor and Perak an alternative to Siamese overlordship, which they took advantage of—to the dismay of Siam.

In 1826, a British East India Company official, Henry Burney, concluded a treaty with Siam which prevented Selangor and Perak from becoming dependencies of Siam. Under the Burney Treaty, Siam promised not to 'molest, attack or disturb' these two states. The treaty also ensured that Siam would not obstruct British commerce in the nortrhern states of Kelantan and Terengganu (see 'The Burney Treaty, Siam and the northern Malay states').

British intervention

In 1842, Britain intervened to restore the sultanate of Kedah. A smaller state was returned as Siam detached Perlis, Kubang Pasu and Setul from Kedah and recognized them as separate and minor kingdoms. Only Kubang Pasu was later returned to Kedah (Setul remained Siamese territory). In the 1860s, a crisis developed over Terengganu and Pahang. Growing British commercial interests clashed with Bangkok's desire to strengthen and extend its influence. In 1862, British ships bombarded Kuala Terengganu, the state capital, to discourage Siamese encroachment into the state and to prevent Siam from interfering in the civil war in Pahang.

However, by the third quarter of the 19th century, Britain's own imperial interests in the Malay Peninsula necessitated intervention in Malay–Siamese affairs. In the 1870s, Britain had brought most of the important states of the Malay Peninsula under its rule and had consolidated its power with the extension of the Residential System to Pahang in 1888 and with the formation of the Federated Malay States in l896 (see 'The formation of the Federated Malay States').

In what has become known as the 'British

Rulers of the Unfederated Malay States

Raja of Perlis, Syed Alwi (r. 1905–43)

Perlis

Kedah

Kelantan

Sultan Muhammad IV (r. 1900–20)

Terengganu

Sultan Abdul Hamid Halim (r. 1882–1943)

Sultan Abu Bakar (r. 1862–95)

Johor

Sultan Zainal Abidin III (r. 1881–1918)

The members of the state council of Kelantan in 1909. The sultan of Kelantan, Muhammad IV, who was recognized by the British as sultan after the 1910 treaty, and the Raja Dewa (formerly Raja Muda) Zainal Abidin are third and fourth from the left, respectively.

Forward Movement', during this period British officials worked to replace Siamese authority in the northern Malay states by coming to an understanding with France over the future of Siam itself. The two European powers decided to use Siam as a buffer between their colonial empires, with each attempting to extend its influence into Siamese territory or to seize as much of it as possible for themselves. In 1902, the Anglo-Siamese Agreement formally recognized Bangkok's right to supervise the foreign relations of Kelantan and Terengganu, but the Siamese advisers appointed in the two states had to be of British nationality. In 1903, W. A. Graham was appointed as Adviser to the sultan of Kelantan. This agreement, which had been hastened by the activities of R. W. Duff, a former British official in Pahang who had obtained a monopoly on mining rights to about one-third of Kelantan, marked the first stage in the British takeover.

In 1909, the process was completed with the signing of the Anglo-Siamese Treaty which transferred Kelantan and Terengganu, together with Kedah and Perlis, to British overlordship. These treaties were signed without the consent of the Malay rulers concerned. Siam agreed to give up jurisdiction over the northern Malay states as a trade-off for securing British guarantees on national sovereignty in the context of French encroachments on its eastern boundary.

British Advisers

Although Perlis and Kedah accepted British Advisers in 1909, Kelantan and Terengganu did so only in 1910 and 1919 respectively. In 1910, Kelantan signed a treaty with the British which recognized Raja Muhammad IV (r. 1900–20) as sultan on condition that he accepted a British Adviser according to the usual terms. Also in 1910, Terengganu signed a treaty

with the British. In place of a British Adviser, Sultan Zainal Abidin III (r. 1881–1918) was to receive a British Agent with the functions and powers of a consular official. Terengganu's independence lasted for another eight years. During this period, British influence was exerted to persuade Kedah, Perlis, Kelantan and Terengganu to join the Federated Malay States, but the pressure was successfully resisted right up to the outbreak of war in 1941.

In these four northern states and in Johor (which did not receive a British Adviser until 1914)— collectively known as the Unfederated Malay States—the Malays enjoyed greater political autonomy than in the Federated Malay States. But British reforms continued to be introduced. These included registration of land titles, collection of land rents and imposition of new taxes on agricultural crops and forest products. There was opposition to these taxes by peasant cultivators and landowners, including members of royalty, resulting in rebellions in Kelantan (1915) and Terengganu (1928). However, these rebellions were crushed by British military might. In the other unfederated states, British reforms were enforced more judiciously.

Benefits to the Malays of the Unfederated Malay States

- The administrative machinery was largely in the hands of Malay officers.

- The Jawi script was widely used for official correspondence in Malay.

- Friday, the Islamic holy day, was the weekly rest day, unlike Sunday in the FMS.

- Johor was allowed to have its own Johor Military Force and fly its own state flag alongside the Union Jack.

Johor, the southern state

Johor was the most modern of the Unfederated Malay States. From 1885 to 1941, Johor enjoyed a special position in its relations with Britain. The 1885 Anglo-Johor Treaty had recognized Temenggong Abu Bakar as sultan (see 'British mediation and the new sultanate in Johor') and accorded him sovereign status on the basis of equality with Britain. The appointment of a consular official to the state was waived because of the cordial relations between the rulers of Britain and Johor; thus it was a relationship based on friendship, not one of suzerainty and dependency.

British officials in Singapore attempted, but failed, to bring Johor under British control. Just before his death in 1895, Sultan Abu Bakar drew up a written constitution to protect the state's independence (see 'Constitutional reforms'). His successor, Sultan Ibrahim, was unwilling to continue receiving informal advice from the British, and in 1909 was forced to accept a British General Adviser, who found he could not rule unimpeded. A threat of deposition by the British was needed before the sultan handed over full control, and in 1914 the General Adviser was given the same powers as the Residents in the Federated Malay States. However, he won some concessions: Johor was allowed to have its own Johor Military Force and to fly its state flag alongside the Union Jack.

Sultan Abu Bakar in 1886 in his coronation robes. He tried to maintain the state's independence after his death by drawing up a written constitution.

Sultan Ibrahim (r. 1895–1959) was unwilling to accept advice from the British, resulting in the appointment of a British General Adviser in 1909.

The 1909 Anglo-Siamese Treaty

The 1909 Anglo-Siamese Treaty ended the traditional Siamese–Malay tributary relations which had existed since the 15th century, and brought about the cession of the four northern Malay dependencies of Siam— Kedah, Perlis, Kelantan, and Terengganu—to Britain. With this treaty, Siam relinquished its suzerain rights and recognized these four Malay states as being under British protection. The treaty marked a turning point in the history of the Malay Peninsula; by relinquishing its suzerainty in these states, Siam had made it possible for the later development of Malaya into a unified, modern state.

Important articles of the Anglo-Siamese Treaty

- Siam agreed to transfer 'all rights of suzerainty, protection, administration whatsoever' over its four Malay dependencies—Kedah, Perlis, Kelantan and Terengganu—to Britain.

- In return, Britain agreed to relinquish its extraterritorial rights over British subjects in Siam.

- Britain also agreed to the abrogation of the 1897 Secret Convention.

- Britain offered Siam a loan of 4 million pounds sterling at 4 per cent interest for the construction of the railway to the Malay Peninsula.

Territories ceded to Britain in 1909

Historical background

The 1909 Anglo-Siamese Treaty was the outcome of lengthy rivalry and conflict of interest between Siam and British colonial authorities dating from 1786 when the British East India Company (EIC) established its Penang base. The Anglo-Dutch Treaty of 1824 confirmed Britain as the sole European power in the Malay Peninsula. The only local power contesting the British advance was Siam, which laid claim over the northern Malay states. The Burney Treaty of 1826 (see 'The Burney Treaty, Siam and the northern Malay states'), signed by Siam and the British government of India, limited Siam's sphere of influence in the Malay Peninsula to Kedah, Kelantan and Terengganu. Up until 1909, Siam's suzerain rights and privileges over these states were questioned by the British authorities, especially after the 1880s when the Forward Party gained influence and control over both the Colonial Office in London and the colonial regime in Singapore.

By the end of the 19th century, London had accepted the British Forward Movement's rationale for the strengthening of Britain's position vis-à-vis Siam. The outcome was the Secret Anglo-Siamese Convention of 1897. In return for British guarantee of Siamese sovereignty in the northern Malay states, including suzerainty over Kelantan and Terengganu, Siam pledged not to part with any of the territories or grant concessions without prior British consent. In 1902, under pressure from both London and Singapore, Siam signed a treaty with Kelantan to replace the tributary relationship with a contractual one modelled on the Residential System.

King Chulalongkorn (r. 1868–1910) adopted a policy of equidistance in dealings with Britain and France. The 1909 treaty was intended to put Anglo-Siamese relations on a new footing and safeguard the sovereignty of Siam.

Reasons for the 1909 treaty

In the late 19th century, four major issues affected the ties between Siam and Britain: the problem of extraterritoriality; the Secret Anglo-Siamese Convention of 1897; Thai suzerainty over the four northern Malay states; and the railway to southern Siam. The objective of the 1909 treaty was to find a common solution to these problems, and thus put Anglo-Siamese relations on a new, tension-free basis. This, in turn, would ensure the success of King Chulalongkorn's nation-building programme.

Siamese–Terengganu tributary relations

Kuala Terengganu, the capital of Terengganu, depicted in the *Illustrated London News* of 29 March 1890. Terengganu's long-reigning sultan, Baginda Omar (1839–76), once resided in the stone fort on top of Bukit Puteri. A large bell in the grounds was used to signal the time for breaking fast during the month of Ramadan.

LEFT: Sultan Zainal Abidin III of Terengganu (r. 1881–1918), photographed c. 1900.

RIGHT: Istana Tengku Nik, built by Sultan Zainal Abidin III in 1881 upon ascending the throne, is all that remains of a much larger palace complex. The building is typically raised on posts and has panelled walls made of teak.

The tributary relationship that existed between Siam and Terengganu from about 1785 to 1909 was successful despite the fact that Siam had no real interests in Terengganu politically, economically or socially. The nature of tributary obligations demanded that as a vassal Terengganu send to Bangkok every three years tributary dues consisting of the *bunga mas* (golden flowers) (90 centimetres high) and the *bunga perak* (silver flowers) (30 centimetres high) together with five kinds of goods: 2–4 rolls of cloth, 100 bushels of sago, 500 pearl shells, 500 bundles of rattan sticks and 100 floor mats. Terengganu was also obliged to give 'wartime' assistance to Bangkok whenever required.

In return for the tributary dues, Siam was obliged to offer Terengganu military and diplomatic assistance when requested, as well as other types of aid. For example, when a large fire in Kuala Terengganu in 1883 caused a great deal of damage, Bangkok sent assistance to relieve the hard-ship of the town's residents who were affected by the fire.

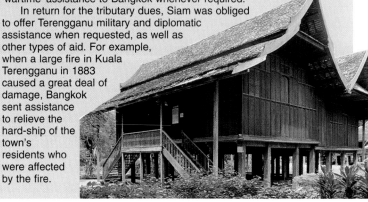

King Chulalongkorn of Siam, who authorized the 1909 Anglo-Siamese Treaty which transferred Siam's rights of suzerainty over the four northern Malay states—Perlis, Kedah, Kelantan and Terengganu—to Britain.

Extraterritoriality

In 1855, Britain obtained extraterritoriality over its subjects in Siam. By the 20th century, it was evident to King Chulalongkorn that as long as Siamese sovereignty remained impaired by this partial loss of judicial authority, Siam would remain a target of Western interference and a second-class nation in the international community. It was also obvious that to regain authority over the subjects of its powerful neighbours, France and Britain, Siam must offer some territory cession in return.

Edward Strobel, the American General Adviser to the Siamese government, persuaded the king to sacrifice Siam's Malay dependencies to Britain in return for British abandonment of its extraterritorial rights in Siam. By ceding these tributaries to Britain, Siam could be assured of British friendship and would advantageously rid itself of the Siamese Malay tributaries, the main source of 'weakness, danger, and annoyance'. Finally the king concurred, and in 1906 Strobel began negotiations for the cession of the four northern Malay states to Britain.

The Secret Anglo-Siamese Convention

The Secret Convention of 1897 was signed by Siam and Britain to safeguard their mutual interests in the northern Malay Peninsula. However, difficulties arose. The British interpreted the convention as giving British economic interests a free hand in the areas of the agreement, causing Siam great concern over the possible reaction of other European powers whose requests for concessions in the area were always rejected, regardless of whether they truly posed a threat to British influence. Siam wished to be released from such unequal obligations. This was another reason for Siamese leaders to concur with Strobel's argument for territory cession as a price to pay for the abolition of this diplomatic faux pas.

The railway project

Among its plans to modernize the country's infrastructure, Siam wanted to build a railway between Bangkok and Trang, a western seaboard province in the northern Malay Peninsula, using German technical and personnel assistance. Britain strongly objected to German involvement in an area which was so sensitive to both its political and economic interests.

To overcome British objections, in April 1907 Strobel proposed that the Federated Malay States (FMS) give Siam a loan of 4 million pounds sterling at 4 per cent interest. In return, the Siamese government would allow the FMS absolute authority over the construction of the railway. However, British objections remained unresolved.

Siamese suzerainty

Siamese suzerainty over the northern Malay states had caused friction between Siam and British officials since the mid-19th century. As King Chulalongkorn's policy of building a nation-state gained momentum, it became increasingly obvious to Siam that its Malay dependencies were hindering the national integration progress. They were also the source of constant conflict with Britain as Straits Settlements officials worked for the elimination of Siamese authority in the Peninsula in spite of the agreements recognizing Siam's suzerainty over the four northern Malay states: the Burney Treaty of 1826; the Secret Anglo-Siamese Convention of 1897; and the 1902 Anglo-Siamese Agreement. Strobel proposed, as a final solution to the obstacles of national integration and the survival of Siam as an independent state, the cession of these four dependencies to Britain. In this way, he thought, Siam could solve all its outstanding difficulties with Britain, regain its judicial sovereignty, and start a new chapter of positive Anglo-Siamese relations.

Treaty negotiations

The principal negotiator for Britain was Ralph Paget, Minister to the Siamese court. Strobel was the Siamese negotiator until his sudden death, when he was replaced by Jens I. Westengard, who was his successor as General Adviser. Negotiations focused on two main aspects: extraterritoriality and a 'readjustment' of political relations in the Malay Peninsula. The negotiations were long and difficult. Britain demanded more territory, while Siam refused to consider ceding any territory other than the four Malay states. Eventually, the two parties arrived at an agreement and the treaty was signed on 10 March 1909.

The rulers' reaction to the treaty

Throughout the lengthy, difficult negotiations for the 1909 Anglo-Siamese Treaty, none of the Malay rulers was informed or consulted. When the treaty was signed, all the rulers felt bitterly betrayed by Siam. The sultan of Kelantan, Muhammad IV, exposed the illegality of the treaty in a letter to the governor of the Straits Settlements.

Sultan Abdul Hamid of Kedah summed up the rulers' frustration and rage against Siam when he said: 'I can forgive the buyer [Britain] who had no obligation to me, but I cannot forgive the seller [Siam].'

Sultan Abdul Hamid Halim Shah of Kedah wearing the Siamese Order of Chulachomklao, which carried the title of Chao Phraya Saiburi.

The elaborate gilt decorations and layers of upswept roofs of Kelantan's oldest functioning Thai temple, Wat Uttamaran at Repek, attest to Kelantan's long association with Thailand.

Constitutional reforms

The traditional consultation process between the sultans and the more powerful of the district chiefs changed after British intervention in the Malay states, when British Residents were appointed to advise the sultans. To restore the chiefs' role in the consultation process, and to include Chinese headmen, state councils were established. The sultans did not take an active part in these councils or the Federal Council, which was later established. Laws were passed by the councils and the sultan's assent given. Johor and Terengganu, fearing a British takeover of their states, promulgated state constitutions to forestall that possibility.

Prior to British intervention in the Malay states and the establishment of state councils, there was already a Legislative Council in Singapore. The only local representative in 1873 was Hoo Ah Kay, nicknamed Whampoa by the British, who is standing second from right. On his right is J. W. W. Birch, who was appointed as the first Resident of Perak in 1874 and murdered in 1875.

A page from the *Sejarah Melayu* (the Malay Annals), a historical text which tells the story of the rise and fall of the Melaka sultanate, from its founding to the time of Portuguese conquest in 1511.

Government by district chiefs

The present system of constitutional monarchy in Malaysia evolved through a combination of Malay custom and Western influence. In the precolonial semifeudal Malay political system, the Malay chiefs were more powerful than the rulers. Consequently, in the 19th century the Malay states frequently lapsed into anarchy and civil wars (see 'Civil wars and British intervention'). In states such as Selangor, Perak and Negeri Sembilan, the chiefs were busily engaged in succession disputes in which they often backed royal candidates who were weak and pliant. The chiefs disliked candidates who showed too much authority or dared to antagonize them. In almost all states, there was a decentralized system of local government by district chiefs, and thus the sultans could exercise little real power.

Ideal ruler

To the chiefs and advisers, the ideal ruler was one who did not interfere in government affairs. Although he was head of state and of the Islamic religion, the sultan was expected to consult with his

chiefs on every major policy, and both sides had to agree before any decision was made (see 'The Malay *kerajaan*'). Although some rulers—such as Baginda Omar of Terengganu (r. 1839–76) and Sultan Muhammad II of Kelantan (r. 1838–86)—had been able to govern their states with a strong hand, most accepted their role as largely ceremonial and symbolic rather than executive. Although the sultan held an exalted position, he could not abuse his powers arbitrarily. He was a fount of justice, and the supreme authority in the judicial system.

The *Sejarah Melayu* (the Malay Annals), in describing the correct ruler–chief relationship in 15th-century Melaka, reminded the rulers that 'No ruler, however great his wisdom and understanding, shall prosper or succeed in doing justice unless he consults with those in authority under him. For rulers are like fire and their ministers are like firewood and fire needs wood to produce a flame.'

The ministers and the rulers had specific but complementary duties, and were expected to respect each other's roles. In the Johor–Riau–Lingga sultanate, under the Bugis–Malay pact, the Malay sultan agreed to allow the Bugis chiefs to rule on his behalf, while the sultan remained the ceremonial head of state. The Johor chronicles, *Salasilah Melayu dan Bugis*, likened the role of the Malay ruler to that of a woman: 'And the Yamtuan Besar must be like a woman only, when asked to partake of a meal, then he partakes of the meal; And the Yamtuan Muda is like a man; and if there arises any matter or discussion only the views of the Yamtuan Muda would prevail.'

Johor state constitution

The Johor state constitution of 1895, entitled *Undang-Undang Tubuh Kerajaan Johor 1895*, containing 64 articles, was adopted by the state council and approved by Sultan Abu Bakar (r. 1862–95) just before his death. It is an extraordinary document because, for the first time, a constitution curbed the powers of a sultan. Anticipating the appointment of a British Adviser, Article 15 of the constitution barred the sultan, his heirs and successors from handing the state over to any European power. If the sultan flouted this provision, he would forfeit the loyalty of his subjects, which implied that he would be removed from office; and if any member of the royal family violated this provision, he or she would be punished. Other articles attempted to define the conduct of the ruler, his annual expenditure, and his relations with his ministers.

Coat of arms at Sultan Ibrahim Building, Johor Bahru.

On 22 April 1908, Sultan Abu Bakar's successor, Sultan Ibrahim (r. 1895–1959), promulgated an amendment to the constitution which upheld the rule of law and further curbed his own powers. The amendment declared that neither the sultan nor his ministers should attempt to interfere with the courts, and reiterated that no one should be detained or imprisoned except by the process of law. The amendment also declared: 'The sultan should conduct himself with due respect and justice to the people, showing love and consideration to all of them and rule according to the law. He must uphold the Islamic religion and remember that he has been appointed to this high office by the people with the belief that he will fulfil all their expectations.'

The rulers' new role

When the British began to intervene in the Malay states in 1874, they signed treaties with the rulers by which each ruler agreed to the appointment of a British Resident in his state, and to seek and accept the Resident's advice (see 'Sultans and Residents'). This was not very different from the Malay–Bugis pact of Johor–Riau–Lingga. However, the British Resident held consultations with the sultan and attempted to involve him in decision-making.

The purpose of the state councils, established initially in Selangor and Perak in 1877, was to bring into the consultation process not only the sultans but also the Malay district chiefs and the Chinese headmen. The decisions of these council meetings, presided over by the sultan, made the rulers familiar with procedures and legislation.

Although the presence of the rulers at council meetings both added to the prestige of the councils and enhanced their personal status, most felt the need to say little but to listen more. Only a few seemed keen to participate in the proceedings. From 1909 to 1926, however, the state councils of the Federated Malay States (FMS) of Negeri Sembilan, Selangor, Perak and Pahang lost power as the rulers had become members of the Federal Council, which made decisions on behalf of the four states.

The rulers' passivity during the Federal Council proceedings was very noticeable, and eventually it was agreed that they need not attend the council meetings. Unlike previously, they were also not required to attend their own state council meetings. In 1932, the state councils were reconstituted and revived as legislative bodies with representatives of various interests and ethnic groups.

The Residents continued to consult the rulers, and the state councils discussed and passed laws. A sultan was required to give his assent to legislation only after it had been passed by the state council. There is no known case of any sultan refusing to give his consent. The normal procedure was for the sultan to affix his signature and seal to the bill, which would then be gazetted and become law.

Thus, like English constitutional law, under Malay law a sovereign could make laws, but only on the advice of his legislature. This legal reform during British rule was an important measure towards the transformation of the Malay rulers into constitutional monarchs, although no state constitutions had been drafted for the individual Federated Malay States. However, it did not differ from the old Malay custom in practice, as all laws still appeared in the name of the sultan.

Unfederated Malay States

An almost identical transformation was taking place within the Unfederated Malay States of Kedah, Perlis, Kelantan, Terengganu and Johor (see 'The Unfederated Malay States'). Ruler-in-council meetings were still held in these states. However, they enjoyed greater political autonomy than the FMS. Consequently, their rulers and state councils were anxious to retain as many as possible of these political powers. Fearing that the British might intervene and usurp the powers of their rulers, or force them to agree to British annexation of their states, the state councils of Johor and Terengganu, in 1895 and 1911 respectively, drafted and adopted their own state constitutions. In these documents, the rulers virtually surrendered their powers on

Perak State Council

Following British intervention in the Malay states from 1874, the signing of treaties and the appointment of British Residents to advise the sultans, state councils were established as law-making and administrative bodies. Perak, as the first state in which Britain intervened, was the first to receive a British Resident, after the signing of the Pangkor Treaty in 1874, with the appointment of J. W. W. Birch. After Birch's brutal murder in 1875 and a stay of only a few months by J. G. Davidson, Hugh Low was appointed as Resident in 1877. During his 12 years in Perak, Low went on to establish an effective administrative and tax collection system, providing a model for the other states. The Perak State Council, set up in 1877, was chaired by the Perak ruler, Sultan Idris (r. 1887–1916), and included the Resident, Malay notables and leaders of the Chinese community. Although he was obliged to accept the advice of the Resident in matters other than those relating to Islam and Malay custom, his role as chairman of the council gave a certain amount of power to the sultan. As a result, when this power diminished after the formation of the Federated Malay States and the centralization of power, Sultan Idris—originally a supporter of the British—became a vocal critic of the colonial government at meetings such as the Malay Durbars.

Sultan Idris of Perak (r. 1887–1916) pictured with members of his household and staff in 1897, in front of his new palace, Istana Negara, in Kuala Kangsar, which was finished for the holding of the first Malay Durbar.

The members of the 1918 Perak State Council with Sultan Iskandar (r. 1918–38) and the British Resident, W. G. Maxwell, seated in the centre.

INSET: Sultan Iskandar, son of Sultan Idris, who succeeded to the throne after the death of Sultan Abdul Jalil (r. 1916–18).

certain matters to their respective state councils.

The Johor constitution transformed the state's monarchy into the first constitutional monarchy in Malaya. Although Johor and Terengganu were the only states to promulgate constitutions, the British Resident's practice of consultation with his state ruler and the reconstitution of the state councils in 1932 already suggested the desire of the other rulers to become constitutional monarchs. This duly happened when their state constitutions were promulgated for the first time under the Federation of Malaya Agreement and the state agreements,

A watercolour of three British ships, the *Vixen, Pluto* and *Nemesis,* at anchor in Brunei harbour in August 1845 by Edward Hodges Cree, a Royal Navy surgeon. A British squadron of eight ships had gone to Brunei to seek the release of two Lascar seamen detained there.

'Keeney-Ballo', from F. S. Marryat, *Borneo and the Indian Archipelago* (1849). A view of Mount Kinabalu, the highest mountain in Southeast Asia, was probably used as a navigation aid by ships travelling along the coast of North Borneo.

RIGHT: A map entitled 'Part of the Malayan Archipelago', from Henry Keppel, *The Expedition to Borneo of HMS Dido* (1846), clearly showing the long mountain range running from Mount Kinabalu in the north.

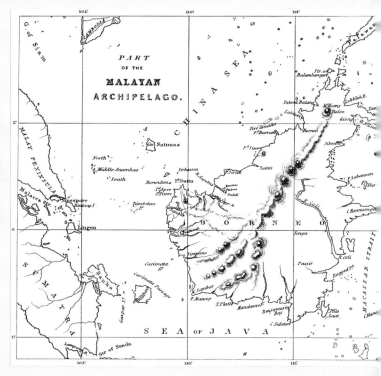

'Mr Brooke's First Residence', from Spenser St John's *Life in the Forests of the Far East* (1863), shows a group of timber structures with thatched roofs located on the east bank of the Sarawak River. When Brooke became rajah of Sarawak in 1841, Kuching was a small village.

SARAWAK AND SABAH

The present territorial boundaries of Sarawak and Sabah evolved gradually. During Brooke rule, Sarawak expanded northwards by acquiring territory from the sultanate of Brunei. The state of Sabah (North Borneo) came into existence with the British North Borneo Company's acquisition and incorporation of territories on the north-west coast of Borneo from the sultanate of Brunei as well as territories on the east coast from the sultanate of Sulu. Both Sarawak and Sabah were run as British private enterprises and the British government did not afford them official protection until 1888 when Sarawak, Sabah and Brunei were made British protectorates. This was largely to check attempted interference from foreigners in the region's affairs.

As James Brookes' offer of Sarawak to the British government in 1841 had been rejected, to secure a British navy presence he persuaded Sultan Omar Ali of Brunei to offer Labuan to the British as a naval base. This offer was accepted in 1846, and Labuan became a British colony with its own governor.

Sabah was initially acquired in 1865 by the United States consul in Brunei, Charles Lee Moses, who later sold his lease to Baron von Overbeck, an Austrian businessman. The baron then purchased the area from the sultan of Brunei in return for annual payments, and also acquired an additional area from the sultan of Sulu. Following the intervention of the British government, he transferred his titles to Alfred Dent, a British businessman who set up the British North Borneo Company to administer the territory. The first station was opened at Sandakan under Resident William Pryer. Its policies were initially solely directed towards exploiting Sabah's mineral resources, believing the area to have large gold deposits. However, lack of revenue resulted in tax collection from the local population, an unpopular move which led to armed rebellions. Only after 1900 did commercial agriculture succeed.

Between 1867 and 1941, Sarawak was more successful than North Borneo in exploiting its mineral resources. Five minerals—antimony, mercury, gold, coal and petroleum—played an important role in the economic development of the two states. In Sarawak, James Brooke established monopolies for himself, which later passed to the Borneo Company. After his attempt to tax the exclusively Chinese gold-mining industry led to the 1857 uprising, the Borneo Company also took over gold mining. Petroleum production in Miri began in 1913. The British North Borneo Company's expectations of rich mineral resources were not realized, although it had invested capital, labour and settlement for exploration. Coal deposits in Sandakan, and also on Labuan were worked, but heavy production costs later forced mine closures.

In both territories, a plural society emerged. The Brookes adopted a conscious 'divide and rule' policy, segregating the various ethnic groups and dividing political and economic activities along racial lines. Education was left to Christian missions. In Sabah, the Company relied on native chiefs and headmen to deal with the local people, but the political and economic development of the indigenous communities was neglected. With the introduction of commercial agriculture, foreign workers were imported because of the labour shortage.

Chinese gold miners at Bau, near Kuching.

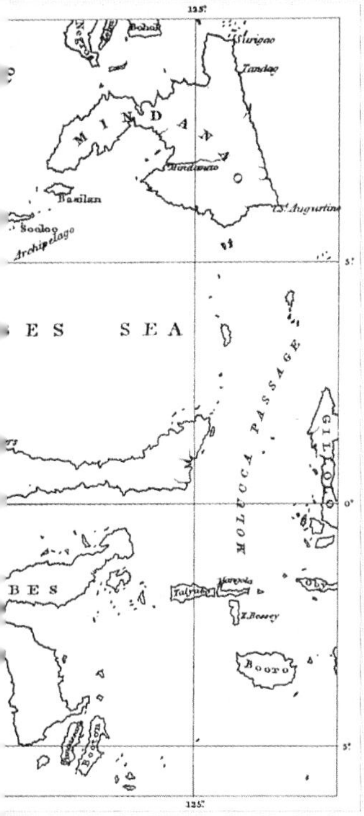

The white rajah Brooke government of Sarawak issued its own banknotes, coins and stamps. The 50-dollar note shown here carries the portrait of Charles Brooke, the second rajah.

There had long been reports of oil seepage from the ground around Miri, but it was not until 1913 that oil production began.

The territorial expansion of Sarawak

The area called 'Sarawak' which was acquired by James Brooke in 1841 from Raja Muda Hassim was only a small part (the later First Division) of the present-day state of Sarawak. Additional areas were acquired between 1853 and 1905 by James Brooke and his successor, his nephew Charles Brooke, from three successive sultans of Brunei— Omar Ali, Abdul Mumin and Hashim. From the early 16th century, the sultanate of Brunei had claimed—and to varying degrees exerted— political authority over the entire area of northwest Borneo.

An artist's impression of James Brooke at the court of the sultan of Brunei. All of present-day Sarawak was obtained over a period of time by James and Charles Brooke from the Brunei sultanate.

Nineteenth-century Brunei rulers

Sultan Omar Ali (r. 1828–52)

Sultan Abdul Mumin (r. 1852–85)

Sultan Hashim (r. 1885–1906)

Sarawak Proper

In return for his assistance in suppressing an uprising in Sarawak, the English adventurer James Brooke was bestowed the title of rajah of Sarawak in September 1841 by Raja Muda Hassim, the Brunei governor of Sarawak (see 'James Brooke: The white rajah of Sarawak'). Sultan Omar Ali of Brunei subsequently ratified the agreement which had been made between Brooke and Raja Muda Hassim and ceded to Brooke the territory later known as 'Sarawak Proper', which covered what is now the First Division of the state. It extended from Tanjung (Cape) Datu in the west to the Samarahan River in the east, and included all the hinterland as far as the mountain watershed. The area comprised the Lundu, Sarawak and Samarahan river basins.

Sadong, Batang Lupar, Saribas and Kalaka

Brooke achieved informal but effective control over the Batang Lupar and Saribas rivers and their tributaries by the late 1840s. This was made possible with British naval assistance provided for the suppression of 'piracy'. Expeditions in the boats of HMS *Dido*, commanded by Captain Henry Keppel,

up the Batang Lupar and the Saribas in 1843 and 1844 crippled resistance there. Later, in July 1849, Admiral Sir Arthur Farquhar crushed a large Dayak force at the 'battle' of Beting Marau near the estuary of the Saribas River. In August 1853, James Brooke persuaded Omar Ali's successor, Sultan Abdul Mumin, to cede to him the Sadong, Batang Lupar, Saribas and Kalaka rivers in return for half of any surplus revenue that he obtained in the district.

The 1857 Chinese rebellion

James Brooke's acquisition of the upper Sarawak River area in 1841, together with continued migration of Chinese miners from Montradok and other settlements in Dutch West Borneo, brought about an inevitable conflict with the Chinese gold miners of the Bau area whose *kongsi* (cooperative body) wished to maintain its political autonomy. When Brooke chose to emphasize his authority over the kongsi by punishing one of its members for a crime, the Bau miners rebelled and took control of Kuching for several days in February 1857. The subsequent defeat and harassment of the rebels brought to an end any further Chinese challenge to Brooke's government.

The Rajang

James Brooke's first foothold in the Rajang River area was established in 1851 when his younger nephew, Charles Brooke, initiated the building of a fort at Kanowit as a means of controlling the Dayak peoples along the lower Rajang River. Taking advantage of a rebellion against Brunei authority by some Malay leaders, James Brooke obtained authority from Sultan Abdul Mumin in August 1853 to restore order in the area. This was put into effect in January 1856 when Charles Brooke built a fort at Sarikei and installed Charles Fox there as Resident. When Fox and Henry Steele, the Resident of Kanowit, were brutally murdered by Kanowit tribesmen in 1859, Charles Brooke led a punitive expedition against them, consolidating informal Brooke authority in the area.

Territorial expansion of Sarawak 1841–1905

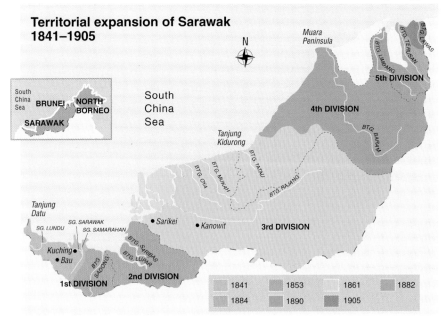

South China Sea

BRUNEI

NORTH BORNEO

SARAWAK

South China Sea

Muara Peninsula

BTG. LAWAS

BTG. TERUSAN

BTG. LIMBANG

5th DIVISION

4th DIVISION

Tanjung Kidurong

BTG. BARAM

BTG. TATAU

BTG. MUKAH

BTG. OYA

BTG. RAJANG

Tanjung Datu

SG. SARAWAK

SG. LUNDU

SG. SAMARAHAN

Sarikei

Kanowit

3rd DIVISION

Kuching

Bau

BTG. SADONG

BTG. SARIBAS

BTG. LUPAR

2nd DIVISION

1st DIVISION

| 1841 | 1853 | 1861 | 1882 |
| 1884 | 1890 | 1905 | |

HMS *Dido*, commanded by Captain Henry Keppel, whose boats were used in attacks on the Dayaks along the rivers of Sarawak in 1843 and 1844. *INSET*: Captain Henry Keppel.

The attack on the village of Padeh in June 1843 by the boats of HMS *Dido*, commanded by Captain Henry Keppel, and James Brooke's forces.

A surprise raid on the 'pirate' village of Kanowit in June 1846 by Admiral Sir Thomas Cochrane's *Phlegethon*.

Mukah

The next extension of territory was in August 1861 when the sultan of Brunei ceded to Brooke the sago-producing area of the Rajang, Oya, Mukah, Tatau and Bintulu rivers for an annual payment of Straits $4,500. The trade in sago, which was sent to Kuching for processing and exported to Singapore, had become the principal source of wealth after the collapse of the antimony market (see 'Antimony mining and the sago industry of Sarawak'). When the Brunei governor of Mukah closed the port to Kuching traders, the rajah's elder nephew, Brooke Brooke, led an expedition to attack the fortifications there in July 1860. After this was thwarted at the last moment by the British Governor of Labuan, G. W. Edwardes, the rajah protested to the Foreign Office. In early 1861, he went by British warship to Mukah where all resistance quickly crumbled.

Baram and Trusan

On his accession to the raj after his uncle's death in 1868, Charles Brooke was anxious to bring the Baram River under his control, but was forestalled by the actions of Charles Lee Moses, the United States consul in Brunei, who acquired and promptly sold a lease of most of Brunei's remaining territory. Baron von Overbeck, an Austrian adventurer, later purchased the entire area in return for annual payments to the sultan of Brunei and the sultan of Sulu (who also claimed rights of part of the territory). Following British intervention, Overbeck transferred his rights to the British North Borneo Company, which took over North Borneo in 1881 (see 'Sabah under chartered company rule').

As compensation, the rajah, who was incensed at this arrangement, was allowed to acquire the Baram River in the following year. He subsequently acquired the Trusan River in early 1885 after his senior officer, F. R. O. Maxwell, used the murder of 20 Sarawak produce collectors to pressure the Pengiran Temenggong, the holder of *tulin* (personal property) rights there, into surrendering these in return for an annual payment of Straits $4,500.

Limbang and Lawas

The Limbang River was annexed unilaterally by Charles Brooke on 17 March 1890 after a series of rebellions there against the authority of the new sultan of Brunei, Hashim, and an invitation from the local chiefs to assume control. The Foreign Office stipulated that Brooke make an annual payment of $6,000 to the sultan, who continued to claim ownership over the territory. Sarawak achieved its final borders in January 1905 after Charles Brooke persuaded the British North Borneo Company to abandon its claims to the Lawas River, which it had leased from relatives of the sultan in 1902.

Charles Brooke wanted to acquire by purchase all that remained of Brunei with the exception of the capital itself. In May 1885, he had tried to achieve this by offering the Pengiran Temenggong (later Sultan Hashim) an annual payment of Straits $14,500. He had to be satisfied, instead, with acquiring from the British North Borneo Company in 1888 the lease to the tip of the Muara Peninsula, where he established a colliery. In 1893, he had made an unsuccessful attempt to buy out the British North Borneo Company.

To maintain peace and collect duties, Brooke built forts at the river mouths—such as this one at Marudi on the Baram River—which were staffed by European officers and native policemen.

The Brookes and Sarawak's plural society

When James Brooke gained his foothold in Sarawak in 1841, he assumed authority over a polyglot population of Malays, Chinese, Iban and Bidayuh, with the two latter groups making up the clear majority. Territorial expansion during his reign, and that of his nephew Charles Brooke, increased the state's geographical size and added more indigenous groups. However, the policy of 'divide and rule', which created a division of labour or residence according to ethnic group, never wavered.

An Iban group attired in war dress and carrying spears, c. 1880s. This is one of the many photographs of the people of Sarawak taken by Charles Hose, a district officer who took a keen interest in the local groups and their customs.

The Brooke dynasty, 1841–1946

The three white rajahs of Sarawak (from top): James Brooke (r. 1841–68); his nephew Charles Brooke (r. 1868–1917); Charles' son, Vyner Brooke (r. 1917–46).

In Sarawak, Chinese traders travelled to the longhouses of the interior tribes to buy camphor and other forest products which were profitable items for export.

The ethnic division of labour

Despite the increase in the number of indigenous groups during the Brookes' reign, the basic ethnic proportions of Malays, Chinese and non-Muslim natives were not substantially altered. The essential pattern of Brooke rule, as established by the first rajah, was to use the traditional Malay élite (*perabangan*) of the Sarawak River area as the second level of leadership under a European ruling class, having first abolished their feudal rights and made them paid state officials.

Malay was the effective language of government, and the Brookes were pledged to uphold Islam, the religion of the Malays. The Native Officer Service was drawn from the sons of hereditary chiefs (*datu*) to whom the Bidayuh, in particular, had traditionally paid homage. The Iban, who lived in the interior as cultivators and collectors of jungle produce, were also warriors who could be pressed into service against the rajah's enemies when there was any prospect of looting and head-hunting.

The Chinese originally came overland as gold miners from Dutch West Borneo, but their numbers were swelled by entrepreneurs from Singapore and coolie immigrants from southern China who continued to arrive until the 1930s. They were to become the traders, artisans and unskilled workers who would help to convert Sarawak's natural resources into wealth. From the 1890s, Methodist Chinese from Fujian province were actively encouraged to settle as farmers in the Rajang River area in order to foster padi production and impart their techniques of cultivation to the Iban.

A small number of Javanese and Indians were also imported as plantation workers. Apart from a handful of Muslim Indian traders from Penang and Singapore, who settled in the main towns, the import and export trade was monopolized by Chinese, who also controlled the marketing of rubber, pepper and other cash crops.

During the rubber boom, the more adaptive Iban of the Saribas area could afford to employ Chinese to tap their rubber and build their longhouses. By the mid-1930s, a few Iban were being recruited into the Police and the Native

Officer Service, but clerical positions with the government, banks and other foreign-owned commercial enterprises were dominated by English-educated Chinese. Despite an English education, many of the Iban could not find appropriate employment in Sarawak and were forced to move to the Malay Peninsula and elsewhere.

'Divide and rule'

Physical force had played a vital part in bringing together these diverse groups under a single political authority, and the Brookes were not averse to exploiting traditional animosities for their own purposes in a 'divide and rule' strategy. They used the Balau and Sebuyau Iban to quell the Iban of the Batang Lupar and Saribas in the 1840s.

The Brookes encouraged the Malays and Iban to hunt down Chinese rebels in the wake of the 1857

European missionaries

Francis Thomas McDougall, who started an Anglican mission in Sarawak at the request of James Brooke, and his wife Harriette.

The Brookes also exploited the powerful status accorded to Europeans as members of a new and technologically dominant master class in Asia. European missionaries, principally Anglican and Catholic, were invited to Sarawak by the rajah and were allocated areas which would benefit the interests of the Iban by educating them in European ways. Most importantly, the Brookes provided a system of personal and informal government (*perentah*, rather than the more formal *kerajaan*), which offered the basic rudiments of justice and good order which had been lacking under earlier Brunei rule.

The best known of these missionaries was Francis McDougall, who was asked by Rajah James Brooke to start an Anglican mission in Sarawak. McDougall and his wife Harriette built the first church in Kuching and a mission house, educating children and prospective converts. McDougall was consecrated as Bishop of Labuan and Sarawak in 1856.

Chinese rebellion. They sometimes intervened to separate settled groups of Malays and Iban whose political cooperation promised to upset the rajah's tenuous power position, as had happened in the mid-1840s and the late 1850s. The rajahs also used the Iban against the Kayan, who were their traditional enemies, in the 1860s and subsequently demarcated the areas where each group was permitted to settle or collect jungle produce. Iban expansionism was, in this manner, stemmed.

Pax Brookeana

The system of law codified in Sarawak by James Brooke in 1843 was based on the laws of Brunei, but modified by British liberal principles which opposed institutions such as slavery and head-hunting, and punishments like amputation. Islamic courts were allowed to administer *syariah* law for the Muslims, and the Chinese were permitted their own courts for the administration of customary law as well as to judge commercial cases.

In the interior amongst the Iban and other indigenous non-Muslim peoples, the British officers adjudicated in cases involving property and other disputes. *Adat* (indigenous custom) was recognized except when it directly contravened what was seen as 'civilized' behaviour. By contrast with other colonial Southeast Asian societies where the market-driven economy promoted ethnic interdependence, it was this pax Brookeana that provided the social cement of Brooke rule.

The smallholder system

Unlike other multiracial Southeast Asian societies such as Indonesia and the Malay Peninsula in the 1920s and 1930s, the economy of Sarawak (with the conspicuous exception of petroleum) was not based on foreign-owned companies employing imported labourers. Its foundation was indigenous and Chinese smallholder production of rubber, pepper and other agricultural crops, together with the collection of jungle produce.

There was no need for a powerful central government to provide strict physical control of the people: the smallholder economy did not give rise to urbanization and a landless proletariat. The only industrial unrest before World War II occurred amongst Chinese oilfield workers at Miri.

The broad loyalty of Sarawak's diverse peoples to the white rajahs was a tribute to a modified system of indirect rule and minimalist intervention developed by a small group of dedicated Englishmen who believed that Sarawak was completely different from Java, the Malay states, Burma and India.

An 'anthropological exhibition'
One of the criticisms of the Brookes and their officers was that, in the style of human zoo-keepers, they artificially maintained racial and cultural diversity. Education, for example, was largely left to the Christian missions. Although resistance to change of the kind that was taking place in Malaya tended to preserve the European power position, it also fulfilled the Brooke commitment to act as trustees for the 'rights of the natives', particularly the right to own land.

A Sebuyan Dayak from Lundu, equipped for hunting with his sword and spear.

A sketch by Thomas S. Chapman which appeared in his book, *A Short Trip to Sarawak* (1870). The caption reads: 'Tourist sets off in Resident's boat to visit Dyaks (Iban) up country'. In the 19th and early 20th centuries, tourists who came to Sarawak thought of the local peoples as anthropological 'exhibits'.

One indication of the success of the Brookes' rule of Sarawak and their popularity was the strong movement after 1946 to repeal the 1946 British annexation of Sarawak and to restore the Brookes to power. This movement was supported particularly by the Malays, whose position had been relatively privileged during the period of Brooke rule. Another indication of the success of Brooke rule of Sarawak was the positive understanding of the term 'native'.

Miscegenation

Both James and Charles Brooke encouraged intermarriage between Chinese men and Iban women, believing that their hybrid offspring would have the potential to form an indigenous ruling class in Sarawak. With little encouragement, immigrant Malays intermarried with native Bidayuh and Melanau women to form a significant Malayo-Muslim community in the state. However, due in part to the Brookes' policy of not employing married European officers, miscegenation (inter-breeding between different races) was common between European officers and local women. By the time of the Japanese invasion in December 1941, there was thus an educated Eurasian élite which was demanding equal status with Europeans.

In 1898, a peacemaking ceremony was held at Marudi (Claudetown) on the Baram River to bring to an end blood feuds between the various ethnic groups. Charles Hose, district officer of the Baram region, photographed the historic occasion.

Sabah under chartered company rule

Most of the territory of North Borneo (present-day Sabah) was first acquired from Brunei by American adventurers in 1865. It was then sold to a consul of Austria-Hungary before being acquired by Alfred Dent, a Hong Kong merchant, who set up the British North Borneo Company to administer the territory. Governing proved difficult because of the lack of revenue, compounded by opposition from indigenous people. Only slowly was infrastructure built so as to aid development.

Spheres of control in North Borneo in the 19th century

Brunei sphere of control
Sulu sphere of control
Independent communities

South China Sea · Palawan · Balabac · Balabac Strait · Banggi · Kimanis Bay · Sulu Sea · Jolo · Sandakan · North Borneo · Labuan

South China Sea · BRUNEI · NORTH BORNEO · SARAWAK

0   50 km

Alfred Dent, founder of the British North Borneo Company, which was incorporated in 1881 to rule North Borneo (now Sabah).

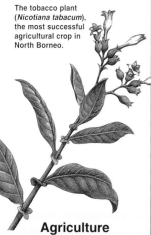

The tobacco plant (*Nicotiana tabacum*), the most successful agricultural crop in North Borneo.

Agriculture

Tobacco was a small-scale crop in Sabah long before the arrival of the British North Borneo Company. After failed attempts with other crops, large tobacco plantations proved more successful. The tobacco leaves were of such high quality that they were exported for use in the cigar industry as cigar wrappers.

The advent of company rule

The sultanates of both Brunei and Sulu had claims over the territory of present-day Sabah. Brunei's claims were stronger on the west coast, Sulu's on the east coast. The position changed in the 1850s when James Brooke asserted Sarawak's independence and expanded it by making cash payments for territory (see 'The territorial expansion of Sarawak'). Brunei's Sultan Abdul Mumin and his heir apparent, Temenggong Hashim, granted a 10-year lease of the area between Kimanis and Sandakan to American adventurers in 1865. That was done perhaps not merely in search of more cash, but also with a view to countering the advance of Brooke rule. Later, the Americans briefly settled in Kimanis.

In 1875, one of the Americans, J. W. Torrey, returned to renew the leases. Temenggong Hashim agreed to the renewal, but the sultan did not. In 1877, Baron von Overbeck, Austria-Hungary's consul in Hong Kong, with the support of Alfred Dent, a British merchant, gained leases to many of the rivers claimed by Brunei. The territory was subject to a right of resumption only if the lease money remained unpaid for three years.

Though it seems Dent was not aware of the Sulu claim, Overbeck went to Meinbung to obtain the sultan of Solo's approval. The Spaniards had occupied Jolo in 1876, and perhaps the sultan hoped for British help if he ceded his claims. Indeed, he consulted W. H. Treacher, the British Consul-General at Labuan, on the amount he should ask. His suggestion of $5,000 per annum was accepted. This agreement proved controversial. It used the word *pajak* (grant), as did the Brunei agreement, but it did not include a retrocession clause.

The lease of North Borneo territory had no official support from the British government, but possibly received some unofficial backing from the Foreign Office. Labuan, off the North Borneo coast, was already a British colony (see 'The Labuan entrepôt and the Borneo protectorate'). The British did not wish to establish another colony in the region, but they wanted to prevent other powers from doing so. Article 10 of the 1847 treaty with Brunei provided against it, but with the decline of the Brunei sultanate and the increased intensity of international rivalry, the article was proving inadequate. It was thought the type of company proposed by Dent and Overbeck would fend off other powers without provoking them unduly. Moreover, Britain would not be committing itself to further territorial acquisition or additional colonial expenditure. In 1881, the British government chartered the British North Borneo Company. It did not assume sovereignty; the sultans were regarded as suzerains.

The establishment of the administration

The backing of the British government, and the subsequent charter, emphasized the Company's main role as government, not commerce. However, Sabah was not a rich territory, and a colonial-type administration could not be sustained from the available revenue. Expenses quickly outran income. The shareholders were not satisfied, nor were the people of North Borneo.

The Company's problems were not merely financial, but also administrative. In the Malay Peninsula, the British used existing state structures, and in Sarawak the rajahs utilized Malay and Iban leaders. North Borneo had neither the cohesion of the former nor the opportunities for securing collaboration available in the latter.

The most successful of the early administrators was William Pryer at Sandakan. In keeping with the Company's aims, he opened up trade in eastern and interior Sabah. However, he could not ensure that trade was fair, and exploitation, indebtedness and impoverishment resulted—not by Europeans, but by Muslim and Chinese traders, unchecked

A Murut warrior. One of the many indigenous peoples of Sabah, the Murut revolted against the British North Borneo Company several times.

chiefs and dishonest police (not European, but not Sabahan either—often Iban or Sikh). Opportunities for petty tyranny increased rather than decreased. In the interior, too, the poll tax was an unwelcome introduction, and collectors abused their authority.

Anti-Company revolts

The Company was weak, but it continued to function because it never faced united opposition from the various indigenous groups. The opposition it faced, however, reflected its inadequacies. The first Murut revolt came in 1888, followed in 1891 by angry reactions to the activities of traders and police, partly through bloodshed and partly through the millenarian Malingkote cult. (Malingkote is an English corruption of the Malay word *malaikat* (angel)). Cult adherents claimed that angels appeared in their dreams, describing the coming of an age of happiness, with plentiful food, no suffering and the rising again of the dead.) The Company's inadequate control of its agents and the influx of traders were also factors in the 'revolt' led by Mat Salleh in the 1890s.

The last major revolt the Company faced was that of the Murut from the south in 1915–17, again with a millenarian aspect. New taxes had been introduced and resented. Above all, the government had once again shown that it was insensitive to the needs and feelings of the people.

Development

In the late 1880s and early 1890s, the government encouraged the tobacco boom. Belatedly, Governor Charles Creagh (1888–95) acted to protect the land rights of the indigenous people. The poor treatment of estate labourers (who were predominantly Chinese) resulted in very high death rates. The tobacco boom quickly collapsed, partly as a result of the tariffs imposed in the USA, and partly because of Sabah's lack of infrastructure.

The future of the Company became uncertain. William C. Cowie, the managing director, advocated a policy of deficit-financing rather than the cost-cutting preferred by Dent, the Company's founder. To improve the infrastructure, a cross-country telegraph was set up, a railway line was laid on the west coast, and a road was built through the Padas gorge. Cowie's focus on development indeed prompted his attempt at a deal with Mat Salleh

The failure of that approach resulted in a major crisis. However, Cowie's policies did bear some fruit, despite the criticisms of Governor Hugh Clifford (1900–1). The Company's dividends, which had never been high, reached 5 per cent in 1909, helped by the growing demand for rubber.

Education was a low priority for the Company, which relied mainly on the missions. The school established by the Company in Jesselton in 1915 for the sons of chiefs was not a success. Vernacular schools did not become popular because, unlike the missions, they did not offer English. The Chinese community established and maintained their own schools.

In the 1930s, Governor Douglas J. Jardine experimented with 'indirect rule'. He established the Native Chiefs Advisory Council in 1935 and a year later set up a native administrative centre on the Keningau plain. But with no tradition of larger government, some people feared that indirect rule would result in rule by the Chinese, who by then numbered 48,000 out of a population of 270,000.

Mat Salleh

Mat Salleh, the son of a Sulu chief and his Bajau wife, with followers from various ethnic groups began a period of armed resistance in 1895 to protest the Company's taking of what he considered were the rights of the indigenous people. As the Company mounted attacks, Mat Salleh retreated, quickly establishing a new fort in his new location. In July 1897, Mat Salleh razed the main west coast trading station on Pulau Gaya. In November 1897, he burnt the Government residency at Ambong. Early in 1898, the Company bombarded Salleh's fort at Ranau, but he escaped to Tambunan.

W. C. Cowie, the Company's director-general came from London in April 1898 to make a peace agreement with Mat Salleh. However, after Mat Salleh concluded that the British had broken the agreement, he began more attacks on government stations. This resulted in a British attack on 1 January 1900, and Mat Salleh was killed on 31 January. However, other leaders continued the struggle until 1903.

The memorial to Mat Salleh erected at Tambunan, on the spot where he was killed by British soldiers, to honour the man considered by the people of Sabah to be a warrior rather than a rebel.

Sandakan

Settlements were established on Sandakan Bay in the 18th century by traders from the Sulu sultanate. British and German traders, who bought Sulu forest produce for the China tea trade, founded a small settlement on an island in the bay in the 1870s. They included W. C. Cowie, who sold guns and ammunition to the sultan of Sulu. The traders later left this settlement, which had become known as Kampung German. It was at this village that William Pryer, first Resident of the east coast, settled. After the village was burnt down, Pryer—not needing the cover the island had provided for gun-runners—moved to the mainland at the mouth of Sandakan Bay and named the new settlement Elopura (beautiful city). However, it soon became known as Sandakan. In 1884, it became the capital of North Borneo, and retained that status until 1946.

An early view of Sandakan from Government House. Sandakan was the capital of Sabah until after World War II.

Government House, Sandakan, in the 1880s, when it was occupied by the first governor of North Borneo, William Hood Treacher.

The Sandakan police barracks, an attractive two-storey timber building.

RIGHT: The police force of the British North Borneo Trading Company rode on water buffaloes, the most common form of transport at that time.

The Labuan entrepôt and the Borneo protectorate

In 1846, at James Brooke's instigation, Britain acquired from the sultan of Brunei the coal-rich island of Labuan. It served Brooke's own plans for the British navy to be close and provide support for his policy in Brunei. The coal deposits proved to be of inferior quality, but the island was retained as a base of operations against piracy. Commercial enterprises failed, and as Labuan was a financial strain on Britain its administration was handed over to the British North Borneo Company in 1890. In 1905, it was returned to the Colonial Office and attached to the Straits Settlements government.

Labuan

South China Sea

Tanjung Aru •

Victoria •

0   2 km

South China Sea   BRUNEI   NORTH BORNEO

SARAWAK

The early years

In 1846, Sultan Omar Ali of Brunei ceded Labuan to Britain and a crown colony was set up. The plan was conceived by James Brooke, who had hoped to reform the Brunei sultanate by exerting British influence and by suppressing piracy. Brooke became the first governor of Labuan. However, his initial policy was already changing, with more emphasis on the independence and expansion of Sarawak.

Labuan became something of a political and economic rival to Sarawak, with British officials supporting Brunei against Sarawak aggression and even opposing its negotiated expansion over the Baram River district. The Anglo-Brunei Treaty of 1847, which bound the sultan not to cede territory without Britain's approval, was one argument for this policy. There was also an economic reason. Due to the poor quality of its coal, the coal companies were never successful. However, Labuan did have some success as an entrepôt. Its trade with Sulu came to involve smuggling and illegal arms sales that led the governor to concentrate on the Brunei rivers, and to back Chinese enterprise there.

The British North Borneo Company

The concessions of North Borneo territory made by Brunei, first to J. W. Torrey and then to Baron von Overbeck and Alfred Dent (see 'Sabah under chartered company rule'), prompted a review of this approach, particularly as Britain's final approval of the British North Borneo Company led to the removal of restrictions on Sarawak's advance. The Colonial Office had doubted the wisdom of retaining Labuan when its coal proved unworkable. Now its commercial role was also under threat.

The British government had adopted Sir James Brooke's venture in Sarawak only reluctantly, and the Colonial Office had opposed the acquisition of Labuan. Forty years later, however, its views had changed. It was still, as before, desirable to keep other powers out of northern Borneo, but it disliked the Foreign Office's issuing of a charter to the British North Borneo Company. The Colonial Office preferred a more regular and responsible form of government in Borneo. In the 1880s, Sarawak was seen as its future nucleus.

The Foreign Office proposal went ahead, and it seemed that the Company and the Brookes would partition the rest of Brunei between them. The risk that another foreign power might intervene in Brunei was an argument for retaining Labuan.

Victoria, the capital of Labuan

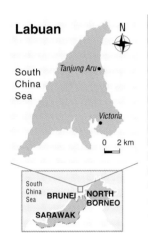

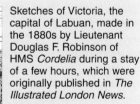

Sketches of Victoria, the capital of Labuan, made in the 1880s by Lieutenant Douglas F. Robinson of HMS *Cordelia* during a stay of a few hours, which were originally published in *The Illustrated London News*.

1. Native houses.
2. A bridge behind the town.
3. A Chinese temple.
4. The bund, with shophouses behind.
5. Government House.
6. Government offices.

The signing of the treaty for the cession of Labuan to the British. It was hoped that a lasting friendship would be established with Britain, and that joint Brunei–British efforts could rid the area of pirates.

The hoisting of the British flag on Labuan on 24 December 1846. The Brunei contingent was led by Pangiran Mumin, who was to succeed Sultan Omar Ali in 1855. The British were led by Captain Rodney Mundy of HMS *Iris*.

The protectorates of 1888

The fear of foreign intervention was also a reason for the agreements of 1888 by which Brunei, Sarawak and North Borneo became British protectorates. The British government took control of their foreign relations, though not their domestic affairs. The agreements did not preclude, but might indeed have facilitated the final partition of Brunei. However, Charles Brooke's acquisition of Limbang in 1890 and Sultan Hashim's refusal to agree to it made that partition less likely, not more.

Colonial Office officials, particularly C. P. Lucas, renewed their plans for Borneo. Sarawak could not now be the basis for a colony, but something like the new Federated Malay States (FMS) (see 'The formation of the Federated Malay States') was considered. The administration of Labuan, then under the British North Borneo Company, would be resumed, a Resident placed in Brunei, and the territories drawn together under British advice. Sultan Hashim accepted a Resident in 1905, and British administration of Labuan was resumed. The proposal went no further, however, above all because Rajah Charles Brooke opposed it.

The interwar period

The accession of the third rajah, Vyner Brooke, in 1917 did not, as had been hoped, make it easier for the British government to extend its influence in Sarawak. The new ruler was as evasive as the old had been obstinate, yet the pressure to intervene was increasing. The administration seemed amateur and autocratic, and there were complaints from British traders there. The 1888 treaty, however, gave the British no right to interfere in domestic matters.

On the Malay Peninsula, Sir Cecil Clementi intensified attempts at decentralization in the Federated Malay States (see 'The decentralization policy'). The aim was a federation of the Straits Settlements, the Federated Malay States and the Unfederated Malay States. Clementi renewed the idea of a similar federation in Borneo, believing that progress in Borneo could be hastened by a loose federation of its four component parts (Sarawak, Brunei, North Borneo and Labuan). The idea made no progress. One obstacle was the position of the raj in Sarawak: it was feared that this might be undermined with the appointment of a Resident. Vyner Brooke preferred collaboration to federation.

Governor Arthur Richards (1930–3) of North Borneo believed it would be better to establish a colonial government than to adopt Clementi's proposal. However, the British government, beset by the Depression, was not prepared to finance a buy-out. Labuan had been attached to the Straits Settlements, and Clementi now proposed that North Borneo join the Settlements, at a price of £1 million. He argued that a link with North Borneo would make it easier for the Straits Settlements 'to retain their proper place' in the proposed all-Malayan federation. The Straits government declined to grant a loan, however, and the British government reaffirmed its negative stance.

The Sarawak constitution

Cooperation between Sarawak and Britain grew, and in 1938 transfer of the administration seemed a possibility. It did not materialize, but in 1941, the centenary of Brooke rule, Vyner Brooke announced a constitution. His motives may have been both personal and financial. The effect was that he ended autocracy, but not by appointing a British adviser. He later accepted a new agreement with the British government, supplementing the 1888 agreement. This allowed for the appointment of a British representative whose advice had to be taken on foreign affairs and defence matters.

The settlement of Labuan

When the small island of Labuan (about 25 miles in circumference) was ceded to Great Britain in 1846, the population numbered about 6,000, chiefly Malays, with small groups of Indian coolies and Dayaks and about 20 Europeans.

The island did not swarm with settlers as the British expected: although fish were bountiful in the surrounding seas and rattan flourished in the interior, the market for Labuan's produce was limited and the local population too poor to buy it. Hardly any traders came to settle on the island, and ships from coastal China, the Philippines and the Celebes (Sulawesi) preferred to sail on to Singapore.

Sketch of a Malay native of Borneo, c. 1847. The British hoped that large numbers of Malays, who occupied nearly the whole coast of Borneo, would settle in Labuan where they would be protected from pirates.

Petroleum and mineral resources in Borneo

An important consideration of the governments of both Sarawak and North Borneo (Sabah) in the 19th and early 20th centuries was the utilization of three main resources: minerals, land and forest products. Sarawak proved to have much richer mineral resources, and thus gained greater rewards from their exploitation. However, there was virtually no difference between Sarawak, a 'private colony', and North Borneo, a chartered company territory, in mining administration because both governments monopolized mineral resources.

A letter, dated 23 August 1846, from Sultan Omar Ali Saifuddin of Brunei to James Brooke, regarding coal concessions in Sarawak.

Sarawak

Five mineral resources—antimony, mercury, gold, coal and petroleum—played an important role in Sarawak's economy during the Brooke period, with each mineral dominating for a period before being supplanted by the next. Antimony was the leading mineral resource until the mid-1880s. Mercury then took over for a short period, followed by coal until 1898, when it was supplanted by gold. In the 1920s, gold gave way to petroleum.

From the outset, James Brooke adopted a policy of monopolization of the mineral resources of the state. He reserved for himself a monopoly on the trade of antimony ore, which was mined at Bau, near Kuching, kept Western interests out of Bintulu, and obtained for himself exclusive rights to mine coal along the whole northwest coast of Borneo.

Brooke's main rivals were Chinese miners who had been mining gold near Pangkalan Tebang in Sarawak since the early 19th century. Initially, Brooke was reluctant to disturb the Chinese *kongsi* (cooperative ventures) which had work and profit-sharing arrangements which were well-suited for mining activity on a small scale, and which enjoyed political autonomy. However, this autonomous existence was ultimately challenged by Brooke, leading to the Chinese uprising of 1857 which resulted in the collapse of the Chinese mining industry, the strengthening of Brooke's position, and the Borneo Company taking over all mineral exploitation in the state.

Bau then came directly under the political control of Kuching and the leaders of the reconstituted kongsi established a working relationship with the rajah and the company. With its superior technology (using cyanide in gold extraction) and capital, and its special relationship with the Brookes, the company took over gold mining. It only surrendered its monopoly rights in Sarawak in 1921 when most of the minerals were finished and it was no longer profitable to work the mines. The gold-mining industry was revived in the 1930s by Chinese miners.

Antimony and cinnabar (mercury sulphide), which was also known as quicksilver, were the company's prime mineral monopolies. Antimony was worked out by the early 20th century, while cinnabar mining was abandoned at the end of the 19th century. Coal mining became important in the 1880s. Charles Brooke was unable to attract investment in the coal sector and turned to the Borneo Company. By 1874, sufficient coal was being mined to supply the government's own vessels. Additionally, the Borneo Company and the Sarawak government contracted to supply coal to the Peninsular and Oriental Steam Navigation Company at Singapore.

Apart from the Sadong mines, coal was also mined on the island of Muara, in Brunei Bay, by the firm of C. C. Cowie & Sons who had obtained sole concession rights from Brunei. In 1888, the Sarawak government purchased Cowie's concession which was transferred to the rajah, who renamed the island Brooketon. While most of Sadong's coal was used locally or exported to Singapore, Brooketon produced bunker coal for steamships.

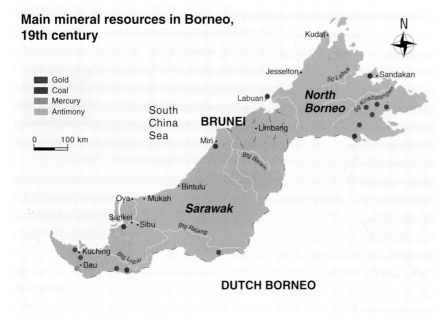

Main mineral resources in Borneo, 19th century

- Gold
- Coal
- Mercury
- Antimony

0   100 km

South China Sea

Kudat

Jesselton

Labuan

Sg Labuk

Sandakan

Sg Kinabatangan

North Borneo

BRUNEI

Limbang

Miri

Btg Baram

Bintulu

Oya   Mukah

Sarawak

Sankei   Sibu

Btg Rajang

Kuching   Btg Lupar

Bau

N

DUTCH BORNEO

LEFT: On 10 August 1910, on Canada Hill in Miri, Sarawak, as curious villagers watched, several Shell oilmen employed the old cable tool method to spud the first oil well, Miri Well No. 1. Drilling by this laborious method was slow. But on 22 December, they struck oil. Initial production was an average of 83 barrels per day. Abandoned in 1972 and now a state monument, Miri Well No. 1, or 'The Grand Old Lady', began the rapid development of the petroleum industry.

The story of oil in Malaya began in Miri, then a small fishing village, in 1882, when the Resident of Baram, Claude Champion de Crespigny, noted in his diary that the local people had discovered 'earth oil'. He made a report of his find to Rajah Charles Brooke, who awarded a concession to the Anglo-Saxon Oil Company to explore for oil and other minerals in the area for a term of 75 years. In 1921, their oil interests were taken over by the Sarawak Oilfields Limited in Kuching.

The first shipment of oil from Miri, in 1913, was taken in drums by lighters to offshore tankers. From 1914, submarine pipelines were laid to an offshore anchorage for loading onto tankers. Peak production was reached in 1929, after which it declined. A small refinery to process oil from the Miri field was built in 1917.

A 1922 advertisement for the Asiatic Petroleum Co.'s 'Fish' brand kerosene and 'Yellow Tin' car cylinder oil, which appeared in *The Straits Times*.

North Borneo

By contrast with Sarawak, North Borneo's mineral wealth offered meagre rewards. Despite Cowie's assumption that the territory was paved with gold and diamonds, coal was the main product, and exploitation was episodic. The British North Borneo Company believed mining would attract capital, labour and settlement into the state, and hired mineralogists to investigate the possibilities.

Early gold mining was carried out by Chinese in the Upper Segama River, and also Europeans. As no significant deposits were discovered, a government proclamation in 1887 forbade entry to any Europeans arriving without means of support. By 1887, only five of the 400 Chinese miners remained. Despite later attempts to find gold by four London companies, and by independent prospectors in 1928 and 1933, there was no commercial production of gold in North Borneo.

Coal deposits were found on Labuan and around Cowie Bay and the Sandakan Bay area. The former, worked from 1890 to 1912, provided fuel for steamships plying the Europe–Australia and Europe–Hong Kong routes. In the Cowie Bay area, a large coalfield was discovered near the Silimpopon River. The Company, in conjunction with Harrisons & Crosfield, formed the Cowie Harbour Coal Company to work the coal. Output rose from a mere 25 tons in 1906 to 87,543 tons in 1922. Annual coal exports averaged 54,000 tons. The colliery shut down in 1931 because of falling prices, heavy production costs, and a declining demand for coal as ships switched to oil.

The only other mineral of any importance was manganese, discovered in Marudu Bay in 1902. It was worked by British interests, but the venture was short-lived.

Chinese gold miners working in an opencast mine at Bau, near Kuching, Sarawak. During the 22-year period between 1899 and 1921, the gold output from the Bau and, later, Bidi mines totalled 983,255 troy ounces. It was valued at Sarawak $25,995,222 and yielded a royalty of $1,466,462. This represented 81 per cent of the recorded gold production of Sarawak from 1865 to 1954.

SARAWAK MINERAL PRODUCTION AND EXPORTS, 1868–1948

YEAR	PRODUCE EXPORTED ($)	MINERAL EXPORTS ($)	% OF MINERAL EXPORTS
1868	N.A.	38,001	—
1878	809,325	83,086	10
1888	1,322,325	118,915	09
1898	3,089,017	323,230	10
1908	5,732,723	1,177,255	21
1918	9,211,459	N.A.	—
1938	23,244,666	12,482,134	54
1948	166,023,615	111,820,069	67

An early fleet of lorry tankers of the Asiatic Petroleum Co. (APC). Formed in 1903, APC did a booming business during World War I when its Singapore depots supplied Allied warships with fuel, and the company dominated the local lubricating oil market.

Labourers waiting to collect their wages at the office of the Shell Company in Lutong, Sarawak, c. 1920. Shell began as a trading company founded by Marcus Samuel Sr in 1833, in London's East End. In the early 20th century, it became involved in the development of the Miri oilfields.

PENANG. NATIVE MARKET.

The various races mostly lived in separate communities and were involved in different occupations. The majority of Malays were farmers and fishermen, and lived in villages. The staple crop was rice, grown in flooded fields near their homes (1). Thousands of Chinese immigrants were employed in opencast mining, such as this mine at Kampar, and lived in housing provided by the mine close to their workplace (2). Many Indian immigrants were employed on rubber plantations to clear the land, plant seedlings and tap the trees. The workers lived on the estate in basic quarters (coolie lines) very different from the hilltop manager's bungalow in this photograph (3).

TOP: The multiracial nature of the population of the Malay Peninsula is clearly seen in this postcard of the Chowrasta Market in Penang issued in the early 20th century.

FAR LEFT TOP: King Edward's School, Taiping, was one of the English schools established in towns. This building, opened in 1906, replaced an earlier thatched-roof structure. At that time, there were 450 pupils, mostly Chinese, although all races were represented.

FAR LEFT BOTTOM: Leprosy was one of the many health problems faced by British officials. In Kuala Lumpur, Dr Ernest Travers opened a new facility outside the city for lepers who had previously been living in unsanitary conditions near the pauper hospital. Here lepers are shown taking their medicine.

LEFT: By the 1920s, brick shophouses, such as these in Petaling Street, had replaced the earlier timber buildings in Kuala Lumpur which were frequently destroyed by fire.

THE BEGINNINGS OF A MODERN STATE

By 1941, a multiracial society had emerged from British efforts to open up Malaya, Sarawak and Sabah for trade and economic development. British rule had brought peoples of different races together and ensured the creation of three territorial states, each with a British-type administration. The new infrastructure facilitated the movement of people and goods, and also integrated states and peoples, but the transformation of ethnic and cultural diversity into political unity had yet to occur.

British rule in Malaya created a modern state, but the idea of a common citizenship came only after World War II. Fortunately, the basis for strengthening multiracial cooperation existed among the peoples in all three territories. The pre-1941 years fostered harmonious interracial living and mutual respect for varied cultures. British policy had always regarded the Malays as the indigenous people, and annexation of the Malay states had been based on treaties with the Malay rulers. The British were thus duty bound to protect Malay rights. However, rapid economic growth brought major changes, including unrestricted immigration of Chinese and Indian labourers and entrepreneurs. With the arrival of female immigrants, the Chinese and Indian populations began to grow by natural increase rather than from immigration. By 1931, the Malay indigenous population had been outnumbered by non-Malay immigrants. Some had already settled permanently, and had begun making political claims to equal status with the Malays. Using their guilds and labour unions, they launched strikes and instigated political agitation.

Consequently, a nascent Malay nationalist movement arose The initial political appeals took on an Islamic aspect, but later changed to a secular basis, focusing on improving Malay livelihood. Pre-1941 Malay nationalism was, however, weak and state Malay associations failed to resolve their basic differences. To appease mounting criticism, the British adopted 'pro-Malay' policies to provide education and jobs and to protect Malay rights, but also met a few non-Malay demands.

Pre-1941 Malaya enjoyed political stability and interracial harmony, although there were wide fluctuations in income levels due to swings in the international economy. The country's prosperity depended on the production and export of tin and rubber. Price booms in 1909–10 and 1925–6 raised incomes to relatively high levels, but tin and rubber prices tumbled during the Great Depression (1929–32), resulting in government restrictions on both the production and export of the two commodities. It became clear that primary commodity production alone could not provide a consistent basis for continued economic growth. World War II and postwar conditions would gradually force state planners towards economic diversification and industrialization. These were changes which had to accompany the postwar constitutional plans and the nationalist aspirations and struggles to forge and achieve multiracial unity, citizenship, nationhood and national independence in Malaya, Sarawak and Sabah, and the eventual formation of Malaysia.

Tourism posters, produced by the Federated Malay States Railway in the 1930s to advertise the sights of the Malay Peninsula, have since been reproduced as postcards.

The growth of a plural society

During the period of British administration, the large-scale immigration of Chinese and Indians changed the population of the Malay Peninsula into that of a plural society (one composed of people of various races, religions, customs, languages, living side by side, but independently, under one political unit). The Malays, as rice farmers and fishermen, lived in the kampongs, the Chinese worked mainly in the tin mines and the towns, while the majority of Indians were on the plantations.

Europeans worked in urban businesses, such as agency houses and banks, and also owned or managed the large rubber estates in rural areas.

The beginnings of a plural society

People of different races, religions and customs began settling in the Malay Peninsula in prehistoric times. In 15th-century Melaka, Malays, Chinese, Indians, Arabs, Sumatrans and Javanese each had their own sections of the city, allotted by the Malay rulers. The immigrants, who were mostly males, never outnumbered the local people. Socialization among the various groups was quite fluid and assimilation was evident, as seen from marriages between members of the immigrant groups and local women. This situation continued during the period of Portuguese and, later, Dutch rule. During this time, society was heterogeneous, but not plural.

After the establishment of the Straits Settlements in 1826, the immigration of Chinese and Indian workers was encouraged to enhance the colonial economy. Progress in the Straits economy spread to the rest of the Malay Peninsula, especially along the west coast, eventually leading to British political intervention. The British observed that economic and also communal development ran along ethnic lines. They allowed this situation to continue as it was convenient for their administration. The population became plural when the various cultural groups began to form political groupings along almost exclusively ethnic lines.

The Malays

From the outset, the British recognized the Malays as the indigenous people of the country and adopted a paternalistic attitude towards them. The Malay rulers were allowed to remain as heads of their states, albeit powerless, and the people had little choice but to remain as farmers and fishermen through land titles and the limited provision (four years) of Malay medium education.

The role of the Malays as farmers was enhanced by immigrants from the Malay Archipelago who were deemed Malay by the British and given equal rights to Malay Reservation lands and educational facilities. As farmers, they remained in the rural areas. Their welfare was looked after by Malay traditional chiefs, *penghulu* (headmen) and *ketua kampung* (kampong chiefs), who were absorbed into the British bureaucracy, together with Malay officers from the traditional élite who formed the Malay Administrative Service of the government.

The Chinese

The Chinese began to arrive in large numbers in the 19th century as a result of the British 'open door' policy in the Straits Settlements and later in the Malay states. The colonial economy wanted tin and rubber in large quantities to satisfy industrial demands in Europe. A large number of Chinese who had earlier been invited by Malay chiefs and rulers

Chinese workers provided the large workforce which was needed for the development of large-scale tin mining.

Four generations of a wealthy Chinese family. The household would have employed a number of Chinese servants, including the three amahs in the front row.

ABOVE: Chinese cobblers providing service by the roadside.

LEFT: The Chinese Residency, built by Lim Teik Soon, was the first four-storey private residence in Penang. It later became the Bellevue Hotel.

RIGHT: Yap Ah Loy, a leading businessman and Kapitan China (leader of the Chinese community) of Kuala Lumpur from 1868 to 1885.

1. Every Malay kampong had its own mosque. This painting of the Masjid Tinggi at Bagan Serai, Perak, is by A. Kasim Abas.

2. A Malay man dressed in traditional dress (*baju Melayu*) of loose shirt and pants, with a folded head- and waistcloth.

3. Malay children in front of a typical traditional kampong timber house with a thatched roof. Wooden shutters replaced windows.

4. Malay boys dressed up for a festival, perhaps leaving a mosque, beside a decorated buffalo cart.

A postcard of three Orang Asli men, the forest-dwelling aboriginal peoples of the Malay Peninsula. Some served as slaves for the Malay aristocracy before the abolition of slavery in the 19th century.

A tableau of Malay ladies in the 1890s demonstrating the art of *tekat* (gold-thread embroidery). Behind them is a display of traditional handwoven silk and cotton textiles.

RIGHT: The daughter-in law of Sultan Idris of Perak (later consort of Sultan Abdul Jalil) (seated), photographed in 1903 with two Malay attendants, who would also have been from the upper classes.

British 'open door' policy on immigrant labour for the sugar and, later, the rubber estates established in the 19th and early 20th centuries.

Unlike the Chinese, who had migrated through their own communal networking, the majority of Indian arrivals were assisted by the British administration. Their migration was largely connected with the development of commercial agriculture, which was almost entirely the preserve of European capitalists who did not have the necessary labour for their estates. The Malays were already seen as rice farmers and fishermen, while the Chinese were considered to be difficult to manage, except by their own kind. Therefore, the most convenient country to tap a large labour force was India, which was already a British colony. The isolation of these labourers in the estates from the other ethnic groups was fairly complete. They were housed on the estates where they worked and, later, when they were able to bring their wives, their children were educated in estate schools with teachers and textbooks brought in from India.

were already mining large areas of land, especially in the western part of the Peninsula. With British political intervention in the Malay states, land and immigration policies that facilitated Chinese participation in the mining sector and businesses connected with it, were introduced. Thousands of Chinese immigrant labourers came to Malaya, worked for some time, and then returned home.

Those who settled were the entrepreneurs and businessmen (towkays). The rest were transients who rarely had to deal directly with the British, but only with their own community leaders, the Kapitan China, who had official social and political recognition from the British. The Chinese workers lived in their own communities in the mining and urban centres. Chinese education classes used Mandarin as the medium of instruction. Throughout the British period, the immigrants remained socially and culturally Chinese, while being actively involved in the colonial economy.

The Indians

Indian traders may have begun visiting the Malay Peninsula as early as the 5th century BCE. Although social and cultural influences were transmitted between them and the Malays, the Indians did not dominate the latter politically or economically. The Indians were also known as one of the important groups of traders in the period of the Melaka sultanate. Many later came to Malaya on their own accord as entrepreneurs, professionals and white-collar workers. However, the number of Indians living in the Malay Peninsula increased greatly only when they responded to the

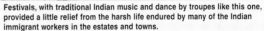

Festivals, with traditional Indian music and dance by troupes like this one, provided a little relief from the harsh life endured by many of the Indian immigrant workers in the estates and towns.

Bullock carts with Indian drivers, such as these, were widely used for the transport of goods.

ABOVE: The Malay State Guides of Perak. The soldiers had originally been recruited from India by Ngah Ibrahim to restore peace after the Chinese feuds.

FAR LEFT: An Indian money-lender, one of many who provided an essential service.

LEFT: A female Indian rubber tapper, one of the many Indian labourers used on rubber estates.

RIGHT: A Hindu temple, built by immigrant Indians, on South Bridge Road, Singapore.

The Malayan economy

The major impetus underlying international economic growth in the 19th and early 20th centuries was the demand from the industrializing countries of the West for raw materials. Malaya, with its ample resources of minerals and land, was particularly well placed to supply this demand. The shortage of labour was overcome with large-scale immigration from China and south India, and the British colonial administration provided centralized government and the necessary infrastructure for development. By World War I, Malaya possessed a fully fledged export economy as the world's leading supplier of tin and rubber.

Railway development in Perak, 1885–96

Kedah

Perai • • Bukit Mertajam

Penang

Perak

Bagan Serai ▼ • • Ulu Sepetang
Port Weld • • • Taiping
Kuala Kangsar • • Sungai Siput
Ipoh •
Batu • • Gopeng
Gajah • • Kampar
Telok • • Tapah
Anson • • Rpad
Slim River ♦
Tanjong Malim ♦

- - Railway
▪ Rubber
  Tin

0   30 km

South
China
Sea

**MALAY
PENINSULA**

Strait
of
Melaka

The basis of the export economy

The British acquisition of the Straits Settlements and the setting up of free ports, which became the centre of a regional trade network, opened the region to the influence of the international economy. Much of the 19th century was spent in a search for commodities with expanding markets, which were mainly in the West.

There was a slow movement of agricultural capital and labour out of the Straits Settlements, which had relatively small areas of cultivable land, into the interior of the Peninsula. Most cultivators were Chinese who relied, for working capital and supplies, on advances from their compatriot merchants in the Straits ports, who in turn put the produce on the world market. European planters gained a foothold in the sugar industry in Province Wellesley and, later, in coffee in Selangor as proprietary planters ; here they used their personal capital resources together with funds garnered from their home country. The predominant method of cultivation was the estate with one or a few crops.

The problem was that international commodity prices were highly unstable. Plantings expanded in response to a boom, but prices could have slumped again by the time the new area was productive. Planters did not have sufficient resources to ride out extended periods of low prices. Also, crops were

Labour supply
Malaya's sparse population, together with the reluctance of villagers to work away from their homes, resulted in a shortage of labour for the mines and plantations. Indian and Chinese workers were imported to meet this demand. The colonial government also organized immigration from India. Chinese immigration was organized privately through a network of agents. Workers from the Dutch East Indies, especially Java and Sumatra, also helped to fulfil the demand for labour.

European planters employed large numbers of Indian immigrant workers to do all the manual labour on their estates. All labourers as well as (in later years) their wives and children were provided with housing on the estate.

Infrastructure development
Apart from the Straits ports and their immediate surroundings, modes of transport and communication in the Malay Peninsula remained rudimentary (mostly riverine) for most of the 19th century. The construction of a network of tracks, bridle paths, roads and, finally, railways, occurred as colonial hegemony spread throughout the Peninsula after 1874. The administration was fortunate in having the tin industry as a major source of tax revenue from which to finance such construction. This obviated the need for foreign borrowing. The first roads and railways (begun in

the 1880s) connected commercial agriculture and tin mines in the interior with coastal ports. In the early 1900s, trunk lines running from the north to the south joined these lines to form a continuous trunk line.

LEFT: The former Malayan Railways building in Penang, which was a major port for the export of tin from Perak.

BELOW: A typical 19th-century Malay village, with coconut trees shading the houses.

susceptible to disease, and some quickly exhausted the soil. Thus, the 19th century saw a succession of 'boom-and-bust' cycles in spices, sugar and coffee. Unlike tin mining, none of these crops provided a firm basis for long-term growth of the economy.

The 20th century
From the late 19th century, the economy became largely dependent on tin and rubber, sometimes called the 'twin high explosives of international trade' because of their price movement volatility. Both high and low prices had widespread effects.

International trading conditions changed greatly in the 1920s and 1930s because of severe slumps in 1920–2 and the Great Depression of 1929–32. The oversupply of both tin and rubber forced prices to drop to unprofitable levels. Imports were reduced, and a sharp rise in unemployment forced many Indian and Chinese labourers to return to their own countries. The government tried to restore export prices by restricting exports of tin and rubber.

However, it was clear by the 1930s that primary commodities could not provide a consistent basis for Malaya's economic growth. Tin was a non-renewable asset, and many of the rubber trees were approaching the end of their economic life.

'The twin high explosives of international trade'

Tin mining

The most consistent export item from Malaya in the 19th century was tin. Following the expansion of large-scale mining in Kinta (Perak) in the 1880s, tin ore exports leapt tenfold from 5000 tonnes a year in the mid-1870s to approximately 50 000 tonnes by the end of the century, making Malaya the world's largest tin producer. Demand came principally from Western industries producing tin plate for canning foods. Traditionally, tin was mined by Malays as a periodic supplement to incomes between rice harvests, but increasingly during the 19th century Chinese enterprise took the lead in the industry. The Chinese were later overtaken by European companies which introduced new technology in the mines.

A pineapple canning factory in Klang, c.1920, which utilized two local products—pineapples and tin.

Bullock carts were used to transport tin ore from mines in the interior to the nearest railway line.

The rubber industry

Malaya's other major export industry, rubber, was based on imported resources. The government in Britain organized the collection of seeds of the rubber tree (*Hevea brasiliensis*) from Brazil. These were germinated at Kew Gardens, and in 1876 seedlings were sent to Ceylon and to Singapore for replanting in their Botanic Gardens. These trees proved successful, but planters in the Malay Peninsula showed little commercial interest in them until rubber prices began to rise rapidly in the early 1900s. The growth of the motor vehicle industry, notably in the USA, created a large demand for rubber tyres, leading to an increase in the price of rubber.

The response to the demand from abroad was unprecedented in the Malay Peninsula. The Chinese agriculturalists were quick to switch from their traditional crops, such as tapioca and gambier, to planting rubber. Western, particularly British,

capital for rubber cultivation was supplied by the agency houses (see 'European agency houses and the Malay states'). In the United Kingdom alone, 260 rubber companies were floated between 1903 and 1912 to acquire estates in Malaya. The indigenous Malays (and immigrants from the Malay Archipelago) were also strongly attracted to planting this crop since they could grow rubber trees on smallholdings without the need for heavy capital investment.

Although rubber prices declined from a peak in 1910 to an all-time low in 1922, the area planted with rubber expanded more or less continuously. The majority of estates were owned by Europeans. By World War I, Malaya had become the world's leading producer of rubber, and in terms of export earnings rubber surpassed tin from around 1916. During the war, the reduced civilian demand in Europe was offset by growth in America. However, the price of rubber fell in the 1920s and during the Great Depression of the 1930s. By the 1930s, also, it was no longer economic to tap many of the old rubber trees.

A cartoon in the 1925 Christmas Day issue of *Straits Produce* takes a satiric look at the rapidly falling rubber prices. They were to continue falling until the early 1930s.

W. W. Bailey tapping Lowlands Rubber, c. 1904. There were an average of 12 latex cups on each tree. Bailey, who was originally a coffee planter, changed to rubber planting when the price of coffee slumped. He was aided in this venture by the agency house Barlow & Co., which had earlier helped the planter export his coffee in return for cash advances.

'A Story Without Words' was published in the magazine *British Malaya* on 15 December 1933. It shows, graphically, the effects of the rubber 'boom-and-bust' cycle on the lifestyle of the people.

The decline
Although rubber prices declined from their peak in 1910, the area planted by all groups expanded more or less continuously to reach 900 000 hectares (2.25 million acres) by 1921.

Year	Price
1910	13 shillings/lb
1922	6 pence/lb
1932	2 1/4 pence/lb

Estates
(an area of more than 40 hectares or 100 acres): 60% .

Ownership:
Europeans : Chinese
75 : 25

Smallholdings
(an area of less than 40 hectares): 40%

Ownership:
Chinese and Indians owned most holdings over 5 hectares, and Malays those less than 5 hectares.

Female workers on an estate sorting rubber seeds collected for planting.

Processed rubber being pressed and packed for the export market.

The development
of urban centres

There was a distinct difference between urbanization in the Malay states before and after the establishment of colonial rule. While previously these centres had been on the coast, under the British the development of urban centres was spurred by the colonial export economy. Towns were established near the mining fields and populated largely by immigrant labourers and, later, by Europeans. The indigenous Malay population was almost never involved in urban developments because they were the least involved in the export economy and its related activities.

Penang fire brigade, c. 1900. Such services were soon a feature of urban centres along with the development of infrastructure and communications.

The development of transport

The job of the Chinese rickshaw pullers was, in many ways, the most pathetic. They earned a living by providing transportation for people prior to the time when motorcars and trams became a common feature.

An adventurous young man on a motorcycle trip from Singapore, across the causeway, to Johor, c. 1924. Two-wheelers became popular after the arrival of cars.

Talbot motorcars were imported by Messrs Aylesbury & Garland to Ipoh, c. 1890s. The company was the first European agency house in the town.

Pre-colonial urban centres

Before the arrival of the Portuguese, Dutch and British, urban centres in the Malay Peninsula were usually situated at river mouths, the focus of the main administrative and economic activities. During the Melaka sultanate in the 15th century, Melaka was a well-known international port dealing with entrepôt trade. Simultaneously, in the north, Kuala Kedah was an important port of call where merchandize was exchanged among Gujarati, local and regional traders. Ports in Terengganu and Kelantan on the east coast were also visited by Chinese traders. However, the various centres developed independently because of the lack of communications.

This isolation of urban centres continued until British rule began. The formation of the Straits Settlements in 1826, the introduction in 1874 of the Residential System and, finally, the 1896 union of Perak, Selangor, Negeri Sembilan and Pahang as the Federated Malay States (FMS), consolidated the development of urban centres.

Urban centres, 1826–1896

From 1826, Singapore overtook Penang to become the leading international port for the Malay Peninsula. Melaka was totally overshadowed by the other two ports because of its poor location. Penang was well sited for the export of tin, while Singapore lay strategically on the China–India trade route. Both served as entrepôt ports for export produce from the hinterland states.

The increasing demand for tin in Europe led to the liberalization of land and immigration policies. This encouraged thousands of Chinese miners to settle in previously undeveloped areas, thereby creating urban centres in the FMS, many of which had already begun to develop before British intervention took place. Among the urban centres which were established as a result of mining activities were Taiping, Matang and Ipoh in Perak; Klang and Kuala Lumpur in Selangor; Seremban in Negeri Sembilan, and Kuantan in Pahang.

More than 90 per cent of the tin produced was exported. Mining towns were connected to ports first by cart tracks, and later by railways. The first railway, linking Taiping with Port Weld (now Kuala Sepetang), was completed in 1885. Later, roads also linked the ports with inland urban centres. At first, houses were erected without proper planning, resulting in crowding and the creation of hazards. Only later was the importance of town planning and maintenance of amenities recognized. The relative importance of the towns was closely related to the mining activities in the area; towns generally declined when miners moved to new fields. Thus, Ipoh became more important than Taiping after the discovery of rich tin deposits in the Kinta Valley.

Urban centres, 1896–1941

The formation of the FMS hastened the development and administration of the states. The British began to synchronize urban development not only within the states of the federation, but also in other parts of the Peninsula. This facilitated further economic exploitation, especially when the rubber industry boomed and eventually replaced tin mining in importance before World War II. More railways and roads were built to link the urban centres with the ports, especially Singapore and Penang. Although still overshadowed by Singapore, Kuala Lumpur, as the capital of the FMS, was rapidly developing. It was linked by roads and railways to Butterworth in the north and Johor Bahru in the south, as well as to Klang and Port Swettenham (Port Klang) on the Selangor coast.

The growth of Penang and Singapore depended largely on the Malayan economy. As the main gateways for Malayan products (tin and rubber), merchant houses and agencies mushroomed in those two ports. Industries were also established to cater for the needs of the burgeoning population. During this period, Singapore dominated Penang because its geographical position enabled it to serve as a regional port; Penang primarily served local needs. However, Penang remained the second most important urban centre until after World War II,

Major urban centres and their development

Penang: Weld Quay in the early 20th century. Penang was the main port for the export of tin from the Perak mines. It also served as one of the major arrival points for manufactured goods and Indian immigrant workers.

Taiping: The Perak Museum, c.1890. Taiping, sited near the tin mines of Kelian Pauh, was the early British administrative centre of Perak.

Kuala Lumpur: A permanent bridge in Market Street (now Leboh Pasar Besar) spanning the Klang River linking the government offices on one side with the town on the other replaced earlier temporary structures.

Port Swettenham: The port (now known as Port Klang) increased in importance after the building of a road and a railway line from Kuala Lumpur. Tin from the Kuala Lumpur mines was exported through the port.

South China Sea

Penang
Taiping
Ipoh
Port Swettenham
Kuala Lumpur
South of Melaka
Melaka
Singapore

Melaka: The town centre. An important port during the 15th century, it was overshadowed by Penang and Singapore by the 19th century.

Singapore: Warehouses along Collyer Quay, c.1890. During the 19th century, its strategic position made Singapore the main entrepôt for the China–India trade.

Ipoh: A 1912 view of the town which replaced Taiping in importance, eventually becoming the capital of Perak.

Urban centres in Selangor

In Selangor, Klang was the administrative and mining centre until the end of the Selangor civil war (1867–73) when Sultan Abdul Samad moved his capital to Kuala Langat. By this time, mining had spread throughout the Selangor valley. Kuala Lumpur became a trading post for the miners in the vicinity. It attracted Chinese and Malay traders, many of whom became wealthy. Kuala Lumpur's apparent prosperity, as well as of the tin-rich surrounding areas, created rivalry between the local people and the Chinese settlers which resulted in the civil wars of the 1870s. This led to British intervention.

By 1887, Kuala Lumpur was connected to other towns by railways and roads, and its export and import activities increased. Building regulations began to be imposed, and amenities were introduced. The population increased from 2,000 in 1878 to 25,000 in 1895. In 1896, Kuala Lumpur was made the new capital of the FMS, and by 1900 the railway linking Kuala Lumpur to Port Swettenham (now Port Klang) was completed. By the time of the 1911 census, the population of Kuala Lumpur was 111,000; Klang 21,000; Port Swettenham and Kuala Kubu 13,000; Kajang and Sungai Besi 9,000; Serendah 7,000; Rawang and Ampang 5,000, and the other centres 1,000. The population continued to rise rapidly throughout the state.

Kuala Lumpur government offices, completed in 1897. In 1880, the administration of Selangor was transferred from Klang to Kuala Lumpur.

Kuala Lumpur's civic leaders, 1884

In 1875, the British confirmed Yap Ah Loy as the Kapitan China (the head of the Chinese community) in Kuala Lumpur. The Kapitan (seated right with hat) is seen here with other government officials and community leaders, including Raja Laut of the Malay community, and Thamboosamy Pillai, a prominent member of the Indian community.

The rubber industry and Indian immigration

The rubber industry not only brought about a transformation of the agricultural economy in Malaya, but also led to a major demographic change in the population. From 1900 to 1920, the rush of planters, capitalists, adventurers and speculators to invest in rubber in the western Malay states established the Malay Peninsula as a primary producer of rubber. By the end of 1909, 399 estates had been planted with 200 000 hectares of rubber, overshadowing other commercial crops.

The Raffles Hotel in Singapore was the popular venue for the 'Planter's Weekend'. As rail travel improved in the early 20th century, this stately hotel, with its bar, billiard room and other recreational facilities, popularly became known as 'The Rendezvous of Planters'. *INSET*: A planter's journal.

Rubber plantations and Indian labour

FROM LEFT: A rubber estate, rubber seeds and the tapping of latex.

Indian labourers carrying buckets of latex to the processing factory.

Coagulating the latex, the first step in the processing of rubber.

The interior of a rubber processing factory on an estate.

Labour recruitment systems

There were two systems used for the recruitment of Indian labourers for plantations in the Malay Peninsula.

The first, the indenture system of labour recruitment, was first associated with sugar estates. Here, a recruiting agent in India supplied the number of labourers required by the Malayan employer. These labourers entered into a contractual relationship with their employer for three years.

The second, the *kangany* recruitment system, evolved as a parallel recruitment system in the 1860s, but it became prominent only after the abolition of the indenture system in 1910. Here, an Indian estate foreman was given the role of a kangany (labour recruiter) to seek labourers from his own village.

The significant difference between the two systems was that the kangany system encouraged a steady movement of families into the Malay Peninsula, thereby improving the gender ratio in the estates. Also, the relationship between the labourers and the kangany was a continuous one as they worked under his supervision and could depend on him for advice and security. Although the kangany system was far less abusive than the indenture system, it was still condemned as a system of labour exploitation by plantation capitalists in the 1930s.

Pre-1890s commercial agriculture

With the extension of British political influence in the Malay states, the development of commercial agriculture became a cornerstone of colonial economic policy. European capital and entrepreneurship, coupled with cheap immigrant labour, were the basis for the development of a plantation economy. The colonial government gave European planters financial assistance and generous land grants at low rentals. Road and railway construction was hastened, and laws were enacted to facilitate a free flow of labour. However, the Chinese dominated the plantation economy until the 1890s. European participation was evident only in sugar cultivation, followed by coffee, which was introduced by planters from Ceylon. In the mid-1890s, coffee was considered the most promising crop for European investors, but by the late 1890s coffee prices had plummeted so low that the industry was completely destroyed. It was at this stage that these planters turned to the cultivation of rubber on a scale that was unprecedented in colonial capitalist enterprise.

The rise of the rubber industry

Originally an experimental commodity, rubber quickly became an export crop which eventually overshadowed the tin-mining industry. Rubber's spectacular rise in Malaya was attributed to the high rubber prices in 1910 because of the phenomenal expansion of the American automobile industry.

Plantations were mostly managed and financed by individual owners. Some were resident planters, while others were absentee owners who employed resident managers. The main concentrations of rubber lay between Kuala Lumpur and Klang in Selangor, along the Matang coastal district of Perak, and around Seremban in Negeri Sembilan.

While the planters laid the foundations of this industry, its development was hastened by the influx of overseas capital. Rubber was a capital intensive industry, and the returns were not immediate. The scarcity of working capital was resolved when, from 1902, planters sold their concessions to joint stock companies floated in London and Shanghai. From 1903 to 1912, nearly 260 companies were floated in London, mainly through the British mercantile firms in the Peninsula which provided the bridge between the estates and the absentee shareholders.

Indian labour at the landing pier in Penang, c. 1905.

| SOUTH INDIAN ARRIVALS AND DEPARTURES AT PENANG, 1909–1938 | | | |
YEAR	ARRIVALS	DEPARTURES	DIFFERENCE
1909	49,817	31,374	+18,443
1920	95,220	55,481	+39,739
1930	69,114	151,735	-82,621
1938	44,207	75,479	-31,272

INDIA

Madras

The majority of Indian labour immigrants to Malaya came from the state of Madras. The volume of inflow and outflow was related to the economic conditions prevailing in the rubber sector. The increase in arrivals from 1910 to 1920 was partly stimulated by the intensive planting programme and also by the need to enhance profitability through increased output. This was followed by an immigration spurt during the price boom of 1925 when European estates, taking advantage of the prosperity, began to increase their revenue-earning potential by further replanting or the purchasing of other planted properties. However, with the hardships that followed the world economic Depression between 1930 and 1933, there was a reversal of flow as a result of massive unemployment and repatriation of labour. When conditions improved in 1934, there was a renewal of the immigration flow but on a scale that was very much lower than during the pre-Depression period.

Aid from the administration

The government should also be credited with much of the initiative for the growth of the rubber industry. In the 1890s, officials such as H. N. Ridley, the Director of the Singapore Botanic Gardens, encouraged the planting of rubber. Land concessions were provided at low cost with minimal conditions, a planters' loan fund was established to assist planters with land but no capital, and infrastructure, such as roads and railways, was extended to the estates.

However, the most significant contribution was in the supply of indentured labour. Rubber planting was labour intensive, needing a constant labour force for tapping as well as maintenance. With the increase in operations from 1903, haphazard labour recruitment was no longer adequate. A new recruitment system was needed to ensure a satisfactory, cheap and regular labour supply. Planters' associations recommended a labour bureau be established by the government, which was already employing large numbers of labourers on infrastructure projects.

In 1907, a semi-official Indian Immigration Committee comprising three government officers and five European planters was appointed by the High Commissioner. Employers paid a levy according to the number of labourers employed. The money was used to pay for all expenses involved in recruiting Indian labourers, including shipping costs and depots in India.

The fund hastened the abolition, in 1910, of the indentured labour system, and also consolidated the *kangany* system (using estate foremen to recruit labour from their own villages) of importing free labour on a large scale. Thus, the government became a joint partner with the planters in the labour recruitment system. The government also became involved in labour supervision and the determination of wage rates and service conditions.

For his contributions to the rubber industry in Malaya, H. N. Ridley (1855–1956) is often called the 'father of the rubber industry'.

Criticism of the labour system

Indian employment in the rubber industry drew criticism from both the Indian government and from local people. The abuses associated with recruiting procedures, accommodation and travel conditions, exploitation by the foreman, and inadequate wage rates were issues frequently raised in conjunction with the rights and status of overseas Indians in Malaya. Local critics came mostly from the Central Indian Association of Malaya, Indian political leaders, and the Agent of the Government of India who supervised and reported on Indian labour conditions. The climax came with the visit in late 1936 of an Indian National Congress politician, V. S. Srinivasa Sastri, who recommended abolition of the kangany system. Coupled with this system was the unwillingness of the United Planters Association of Malaya to restore the wage rates to pre-Depression levels.

Wages could not be raised because of the reduced rubber quota under the International Rubber Regulation Agreement. On 15 June 1938, the Indian government placed a ban on all assisted emigration to Malaya. This marked the beginning of a new phase in both the history of the rubber industry and Indian immigration.

H. N. Ridley initiated the first really successful tapping of rubber in 1897. Each tree was tapped at many points. Later, the one tree one incision system was introduced.

The development of railways

British intervention in the Malay states, which began in 1874, led to the gradual incorporation of the country into a permanent relationship with the expanding British empire and the emergence of an export-oriented economy specializing in tin and rubber. This process was facilitated by the introduction of railways which were specially constructed to carry the Peninsula's exports from the mines and estates to the ports, and to link the growing urban areas throughout the Malay Peninsula.

The three phases of railway development

PHASE I (1885–96)
Short lines in the western half of the Peninsula linked the tin-mining areas with coastal ports from where the ore was shipped overseas.

PHASE II (1897–1909)
The original lines were connected by north–south trunk lines due to the consolidation of British rule and the creation of the FMS in 1896.

PHASE III (1910–31)
The railways were extended to the Unfederated Malay States with the expansion of British influence to those states.

Early transport

Traditionally, the main mode of communication within the Malay Peninsula was by water; the seas and the rivers formed natural highways. Among the factors hindering the development of land transport were dense vegetation and the absence of suitable beasts of burden. Thus, the only means of communication between estuarine settlements and upstream villages were the rivers. Later, a system of footpaths and forest tracks evolved to provide connections between villages and river systems.

The discovery of new deposits of tin in the foothills of the western Malay states in the 1840s resulted in a shift of activity from the river mouths to the inland centres. It was the extraction and removal of tin which provided both the original reason for the building of railways and, by means of export duties levied by state governments, the funds to finance their development.

The phases of development

Three phases may be distinguished in the growth of the railway system in the Malay Peninsula, corresponding approximately to the three stages of British political involvement and the spread of a capitalist economy in Malaya. From short, latitudinal lines (averaging 12.8 kilometres) suited to the localized nature of economic penetration, the railway system grew into a vast network of about 1715 kilometres, covering almost all states and facilitating economic growth on the Peninsula.

Wandering wild elephants, such as this one which derailed a train near Tapah, Perak, in 1894, were a hazard on the new railway tracks.

The construction of a railway tunnel at Bukit Berapit. These backbreaking jobs were done by immigrant labourers, mostly from India.

The Padang Rengas Pass in Taiping was constructed during the second phase of development. *INSET*: A 1930s poster issued by the FMS Railways, now reproduced as a postcard by Raffles Hotel, Singapore.

Phase I, 1885–96

During this period, railways were not planned for integrated development, nor were they regarded as a means to facilitate interstate communication. Rather, they were conceived with limited objectives in mind: to serve the tin mines. Since Perak was the richest tin-bearing area in the Peninsula, it is not surprising that the first railway line was built there. Sir Hugh Low, the Resident of Perak (1877–89), raised the capital for its construction by an additional levy on tin exports, with the support of the Chinese mining community. The line, from Taiping to Port Weld (now Kuala Sepetang), was opened on 1 June 1885. Other lines were subsequently built in Perak's tin-mining areas to carry tin to the ports.

It was generally recognized that Selangor's economic development was being held back by an inadequate transport system. With less revenue from tin mining than was available in Perak, the Selangor government could not spend as much on transport, and therefore concentrated on improving roads and river services. However, neither could provide low-cost transport; later, a line was built from Kuala Lumpur to Klang (completed in 1886) on the grounds that it would be profitable. In 1899, this line was extended to Port Swettenham to carry tin exports from Kuala Lumpur mines.

Although the Pahang and Negeri Sembilan governments also favoured railway construction, funds were not available. In Negeri Sembilan, a concession was given to a private company to build the Sungai Ujong line from Seremban to Port Dickson. Completed in 1891, it was acquired by the FMS Railways in 1908.

The Kuala Lumpur Railway Station was designed by A. B. Hubback. Moorish architectural influences in the form of cupolas, domes, minarets and keyhole arches are its hallmark. Built in 1911, it was the third building housing the station and was preceded by the first phase of railway tracks which linked the capital of the FMS to Port Swettenham.

Keppel Road Railway Station in Singapore, which was opened in 1932. Trains from Kuala Lumpur stopped at Johor Bahru before crossing the Causeway into Woodlands and proceeding to the station which is now on the fringe of the business district. The building's high, barrel-roofed hall features six murals portraying a Westerner's view of life in Malaya.

Phase II, 1897–1909

This phase was motivated by the need for links between inland mining centres and the new areas being opened up for commercial agriculture. In 1896, the Resident-General of the new FMS, Frank Swettenham, proposed a master plan for the extension of the railway. The first section was to be a 'development' line to link the Perak and Selangor railway systems that would run through valuable but undeveloped country. When completed, this line would permit through railway traffic from Perai in the north to Port Swettenham in Selangor. It would also connect with the road to Pahang via Kuala Kubu.

The second section would extend this line to Kuala Lipis, the administrative capital of Pahang, in order to help promote the development of the state's mineral resources.

The third extension was to be from the southern terminus of the railway line at Cheras to Seremban, joining the Sungai Ujong line to provide a direct connection from Perai to Port Dickson.

Swettenham's plan was approved by the Colonial Office which recognized that the administration could not depend on the country's tin assets alone. Wide-ranging transport linkages were necessary for the exploitation of Malaya's vast agricultural potential. Furthermore, in the interests of administrative efficiency, it was important to have rail links between the FMS and the Straits Settlements.

The completion of the west coast extensions in 1903 led to communication via the Province Wellesley (Seberang Perai), Perak and Selangor railway systems. Financed and built by the FMS government, the line was then extended to Johor Bahru in 1909. A ferry service connected Johor Bahru with Woodlands, the northern terminus of the Singapore government railway. The closing of the major gap in the rail link between the FMS and Singapore in 1909 was followed, hardly accidentally, by the extension of British political influence into Johor with the appointment of a General Adviser.

In 1909, the British signed the Anglo-Siamese Treaty with Siam, bringing Perlis, Kedah, Kelantan and Terengganu under British protection. In return, a loan was granted to Siam for the extension of its existing railway line from Bangkok to the Kelantan border to enable the Siamese and FMS railway systems to be linked, extending Britain's trading interests into Siam.

An early 20th-century buffet parlour car attached to the express train that ran between Kuala Lumpur and Singapore. *INSET:* A baggage tag from the Raffles Hotel, Singapore.

Phase III (1910–31)

The rubber industry benefited most from the extension of the railways. Pahang was connected with the other states in the FMS for the first time. The line from Gemas to Kuala Lipis was completed in 1917. In 1931, Gemas was linked to the east coast by a line to Kelantan which linked with the Siam railways. The line on the west coast was extended north to Alor Setar in 1915, then to Kangar and Padang Besar on the border in 1918, to link up with the western branch of the Siamese railway system.

Railway timetables and station hotels were advertised in books and journals. The FMS printed colourful posters in the 1930s which were later part of a series of postcards issued by Raffles Hotel in Singapore.

Borneo railways

While Sarawak and Labuan built short railway lines to transport ore from the mines (and Sarawak's railway also provided passenger services for a time), Borneo's only remaining railway is in Sabah. Built in the early 20th century by the British North Borneo Company for the transport of both goods and passengers, the railway runs along the coast from Kota Kinabalu to Beaufort, from where it climbs the rugged Crocker Range to Tenom. The 150-kilometre-long narrow-gauge line is an engineering feat that took five years to complete.

An early train on the Sabah railway. Steam engines have been reintroduced on the route for tourists and railway enthusiasts. *INSET:* Chinese vendors beside a Sabah train.

Disease and health care services

The role of public health services was crucial to colonial expansion in Malaya. Medical research and public works were geared to fight the diseases which threatened economic development. The pattern of health services which evolved supported the colonial enterprises in the urban areas, while the estates were required to set up their own hospitals. Colonial medical ideology sought to establish the superiority of Western medicine, and blamed the sick for their own ill health.

The Institute for Medical Research in Kuala Lumpur was opened in 1901. The decision to establish the institute was taken by Sir Frank Swettenham, Resident-General of the Federated Malay States, with a view to 'carry out scientific and sustained research into the causes, treatment and prevention of such scourges as beriberi and all forms of malarial fevers'.

Infectious and deficiency diseases

Malaria was virtually uncontrollable in the Federated Malay States (FMS) in the early 20th century and was endemic right up to World War II. It constituted the largest number of hospital cases and was the leading cause of death among the immigrants. Scrub typhus, cholera, diarrhoea, dysentery, smallpox, typhoid, yaws and venereal diseases were also quite common. Some infectious diseases were spread among immigrants on their voyage. In 1918, out of 49 immigrant ships, 11 were infected with smallpox and one with cholera. The Port Quarantine Service, established in 1900, has been credited with cutting out all but minor outbreaks of dangerous infectious diseases by 1911.

Nutritional deficiency diseases were equally widespread, as well as respiratory diseases such as pulmonary tuberculosis, diphtheria and pneumonia. In these cases, protein calorie malnutrition was probably an underlying cause of illness and death. In the estates, the extremely poor living conditions led to high levels of vitamin A deficiency, anaemia and diarrhoea among the labourers.

Workers' living conditions

A diorama at the Singapore History Museum showing a cramped coolie quarter. This typical room in Chinatown in the 19th century shows how landlords crammed as many beds as possible into the space, often renting a single bed to two different persons who worked different shifts.

Numerous immigrant workers died prematurely because of unsanitary and overcrowded working and living conditions. Their subsistence diets caused malnutrition, making them susceptible to infectious diseases. In 1910, 60–90 per cent of the estate workers died during the first year. Sick or dead workers were easily replaced by further immigration, while ill and aged workers were repatriated to their home countries.

Research and public health

Malaria and beriberi were the greatest restraints to economic development in the Malay Peninsula in the early 20th century as they decimated the labour force. Research by government doctors into the causes of these two diseases, therefore, dominated all medical and public health efforts of the colonial administration. The Institute for Medical Research (IMR) was opened in 1901 to spearhead this work.

IMR researchers established that beriberi could be prevented by replacing polished rice with parboiled rice. The IMR also became well known for its work on malaria. Malaya was the first country to successfully apply the knowledge that malaria is spread by the *Anopheles* mosquito for control measures. Malcolm Watson, a British anti-malaria pioneer, aided the government in applying the basic principles of malarial control in Klang by proper drainage, bunding and oiling, which destroyed the mosquito larvae and their breeding grounds.

The two dominant diseases

Beriberi and malaria were the diseases which played the greatest role in decimating the workforce in the rubber and mining industries, and thus threatened the progress of capitalist enterprise and colonialist expansion.

Dr W. Leonard Braddon was the first to make the link between the consumption of polished rice and the cause of beriberi in the early years of the 20th century. Eventually, experiments proved that beriberi could be prevented by substituting polished rice in the diet with parboiled rice. Only later was the lack of thiamine (vitamin B1) identified as the cause of beriberi. This vitamin is found in the outer layers of the rice grain, which were lost in the milling process. Those most affected were the Chinese immigrant tin mine labourers whose work involved great physical exertion and whose diet consisted primarily of polished rice and salted fish as they could not afford to buy fresh meat, fish and vegetables.

The spread of malaria, on the other hand, was exacerbated by the indiscriminate large-scale clearing of forests for mining and rubber cultivation. The successful control methods were based on the work of world researchers. It was once thought that the disease was caused by miasma, the foul air present in swamps. The mosquito-malaria theory came into prominence in the late 19th century, and many scientists worked to prove it, leading to Ronald Ross's discovery of the malaria parasite in the mosquito.

Stamps issued to commemorate the 75th and 100th anniversaries of the Institute for Medical Research.

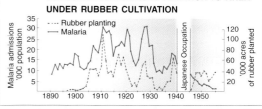

BERIBERI ADMISSIONS TO GOVERNMENT HOSPITALS ('000 POPULATION OF FMS)

MALARIA ADMISSIONS IN RELATION TO AREA UNDER RUBBER CULTIVATION

Top: The European Hospital at Bangsar in Kuala Lumpur, c. 1900s, with its imported equipment, provided treatment to the European community.

Centre: The Tan Tock Seng Hospital in Singapore, one of the pauper hospitals funded by wealthy Chinese for the treatment of the poor.

Bottom: Estate hospitals such as this one provided the only medical facilities available to immigrant plantation workers.

Setting up hospitals

The colonial officers, in the early days of their arrival in the Malay Peninsula, had set up hospitals in the towns and ports for the benefit of the British and their workers. From 1883 to 1910, general hospitals were established in almost all state capitals. In 1889, a pauper hospital was set up on the site of the present Kuala Lumpur General Hospital.

Different hospitals catered for different classes of people. Exclusive European hospitals were set up for the colonial expatriates. In 1910, the European Hospital at Batu Gajah, believed to be one of the best in the region, recorded that 50 per cent of its patients were planters, and out of the 239 cases treated that year, there were only four deaths.

The Chinese population was made to pay for its own pauper hospitals through taxation. At one time, these hospitals in Penang and Singapore were maintained by taxes on pork. The British considered the hospitals the responsibility of the Chinese community because most of the patients were Chinese. Wealthy Chinese donated money for the establishment and running of such hospitals.

In order to ensure that the health of the workers was maintained, various laws were passed. The state Indian Immigration Enactments of 1904 required managers to provide medical facilities for their workers. These, however, proved to be far from adequate. The 1920 FMS report states 'these medical

facilities often consisted of only a shack and a compounder who had picked up the rudiments of medicine along the way'. Even as late as 1918, there were only eight doctors to serve the 1,006 estates, with conditions remaining the same up to World War II.

Maternal and child health

The British colonial medical authorities blamed traditional midwives and mothers for the high incidence of infant mortality in the late 19th and early 20th centuries. Efforts were directed towards making government training and registration compulsory for midwives, and also educating mothers and encouraging them to use Western medical services instead of the traditional midwives.

Before World War II, infant mortality declined, though there were wide variations among ethnic groups and geographical areas. The decline may be attributed to various factors, including anti-malarial measures, the improvement in sanitation facilities, and other public health programmes.

Traditional remedies

The indigenous and immigrant populations all followed their own traditional medical practices, despite attempts by the British to establish the superiority of Western medicine over 'unscientific' traditional cures. Many government reports blamed the people of Malaya for their own ill health. Nevertheless, the British colonialists had an interest in establishing a healthier and more sustainable workforce.

Advances in medicine and public health were of benefit to the progress of colonial enterprise. In addition, as a provider of health care services, the colonial administration legitimized itself as a benevolent guardian of the people.

Traditional remedies, such as those sold by these wayside Indian medicine sellers, were considered by the colonial administrators to be inadequate for controlling disease. The colonial government also considered traditional midwives to be superstitious, unhygienic and lacking in skills, and the mothers, especially in the plantations, as being ignorant of proper hygiene, childcare and infant feeding.

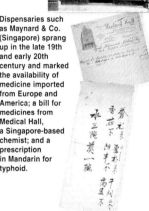

Dispensaries such as Maynard & Co. (Singapore) sprang up in the late 19th and early 20th century and marked the availability of medicine imported from Europe and America; a bill for medicines from Medical Hall, a Singapore-based chemist; and a prescription in Mandarin for typhoid.

Nursing staff of the Government General Hospital in Perak, c. 1908.

Maternal and child health
In the first decade of the 20th century, infant mortality rates continued their upward trend. In the urban areas of the Straits Settlements, they were in the region of 200 per 1,000 live births, rising to over 300 per 1,000 in 1911. The rates in the rural areas were lower, about 150 per 1,000 live births. Infant mortality rates collected at this time were largely estimates, possibly with considerable underreporting of deaths in the first few weeks after birth, particularly in the rural areas.

A vaccination programme at government clinics was part of the official strategy to lower the infant mortality rate. This photograph from the 1938 annual report of the Federated Malay States shows mothers and children at a clinic.

A 1936 vaccination notice issued by the Singapore municipality.

Education and the Malay civil service

At the beginning of the 20th century, the British colonial government in the Federated Malay States (FMS) felt it needed to associate the Malay aristocracy more closely with its administration. The Malay College was thus established at Kuala Kangsar in 1905 to train future administrators. The new administrators were later placed in the Malay Administrative Service (MAS) which was distinctly subordinate to the British-dominated Malayan Civil Service (MCS). In later years, a few MAS officers were promoted into the MCS, and by 1957 many senior government positions—both political and bureaucratic—were occupied by former MAS officers.

Some illustrious MAS and MCS officers
CLOCKWISE FROM TOP: Tan Sri Datuk Dr Mohamad Said with 90-year-old Mr C. Bazell (Principal of the Malay College in the 1930s), in 1974; Tunku Tan Sri Mohamad bin Tunku Besar Burhanuddin, the first Malaysian Principal Establishment officer who later became Chief Secretary; Tan Sri Nik Ahmed Kamil, a brilliant administrator and diplomat, who played a key role in Malaysia's Independence; Tuanku Jaafar Ibni Al-Marhum Tuanku Abdul Rahman, the Yang di-Pertuan of Negeri Sembilan.

The Higher Subordinate Class Scheme of 1910

To find employment for boys of the Malay College, a scheme was drawn up in 1910 in consultation with the first headmaster of the school, William Hargreaves. This first scheme relegated the probationers to comparatively unimportant administrative positions.

Main points of the 1910 Scheme

- Not more than 10 students, who had passed their Standard VII examination, were to be selected each year as probationers for the MAS.

- Probationers were selected by the Resident-General from nominations made by the Residents of the FMS to enter the Special Class, a three-year course at the college on an allowance of $20 per month.

- The subjects offered included English, Malay, office correspondence, typewriting, history and geography of Malaya, law and procedure, surveying and Land Office work, and Official Accounts and Treasury work.

- After graduating, the probationers were appointed as Malay Assistants at the level of Grade III, gaining a three-year seniority, at $600 per year with an annual increment of $60, to a maximum of $720 per year.

The revised 1917 Scheme

This improved the prospects of the officers, who were by then recognized as being an asset to the Service.

- It increased the responsibility of Grade I posts.

- The name of the scheme was changed to the Malay Officers' Scheme.

- Only half of the probationerships were reserved for Malay College students. The others were open to candidates from other English schools who sat for a qualifying test and went before a selection board before being admitted to the Special Course at the Malay College.

The formulation of a policy

The imposition of a modern bureaucratic machinery by the British in the FMS at the end of the 19th century provided little opportunity for the Malay rulers to participate in governing their respective states. The British recognized that this was an anomalous situation because protectorate status, in theory, called for a system of indirect rule. Yet, the

LEFT: The Standard VII examination certificate issued to Raja Abdurrashid bin Sultan Idris in 1907. It is signed by R. J. Wilkinson, the FMS Inspector of Schools.

problem of accepting Malays into the administration was a real one. The language of government in the FMS was English and the administrative structure was alien to the Malays. This prompted certain individuals in the British administration to assert that the Malays were not ready to take their rightful place in the government. Nonetheless, it was generally hoped that with the passage of time more Malays would be found suitable as administrators.

The Malay College was established as a residential school for the sons of the Malay aristocracy to provide an intensive education and to instil discipline through continuous supervision of boys at an impressionable age.

This British domination of the administration in the FMS was in sharp contrast to the situation in the Unfederated Malay States (UMS) of Kedah, Perlis, Terengganu, Kelantan and Johor. Each state in the UMS had its own civil service headed by its ruler. He was assisted by a small number of British officials who held purely advisory positions. In these states, Malay remained the language of administration. Although the British wielded much influence, the rulers of the UMS, unlike their counterparts in the FMS, were in control of their state's day-to-day administration.

It was not until the early 20th century that British officials decided to open up the civil service and give more administrative responsibility in the FMS to the Malay aristocracy as the rightful administrators of the country. The British also realized that the existing English schools in the country were not producing the type of people who were needed by the Civil Service. The Malay College was thus opened in 1905 to prepare the sons of the Malay royalty and nobility for a career in government by English education and training in public administration.

Education at the Malay College
The aim of the founders of the Malay College was to provide a sound moral and scholastic education. The college was run along the lines of an English public school to impart values considered appropriate for a life of service to the public.

Such an education, far from being incongruous in a Malayan setting, was intended to nurture a new breed of educated Malays who could be successfully integrated into the colonial administration.

In the prewar years, the British were confident that the Malay College could produce efficient Malay civil servants, and the college became the main source for their recruitment. Postwar conditions required not only an increased Malay participation in the administration, but also better

qualified officers. By then, a changing social scenario made the traditional role of the Malay College anachronistic.

The Civil Service experience
In 1910, the introduction of the Scheme for the Employment of Malays in the Public Service (Higher Subordinate Class) brought the Malays into the higher echelons of the bureaucracy in the FMS. Until that time, it had been manned almost exclusively by British officials of the MCS. The designation 'Higher Subordinate Class' placed the Malay administrators in a position which was separate from, and subordinate to, the members of the superior MCS scheme.

The MAS was an auxiliary arm of the MCS and its members were perceived as no more than assistants to British officers and were sometimes even dismissed as 'donkey workers'. While the scheme of 1910 made provisions for the promotion of Malay civil servants into the MCS, they were not promoted auto-matically into the higher Service. For this reason, only a small number of Malays achieved that status before World War II.

Malay officers of the MAS served in a range of positions. As land and district administrators, they were concerned with revenue collection, the allocation and distribution of land for settlement, and the development of their district. As law enforcement agents, they assisted the judiciary in hearing and making decisions on minor civil and criminal cases occurring within their district. By the outbreak of World War II, Malay civil servants were holding a range of positions—district officers, senior magistrates, official assignees and Malay assistants to the Secretariat—and were already entrenched in the administration.

Capt. Salleh bin Haji Suliman in the MCS uniform.

The Malay College

A staff member (centre, in wide-brimmed hat) with 'The Moderates', the college football XI, c. 1909. There were always some teachers at the Malay College from English public schools.

Lessons were supplemented with 'character building' activities, such as the cadet corps, shown in this 1914 picture.

A theatre production by Malay College students in 1920. Extracurricular activities were considered essential for the all-round development of the students.

Malay College prefects of 1938 with their headmaster, Mr C. Bazell (centre). The students were given an education modelled on English public schools—the educational mainstay of the English upper class.

The First XI Cricket team, c. 1939. As part of their grooming for a career in the public service of a colonial regime, the students were taught to speak English, adopt British etiquette and acquire the skills required of an administrator.

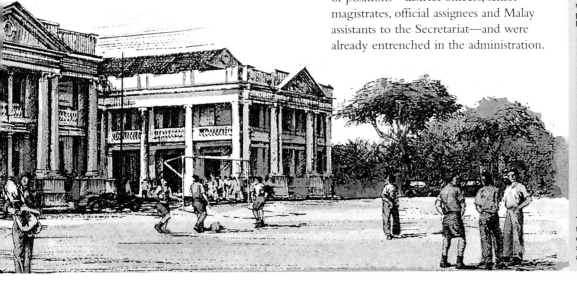

Malay newspapers and literature

The history of Malay newspapers and of Malay literature in the 19th and 20th centuries was intertwined. Both began with publications of Christian missionary organizations, followed by secular publications. During the 19th century, many publications were classics or translations of newspapers (from the local English-language versions) and literary works in other languages. It was not until the 20th century that the emphasis changed to original works, often with an educational aim. Later, social and political criticism became more popular themes.

The staff of the *Singapore Free Press*, a Singapore newspaper which began in 1835 after the repeal of the Gagging Act made a 'free' press possible. In 1907, the company began publication of a Malay language newspaper, *Utusan Melayu*.

INSET: A cartoon about the Singapore Free Press published in *Straits Produce*.

Sayyid Shaikh Al-Hadi, editor and publisher of the reformist journals *Al-Imam*, *Al-Ikhwan* and *Saudara*, pictured with his grandson, c. 1930.

Malay newspapers and periodicals

Bustan Arifin, the first publication with some semblance of a Malay newspaper, began in 1821. Like other early publications, it was the product of a Christian missionary organization. The editor was the Rev. Claudius Henry Thomsen, assisted by the Malay scribe Munshi Abdullah bin Abdul Kadir. The first non-missionary Malay newspaper was the weekly *Jawi Peranakkan*, owned by a group in Singapore led by Penang-born Munshi Muhammad Sa'id bin Dada Muhyiddin and editor Munshi Mohammad Alie bin Golam Al-Hindi. Though it relied on international news from the contemporary English-language media, it survived till 1895 and was the most successful, longest enduring, Malay newspaper before 1941.

During the 1890s, several new newspapers appeared, but all lasted only a short time. These included two in Taiping, and others in Penang as well as Singapore. By the early 20th century, the Malay press began to assume a new form, especially in content and orientation.

Abdul Rahim Kajai, a short story writer and journalist, was editor of *Utusan Melayu*, 1939–41.

New titles such as *Taman Pengetahuan*, *Khazinat al-Ulum* and *Al-Imam* all tried to be more knowledge-based and scholarly, as well as acting as agents of reform. This was most obvious in *Al-Imam*, which urged Muslims to return to the true Islam based on the Qur'an and Sunnah. In their efforts to bring about change, the editors incurred the wrath of Malay leaders whom they accused of being partly responsible for all the ills of Malay society. After the demise of *Al-Imam*, these editors carried on their campaign in later journals, including *Neraca*, *Al-Ikhwan* and *Saudara*.

Early Singapore newspapers, which often began as Malay editions of English papers, gradually assumed distinct identities, publishing articles and letters to the editor, some rather critical of the sociocultural and prevailing political situation. Another newspaper publishing such articles and letters was *Pengasuh*, the first newspaper published on the east coast of the Malay Peninsula. Though published by the Council of Islamic Affairs and Malay Custom of Kelantan, it did not restrict its articles to religious matters or to state affairs.

PRINCIPAL MALAY NEWSPAPERS

DATE	TITLE	FREQUENCY	PLACE	PUBLISHER
1821–2	*Bustan Arifin*	quarterly	Melaka	London Missionary Society
1876–95	*Jawi Peranakkan*	weekly	Singapore	Munshi Muhammad Sa'id bin Dada Muhyiddin
1893–4	*Seri Perak*	weekly	Taiping	Sayyid Abul Hassan bin Burhan
1894	*Surat Khabar Peranakan*	daily	Singapore	Straits Chinese
1894–5	*Bintang Timor*	daily	Singapore	Chinese Christian Association
1894–5	*Tanjong Penagri*	twice weekly	Penang	S. P. S. K. Kaden Sahib
1895–7	*Pemimpin Warita*	weekly	Penang	Khor Teow Han (?)
1895–1906	*Sahabat*	monthly	Singapore	Malayan mission of Methodist English Church
1896–7	*Jajahan Melayu*	weekly	Taiping	Sayyid Abul Hassan bin Burhan
1896–1904	*Pelajaran Skola Agama*	fortnightly	Singapore	Malayan mission of Methodist English Church
1898–9	*Warta Melayu*	monthly	Singapore	Malayan mission of Methodist English Church
1900	*Bintang Timor*	weekly	Penang	Criterion Press (?)
1900–1	*Akhbar Lengkongan Bulan*	weekly	Penang	Kim Seik Hean Press (?)
1900–8	*Chahaya Pulau Pinang*	weekly	Penang	Criterion Press (?)
1904–	*Taman Pengetahuan*	weekly	Singapore	Alwi brothers
1904–	*Khazinat al-Ulum*	monthly	Kuala Lumpur	unknown
1906–8	*Al-Imam*	monthly	Singapore	Al-Imam Printing Co.
1907–21	*Utusan Melayu*	thrice weekly/daily	Singapore	William E. Makepeace
1911–15	*Neraca*	fortnightly	Singapore	Shaikh Abbas bin Mohd Taha
1914–31	*Lembaga Melayu*	daily	Singapore	Malaya Tribune
1918–41	*Pengasuh*	fortnightly	Kota Bharu	Majlis Ugama Islam dan Isti'adat Melayu
1922–5	*Panduan Guru*	quarterly	Penang	Penang Malay Teachers' Association
1924–41	*Majallah Guru*	monthly	KL/Penang	Malay teachers' associations
1925–41	*Warta Ahad*	weekly	Singapore	Sayyid Hussein bin Ali Al-Sagoff
1926–31	*Al-Ikhwan*	monthly	Penang	Sayyid Shaikh Al-Hadi
1928–41	*Saudara*	weekly	Penang	Sayyid Shaikh Al-Hadi
1930–41	*Warta Malaya*	daily	Singapore	Sayyid Hussein bin Ali Al-Sagoff
1931–41	*Majlis*	twice/thrice weekly	Kuala Lumpur	Mohd Amin bin Mohd Yusoff
1939–41	*Utusan Melayu*	daily	Singapore	Utusan Melayu Co.
1939–42	*Utusan Zaman*	weekly	Singapore	Utusan Melayu Co.

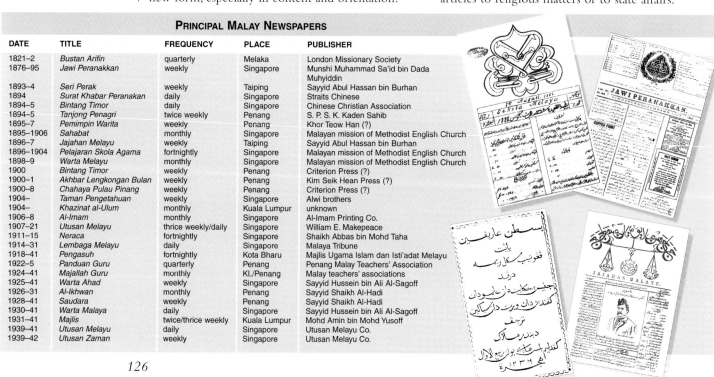

The 1920s also marked more organized activism of vernacular-educated teachers, marked by the appearance of two educational journals *Panduan Guru* and *Majallah Guru*. There had long been a close association between Malay school teachers and newspapers, and these two journals became an influential forum for teachers to air their views. Many of these teachers later became writers, journalists and activists.

Starting with the daily *Warta Malaya* in 1930, Malay newspapers gained momentum in number, variety, coverage and circulation. Many were short-lived, due to either inadequate funding, poor management or lack of support from the readers. Together with the existing titles, these new newspapers became the medium through which journalists and editors such as Muhammad Yunus bin Abdul Hamid, Sayyid Shaikh Al-Hadi, his son Sayyid Alwi, Abdul Wahab bin Abdullah, Onn bin Ja'afar, Sayyid Hussein bin Ali Alsagaf, Othman Kalam, Abdul Rahim Kajai, Ibrahim Haji Yaakob and Ishak Haji Muhammad demonstrated their literary talents and expressed their views. The new publications ranged from the general to the more religiously focused.

Of about 183 Malay periodicals published in the Malay Peninsula and Singapore prior to 1941, fewer than half were from the Malay states. Of these, most appeared in Johor, Perak and Kelantan; none were in Pahang or Perlis. It was not until the 1930s that Malay newspapers and periodical publications began to be a common phenomenon in the Peninsular Malay states. This was due both to the persistence of the traditional way of life and the rather late intro-duction of modern educational and social amenities conducive to newspaper production. Morover, periodicals published in Penang and Singapore were easily obtainable in all the states.

Malay literature

Malay literature of the 19th and 20th centuries also began with the activities of Christian missionaries and the setting up of the first printing press in Penang in 1806. It grew hand in hand with Malay newspapers and journalism. Many of those involved in literature were also journalists or involved with newspaper production. The introduction of periodicals and newspapers brought variety to written Malay, though the formalistic or *hikayat* style of the old literature was not immediately replaced. New Malay literature can be said to have begun with Munshi Abdullah bin Abdul Kadir. Malay literary works during the 19th century were mostly confined to the publication of a limited number of the classics, reports of travel, and adapted translations from Arabic, Tamil, Hindustani and English. The story of Robinson Crusoe, for example, appeared serially in the

quarterly *Chermin Mata* as early as 1858-9, and *Hikayat Bakawali*, an adaptation from a Hindustani version, was produced by Sayyid Muhammad bin Sayyid Abdul Kadir in 1875. An adaptation of Aesop's fables, *Hikayat Penerang Hati*, was produced by Alang Ahmad bin Muhammad Yunus in 1896.

Only in the early 1920s did original story writing appear in a new prose form in periodicals. In 1920, *Pengasuh* published the didactic story 'Kecelakaan Pemalas' and also the political allegory 'Tangisan Tekukur di dalam Sangkarnya'. The latter was among the earliest Malay writings to express a longing for independence from British 'protection'.

A novel by Ishak Haji Muhammad entitled *Putera Gunung Tahan* (The Prince of Tahan Mountain) criticized both Malay feudal leaders and the colonial rulers.

With the publication of works such as *Hikayat Setia Asyik kepada Maksyuknya, atau Syafik Affendi dengan Faridah Hanum* by Sayyid Shaikh Al-Hadi (1925–6), *Hikayat Percintaan Kasih Kemudaan* by Ahmad Kotot (1927), and *Kawan Benar* (1927) and *Iakah Salmah* (1928) by Ahmad Rasyid Talu, the 1920s also marked the beginning of modern novels written in popular Malay which dealt with everyday people and their lives.

In this period, many short stories and novels dealt with social and cultural themes and, though in veiled form, politics. Well-known writers such as Sayyid Shaikh Al-Hadi, Abdul Rahim Kajai, Onn Ja'afar, Syamsuddin Salleh, Muhammad Yusuf Ahmad and Ishak Haji Muhammad were also writing for newspapers and periodicals. Others who achieved fame later, such as Harun Aminurrasyid and Abdul Samad Ahmad, began their writing career in this period while they were pursuing careers as teachers or journalists, or during their student days.

As the new writing style became more popular as a result of the spread of vernacular education and publishing, literary activities—which had earlier been the preserve of the more urban Straits Chinese community—gradually came to be dominated by Malay writers. Among these was Ishak Haji Muhammad, whose novel *Putera Gunung Tahan* (1937) was critical of both Malay feudal leadership and British colonial manoeuvres in Malaya.

Munshi Abdullah

Munshi Abdullah bin Abdul Kadir (1796–1854) was a third-generation Melakan of Yemeni and Indian origins who was fluent in several languages. He was not only a writer of original works but also a translator, scribe of Malay letters and teacher of Malay to colonial officers, including Stamford Raffles, and visiting merchants. In his later years, he taught at the Raffles Institution. Munshi Abdullah's original works include prose (*Hikayat Abdullah bin Abdul Kadir Munsyi*—his auto-biography and the earliest and most vivid account of life in early Singapore by an Asian—and two accounts of his travels), as well as poetry (*Sya'ir Singapura Terbakar* and *Sya'ir Kampung Gelam Terbakar*). Abdullah also made available classical works in Malay, for example *Sejarah Melayu* (Malay Annals), as well as books in other languages.

ABOVE: Frontispiece in Jawi script from the first edition of *Hikayat Abdullah*, published by the Mission Press in Singapore in 1849.

RIGHT: A page from *Hikayat Abdullah*.

Munshi Ibrahim (1780–?) was, like Munshi Abdullah, of Indian extraction. The son of a Penang merchant, he worked for colonial officers in Penang before moving with Stamford Raffles to Melaka in 1810. It was Ibrahim who recruited Abdullah, among others, as a copyist for Raffles. Ibrahim's duties included writing letters in Malay for Raffles and making copies for the British East India Company archives.

TOP: *Chermin Mata bagi Segala Orang Yang Menuntut Pengetahuan* (the story of Robinson Crusoe), edited and produced in 1858 by B. P. Keasberry in Singapore. Such stories, originally produced as beautifully decorated manuscripts, were printed and sold cheaply in large numbers towards the end of the 19th century. After that, they were replaced by romanized Malay versions.

BOTTOM: An illustration from *Cherita Orang Yang Chari Selamat* (a translation of *Pilgrim's Progress*). Many translations of classics were published in the 19th century.

The origins of a Malay nationalist movement

A Malay nationalist movement was slow to develop in the Malay Peninsula because of the separate identities of the various states, and because some states felt British protection was advantageous to them. The movement started at the beginning of the 20th century, but was still developing at the outbreak of World War II. The initial catalyst to the movement was a publication, Al-Imam. Other Malay newspapers also played a major role. Only with the emergence of an educated Malay élite and the formation of state associations did the movement progress.

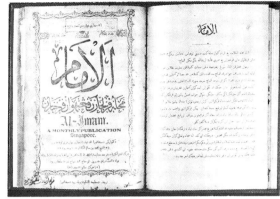

An issue of *Al-Imam*, a monthly journal published in Singapore from 1906 to 1908. It was edited by Sayyid Shaikh Al-Hadi, a Melaka-born Malay of Arabic descent, who was influenced by the nationalist movement in the Middle East.

Shaikh Mohd Tahir bin Jalaluddin al-Azhari, a Sumatran-born Malay nationalist who studied in Mecca and Cairo. He was one of the four founders of the reformist journal *Al-Imam*, to which he was a regular contributor.

The early beginnings

In the Malay Peninsula, the first decade of the 20th century witnessed the first stirrings of nationalist consciousness, as was seen in *Al-Imam*, a monthly journal published in Singapore from 1906 to 1908. Ironically, Malay nationalist consciousness was at that time promoted by several who could hardly be classified as Malay: Shaikh Mohd Tahir bin Jalaluddin al-Azhari was from Minangkabau, Sayyid Shaikh Al-Hadi was a Melaka-born Malay-Arab, Haji Abbas bin Mohd Taha was from Singapore and Shaikh Mohd Salim Al-Kalali was an Acehnese.

This nascent consciousness manifested itself through articles criticizing the dismal economic conditions of the Malays vis-à-vis the non-Malays in the Malay Peninsula, the indifferent attitude of the Malay rulers towards their subjects, and calls to Malays to rely on themselves through the formation of self-awareness associations and the promotion of education. The medium for such views was Islam which, the nationalists believed, if observed faithfully would liberate the believers from poverty, ignorance and exploitation. There was never any attempt to ferment dissatisfaction against British colonialism or to advocate independence.

There was no genuine anticolonial nationalist spirit within the Malay community because the Malays were divided into nine states, each with its own sultan. Malay political ideology at this stage was focused on the *kerajaan* (monarchy), and the Malays saw themselves as subjects of a particular ruler and not as citizens of a nation. Furthermore,

the large numbers of non-Malays resident in the Malay states made many Malays feel that British colonial protection was necessary to ensure they were not swamped by the non-Malays. However, the economic, social and political backwardness of the Malay communities led to the emergence of a number of Malay organizations to cater to Malay needs and to stress Malay ethnic identity.

The Malay press

The emergence of a Malay press was an important factor in fostering Pan-Malayan Malay awareness. In the 1930s, the Malay states saw the emergence of newspapers such as *Warta Malaya* (News of Malaya), *Saudara* (Friend), *Utusan Melayu* (Malay News), *Majlis* (Council), *Bumiputra* (Son of the Soil), *Suara Benar* (True Voice), *Tanah Melayu* (Malay Land), *Berita Sekolah* (School News), *Warta Kinta* (Kinta News), *Chahaya Singapura* (Light of Singapore) and *Persahabatan* (Friendship). All of these newspapers vigorously defended Malay rights against what was perceived as encroachment by non-Malays, mainly Chinese immigrants.

Abdul Rahim Kajai, a journalist, rejected Islam as a means of fostering brotherhood bonds between Muslim Malays and Muslim Indians and Arabs who were effectively marginalized within the Malay community by such derogatory terms as DKK (*darah keturunan Keling*—of Indian descent) or DKA (*darah keturunan Arab*—of Arab descent), respectively. For Rahim Kajai, only Malays of patriarchal Malay descent could be classified as Malays.

Pan-Malayan Malay organizations

Pan-Malayan Malay organizations which attempted to lay the foundations for a nationalist movement within the various Malay communities of the nine Malay states found that they had to battle against the overwhelming sentiment of state parochialism. However, attempts were made to promote national consciousness by utilizing the medium of Malay.

The Persaudaraan Sahabat Pena Malaya (PASPAM), established in Penang in 1934, was perhaps the most influential in fostering some degree of unity by promoting an interest in Malay language and literature, a love of reading and the

The presentation of colours to the Malayan Volunteer Infantry by Sultan Abdullah of Pahang on the occasion of his birthday in 1923. The nationalists felt that loyalties to state rulers were hindering the development of a national identity.

establishment of a Malay library. PASPAM made deliberate efforts to forswear any political activities, instead promoting only cultural and social aims.

However, the organization floundered because of Malay ethnic chauvinism. Although membership of PASPAM had increased steadily since its inception, the tension between its Straits Chinese-dominated headquarters in Penang and the purely Malay branches in the Malay states led, by 1937, to a serious rift within the organization.

The split between the Malays and the Indian and Arab Muslims who, because of their wealth and capabilities, assumed leadership roles in PASPAM, could not be avoided as Malay ethnic chauvinists increasingly questioned the role of the Indian and Arab Muslims within the Malay community. Despite being Muslims and adopting the Malay language and culture, both the Indian and Arab communities were marginalized by the Malays.

The rise of a Malay élite

The 1920s and the 1930s saw a steady stream of graduates from the Sultan Idris Training College in Tanjung Malim and the growth of a Malay 'élite' which shared common educational and political inclinations. These young Malays rejected Indian and Arab Muslim claims to be a part of the Malay community by virtue of religious ties. Nevertheless, an awareness of the exclusiveness of the Malay community did not lead to pan-Malayan Malay political unity. State parochial sentiments were the norm, as seen by the formation of the various state associations, each emphasizing state loyalties.

The first state association, the Kesatuan Melayu Singapura (Singapore Malay Union), was formed in 1926. This was followed by the Persatuan Melayu Pahang (Pahang Malay Association) in March 1938, and the Persatuan Melayu Selangor (Selangor Malay Association) in June 1938. By 1939, Negeri Sembilan also had a state association. Most of these associations were founded by people with some connection to royalty who were loyal to their sultan and were strong supporters of the British.

Pan-Malayan Malay congresses

With insurmountable state parochialism and squabbles over Malay identity and characteristics, attempts to unite the various Malay communities politically and to develop a pan-Malayan Malay nationalist movement ended in abject failure. The first Pan-Malayan Malay Congress of Malay associations, held in Kuala Lumpur in 1939, quibbled over the ethnic credential of two Malay associations from Penang. One of these was the Kesatuan Melayu Singapura, Chawangan Pulau Pinang (Malay Union of Singapore, Penang Branch), whose members were mostly Jawi Peranakan (Indian/Malay). The other was the

Sultan Idris Training College

The Sultan Idris Training College at Tanjung Malim, Perak, was opened in 1922 to train village Malays as teachers for the kampong schools. Although the students came from all states, they were discouraged from identifying with their state and instead encouraged to adopt a wider Malay identity. Despite the deliberate inclusion of practical skills in the curriculum, for several decades the college was a centre of Malay intellectual life. The staff, many of whom wrote for newspapers and journals, nurtured the development of modern Malay language and literature. They thus stimulated the growth of Malay nationalism and produced a new genre of leaders who had strong roots within Malay society.

The campus of Sultan Idris Training College in the 1920s. The college has expanded into a university for teacher training.

RIGHT: O. T. Dussek, the first headmaster of Sultan Idris Training College (1922–36). His vision of the college was of a 'vernacular university in embryo'. There were few other Europeans on the college staff, and most served only brief terms.

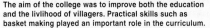

The aim of the college was to improve both the education and the livlihood of villagers. Practical skills such as basket making played an important role in the curriculum.

Emphasis was placed on health. Physiology and hygiene were among the subjects taught to the college students. Sport and exercise were also considered important.

Persatuan Melayu Pulau Pinang, whose members were purebred Malays. Although the dispute was settled at the congress in favour of the Persatuan Melayu Pulau Pinang, a legacy of bitterness and uncertainty remained.

The second Pan-Malayan Malay Congress, held in Singapore in 1940, saw the attendance of Malay state associations from Johor, Kelantan, Perak, Sarawak and Brunei. However, the congress both failed to arrive at an acceptable definition of what constituted a Malay, and was unwilling to make a clear commitment on political involvement in struggling for the Malay community.

There were some attempts to build a politically motivated pan-Malayan Malay organization. In 1938, Malay radicals including Ibrahim Yaacob and Ishak Haji Muhammad started the Kesatuan Melayu Muda (Young Malays Union) aimed at uniting the Malay Peninsula and the Dutch territories in Indonesia in an Indonesia Raya (Greater Indonesia) or Melayu Raya (Greater Malay Unity). The Malay radicals were mainly commoners with few ties to Malay royalty, whom they despised as collaborators of colonialism. However, the Japanese invasion of Malaya in 1941 abruptly ended the political aims of the Kesatuan Melayu Muda and rendered the state associations useless.

Mohd Eunos bin Abdullah, one of the founders (and the first president) of the Kesatuan Melayu Singapura (Singapore Malays Union), the first Malay state association, established in 1926.

An article written by Ishak Haji Muhammad, co-founder of the Kesatuan Melayu Muda (Young Malays Union), about the role of *Utusan Melayu*. Considered to be the first truly Malay newspaper, the article was published in the first issue of *Utusan Melayu* on 29 May 1939.

The labour movement and radical politics

The development of a labour movement in Malaya before World War II was primarily an immigrant phenomenon. Malay wage labour was relatively insignificant; those employed in the estates and mines were casual labourers recruited only when cheaper immigrant labour was not available. On the whole, the labour movement stemmed from socioeconomic grievances among the Chinese and Indian labourers associated with low wages, inflationary pressures and exploitation.

The Loo Pan Hong or Carpenters' Kongsi in Love Lane, Penang, which was the association for the training and welfare of Chinese carpenters and other craftsmen.

Labour unrest

The militancy and violence of the labour strikes in the 1930s were a result of nationalist influences from China and India. Chinese labourers were recruited by left-wing organizations for their own political ends. Indian labour turbulence in the late 1930s was a direct response to the growing nationalist movement in India. Radical and nationalist politics had worsened communal mobilization, and hindered the forging of an alliance of Chinese and Indian workers. The ethnic-based labour movements were due to fundamental differences in labour recruitment as well as working conditions and wage payment between Chinese and Indians.

Indian labour

In contrast to the Chinese, most Indian workers worked in the estates and were answerable directly to their employers. Labour discipline was ensured by the *kangany* (recruiting agent and foreman) (see 'The rubber industry and Indian immigration'). His paternalistic role made it possible for the management to pay lower wages to the Indians than the Chinese. The Indian wage structure, unlike the Chinese (which fluctuated with labour market forces), was based on the principle of a standard wage pegged to a cost of living index determined by the Indian Immigration Committee. In theory, the standard wage protected the welfare of the Indian labourers, but enforcement was haphazard and often was not related to the state of the economy in the Malay Peninsula.

A *kangany* licence, which gave the holder (an estate foreman) the right to recruit labourers in India.

The *kangany* on Sungai Wangie Estate, c. 1914. Their role was the recruitment and supervision of estate labour.

Rubber tappers carrying buckets of latex to the estate factory in the early 20th century. In the foreground, a worker and a manager are collecting rubber seeds.

Workers' quarters (known as coolie lines) of a rubber estate in Selangor. Such housing was in stark contrast to the hilltop bungalows of estate managers.

Pay day on a rubber estate. Rubber tappers were paid according to their production. Rainy days, when trees could not be tapped, meant no wages.

The factory and labour force of Gula estate in Perak. In 1907, a workforce of 1,521 coolies (Indians, Malays and Javanese) was employed on the estate, which had 1000 hectares of sugar, 230 hectares of para rubber and 15 hectares of rambong rubber. An estate hospital was staffed by a doctor and dresser.

Radical politics and Chinese labour

Chinese labour politics developed in response to political changes in China, resulting in a growing nationalist fervour amongst the immigrant Chinese. The labour community was the earliest to respond to the movement for the regeneration of China.

Communist agents from China built a network of illegal labour unions in Singapore and the Malay Peninsula. Night schools for teaching Mandarin to workers became centres for disseminating anti-capitalist and anti-imperialist propaganda. Acts of violence and terrorism were also advocated.

The Depression and its aftermath

The Great Depression marked a turning point in Malayan labour history. The free flow of Chinese and Indian immigration ended, unemployment was rampant, surplus labour was repatriated and wages were reduced to a bare minimum. However, a more permanent labour force was the result. Economic recovery in 1934 was followed by a series of strikes which began with the skilled craftsmen in towns and eventually spread to all sectors of the economy. The causes were a much reduced labour force, the government's reluctance to resume free immigration and labourers' awareness of their bargaining power.

The strikes, which were mostly of Chinese labourers, spread to rubber estates, factories and mines in early 1937. Many Chinese immigrants had worked off their debts and were aware of their rights. The initial unrest was largely spontaneous, with little political instigation. Only with the involvement of the Malayan Communist Party (MCP) was there a sense of cohesion and direction.

Communist influence

The MCP began mobilizing Chinese workers through its front organization, the Malayan General Labour Union (MGLU). A network of trade unions was established. Although the MCP wanted to recruit labour from all the ethnic groups in the Peninsula, it had neither the financial resources nor

N. Raghavan, president of the Central Indian Association of Malaya (CIAM), the leading organization behind the 1941 Indian labour strikes on estates in the Klang district.

the personnel to recruit the Indian estate workers or the Malay peasants. Thus it was forced to restrict its activities to the Chinese workforce.

The MCP's efforts to mobilize workers gained momentum during 1934–7 when it formed unions among building labourers, transport workers and mechanics. In 1936, when labour unrest spread to Selangor and Negeri Sembilan, the MCP organized trade unions among the rubber tappers, miners and factory workers in those states.

The MCP continued consolidating its position over Chinese labour after the commencement of the Sino-Japanese war in July 1937. It blended its labour strategy with resurgent overseas Chinese nationalism by giving support to the Chinese Anti-Japanese National Salvation Movement. Workers collected relief funds for the Chinese government and also enforced the boycott of imported Japanese goods. The spirit of solidarity engendered by these activities encouraged workers to form mutual help societies for arbitration in industrial disputes.

Politics and Indian labour
During the 1930s, the influence of the nationalist movement in India began to mould public opinion among the Indian immigrants in the Malay Peninsula. Indian associations, previously merely social organizations, became more aware of the need for communal solidarity. The societies also felt it was necessary to identify themselves with the labouring class to enhance the status of the Indian community in the Peninsula as a whole. However, only with the founding of the Central Indian Association of Malaya (CIAM) in 1936 did the position of the Indian labourers become cohesive. Neelakandar Aiyer, the secretary of the association, publicly criticized the exploitation of Indian labour. The CIAM also condemned the report by Srinivasa Sastri, a liberal Congress politician from India who visited the Malay Peninsula in 1936 to investigate complaints about the conditions under which Indian labourers worked and lived in the estates.

A more militant turn developed in 1938 after the visit in 1937 of Pandit Jawaharlal Nehru, president of the Indian Congress Party. The CIAM's

appeal to the Indian government resulted in June 1938 in a ban on the emigration of assisted labourers from India to the Malay Peninsula. With the outbreak of World War II in September 1939, and the consequent rise in the cost of living, the president of CIAM, N. Raghavani, rallied the Indian labourers by championing the cause of wage parity between the Chinese and Indian plantation workers. New workers' associations were established in the districts near estates which employed large numbers of Indian workers.

Labour strikes and government reaction
Labour strikes by the Indian and Chinese workers during the post-Depression period were inevitably the result of the workers' socioeconomic grievances and of radical politics. The 1937 Chinese labour strikes in Selangor were followed by a wave of labour unrest among Indian estate workers in the Klang district of Selangor in 1941. These strikes, which were uncharacteristically militant and violent, forced the government to use police and military force to restore order in the state. Significantly, the strikes from 1937 to 1941 played a decisive role in changing official attitudes towards workers' associations as a means of averting labour conflicts.

Previously it had been thought that the conciliatory roles of the Labour Department and the Chinese Protectorate were adequate for the resolution of all labour disputes and for maintaining stable industrial relations. Because employers were opposed to the formal recognition of trade unions, the government did little to review any legislation that might possibly lead to the formation of trade unions by the workers. Although the lessons learnt from the strikes of the 1930s were taken to heart by the government immediately, the Trade Union Ordinance of 1940 was not intended to protect the interests of labourers. Rather, the act was aimed at preventing outside agitators using estate labourers for their own political ends.

Pandit Jawaharlal Nehru, the president of the Congress Party of India, addressing the local Indian community at the padang in Kuala Kangsar, Perak in 1937. Immigrant workers were influenced by the nationalist movement in their home countries in the 1930s.

Female immigration and permanent settlement

Female immigration to the Malay Peninsula from the Malay Archipelago, China and India increased dramatically in the early 20th century, changing the 19th-century demographic profile of a predominantly male immigrant workforce. Many women contributed directly to the economy, as paid and unpaid labour, in tin mines, the agricultural sector, and in various types of work in urban areas. They played an even larger role as wives and mothers, nurturing families and transforming a transient male workforce into settled communities.

Numbers and distribution

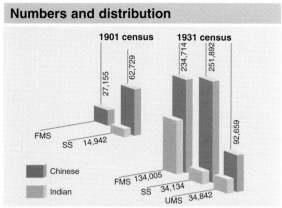

FEMALES PER 1,000 MALES

	1911	1921	1931	1947
Chinese	215	371	486	815
Indians	320	424	456	616

NUMBER OF CHILDREN BELOW 15

	1931	1947
Malays	746,143	1,030,559
Chinese	433,416	1,020,685
Indians	153,957	203,313

Migration of female workers

19th-century immigration

Historically, the Malay Peninsula has been a focus of migration and settlement by peoples from the neighbouring islands of the Malay Archipelago, especially Sumatra and Java. From the mid-19th century, a huge influx of immigrants from China and India added to this traditional migratory flow.

Immigration from all three sources followed a similar pattern. Young adult males came in waves during periods of intense economic growth. The women came later, usually in smaller numbers. In the 19th century, only one in every ten Indian or Chinese arrivals was female, but immigrants from the Malay Archipelago included more women.

From the mid-19th century, thousands of male immigrants from China and India arrived to work in the tin mines and rubber plantations. Many were unmarried. Married workers could not bring their families because of low wages, harsh working conditions and cramped living quarters.

Prostitution

Prostitution increased in the Malay Peninsula after the arrival of immigrants. Young girls were bought, kidnapped or tricked into coming by syndicates and employers of male workers. Yap Ah Loy, the tin magnate who became the Kapitan China of Kuala Lumpur, is reported to have had 300 prostitutes in his brothels in 1883. In 1889, the Straits Settlements had 3,673 registered prostitutes in a Chinese female population of fewer than 30,000. The women lived and worked in sordid, inhumane conditions—worlds apart from the lives led by the wives of successful traders.

To Yap Ah Loy, brothels were a business activity like any other, providing a service to customers.

BELOW: Brothels set up by Japanese prostitues were first opened in 1877.

20th-century immigration

Female immigration increased dramatically in the early 20th century. In 1923, the government of India stipulated that there should be one female emigrant for every 1.5 males. Also, amendments to the Labour Code in Malaya required the provision of rooms for married couples as well as child-care and schooling facilities. The numbers of women and children arriving increased and by the 1920s, women accounted for 30 per cent of all arrivals from India.

Female arrivals from China, a steady trickle since 1850, increased dramatically after the 1933 Aliens Ordinance set a quota for male immigrants. This Act stimulated the recruitment of female workers and encouraged the men to bring in their wives and children. Between 1934 and 1938, when a limit was placed on female immigrants, there was a net migrational gain of 190,000 Chinese women.

The early 20th century also saw a surge in the arrival of women from the Malay Archipelago, especially Java. They came with their husbands to work in smallholdings and plantations in Perak, Selangor and especially Johor where, by 1931, such immigrants outnumbered the indigenes.

Economic and social contributions

Many women and children joined the labour force. The Indian women worked as tappers and weeders in rubber estates, constituting 43 per cent of the sector's workforce in the 1940s. Those in the towns worked mainly as domestic servants and labourers, with only a few employed as professionals .

Chinese women worked as *dulang* washers or as casual labourers in rubber estates besides growing vegetable and rearing livestock. In towns, they were domestic servants, hawkers, shop assistants, nurses, and teachers. By the 1940s, nearly 54 per cent of the Chinese workforce were women and children. The unwaged work of women in smallholding or peasant families was an important part of farming activities, contributing to household income.

The socioeconomic contribution of women's work in the home was often not recognized, but as wives and mothers female immigrants contributed to a major demographic transformation. With the arrival of more women, more children were born and raised locally, families took root and the transition towards permanent settlement began.

The female immigrants

Chinese

There had been a steady trickle of Chinese women arriving in the Malay Peninsula since the 1850 Convention of Peking allowed wives to leave China to join their husbands abroad. Female arrivals increased dramatically after the 1933 Aliens Ordinance set a quota for male immigrants. This stimulated the recruitment of female workers and encouraged men to bring in their wives and children. Between 1934 and 1938, when a limit was placed on female immigrants, there was a net migrational gain of 190,000 Chinese women. As more Chinese moved into the agricultural sector in the 1930s, the proportion of women in the Chinese estate workforce increased from 20 per cent in 1937 to 33.5 per cent in 1947. By the 1940s, female and child workers constituted nearly 54 per cent of the total Chinese workforce, with women in the towns employed in a wide range of occupations.

1. Large numbers of Cantonese women came to the Malay Peninsula by ship from the mid-19th century onwards to join their husbands.

2. The number of Chinese women working as dulang washers increased from around 12,000 in 1936 to nearly 23,000 in 1946. By then they produced 25.4 per cent of the total tin output.

3. A diorama showing a group of female workers from Samsui, a district in the coastal province of Guangdong in South China. These women were well known for doing heavy manual work.

4. Many Chinese women living in towns worked as domestic helpers.

5. There was a great demand for trained, English-speaking Chinese amahs. The samfoo-clad women looked after the children of Europeans living in Malaya.

Indian

By 1931 there were 482 Indian women to every 1,000 men in Malaya, improving further to 637 per 1,000 by 1947.

The immigration of Indian women increased sharply in the 1920s and 1930s, after the indenture system of labour recruitment was banned (see 'The rubber industry and Indian immigration'). In 1923, the Indian government stipulated that there should be one female emigrant for every 1.5 males. Also, improvements in the Malayan Labour Code required employers to provide separate rooms for married couples, as well as some child care and schooling facilities. These new laws encouraged the influx of women and children to the plantations. In the 1920s, Indian women accounted for 30 per cent of all arrivals, and caused a sharp increase in the percentage of Indian women in the plantation workforce, which reached 63 per cent in the 1940s.

As wives and as mothers, women contributed to a major demographic transformation.

Multiple school systems in a plural society

A multiple system of schools teaching in different languages and nurturing different cultural and political identities developed in colonial Malaya, reflecting and further exacerbating social fragmentation between the various ethnic groups. Malay children studied in pondok, madrasah or Malay primary schools, while Chinese and Indian children went to schools which used their respective mother tongues. A small multiracial élite in the towns attended English schools which provided them with a channel to the only higher education available locally up to 1941.

Pondok (hut) schools were set up in Malay kampongs by Islamic scholars to provide religious education to the children. Pupils often provided domestic services, or ran errands, for teachers instead of paying fees.

Malay children on their way to school. In the colonial era, Malay-medium schools provided only four years of basic education. To gain higher education, Malay children had to be selected for special English classes before moving to an English-medium school.

An early 20th-century kampong school in Sepri, Rembau, Negeri Sembilan. Such schools provided Malay children with four years of basic education.

Pondok and madrasah

After the advent of Islam in the Malay Peninsula, education among the Malays became equated with religious learning. Islamic teachers came from Mecca, Egypt, or neighbouring Patani and Aceh. The more renowned were employed by the Malay rulers as court advisers or as tutors for the royal family. In the villages, classes were conducted by the *imam* (religious leader) or local teachers in mosques, *surau* (prayer rooms) or the teacher's home.

From the 17th century, a formal system of religious teaching began in *pondok* (hut) schools, often sited near mosques or on land endowed for religious purposes. Pupils lived in huts surrounding the teacher's home, and ran errands for him in return for the privilege of studying under him. Kelantan, Kedah and Terengganu had many pondok schools, some of which received royal patronage.

In the early 20th century, young scholars, inspired by reform movements in West Asia, set up *madrasah* (religious schools) to teach what they considered a 'truer' and more enlightened form of Islam. Starting from Singapore and Penang, the reformist movement spread into the Malay states. Some madrasah were short-lived, but others survived for several decades as centres of Islamic education. A few, for example the Maahad Il-Ihya

Assarif in Perak, became the nuclei for an Islam-centred political activism which posed a challenge to the English-educated Malays' claims to political leadership in the postwar years.

Secular Malay education

The British began establishing free Malay medium primary schools in the 1870s. Initial antagonism towards these schools, which were perceived as foreign and divorced from religious learning, was overcome by providing after-school Qur'an classes. With wider acceptance, there was a marked increase in the number of these schools in the 1920s.

The Malay schools provided just four years of tuition and taught little more than basic literacy and numeracy skills. A teachers' training course was the only form of post-primary Malay education available. Thus, Malay schools offered no access to social mobility or higher education except to the few recruited to train as teachers or to continue their education in English through special classes.

Limited though it was, Malay education was a catalyst for social and political change. Malay girls gained access to formal education in 1885, and by 1935 there were 150 girls schools as well as a training college for female Malay teachers. Sultan Idris Training College, set up in 1922 for male students, became a centre of Malay intellectual life.

Chinese education was not provided by the British authorities, forcing the Chinese community to establish and manage their own schools.

The first batch of student-teachers who graduated in 1930 from Fukien Girls' School in Penang, later renamed the Penang Chinese Girls' School.

Schools for the children of immigrants

The British did not provide educational facilities for the children of Chinese and Indian immigrants. The Chinese began to establish their own schools from the early 19th century. As the population grew, more schools were set up. Although a few schools received meagre aid from the government after 1924, almost all were established, funded and managed by local Chinese leaders or organizations. The Chinese schools provided a basic primary education, and by the 1930s the larger urban schools had begun to provide secondary education.

Indian children living on estates had no access to schools until the 1923 Labour Code compelled employers to provide educational facilities. Estate schools, often housed in makeshift buildings and with untrained teachers, were usually badly run. Yet this was the only form of schooling available to more than 70 per cent of Indian children. Urban children were more fortunate as schools set up in towns by religious or social organizations were better managed.

The Chinese and Indian schools ful-filled a basic need neglected by the colonial state, but they engendered in their students strong linguistic, cultural and even political ties with the country of their forefathers. Most Indian schools taught in Tamil using textbooks from India. Similarly, the Chinese schools imported both teachers and textbooks, and patterned their curriculum on that used in China.

The emergence of a Westernized élite

The first English schools were set up in the Straits Settlements early in the 19th century, among them the Penang Free School (1816) and the Malacca Free School (1826). Temenggong Abu Bakar started an English school in Johor in 1864. English schools were then set up in other Malay states, for example, King Edward VII School in Taiping (1883) and Victoria Institution in Kuala Lumpur (1894).

By the 1880s, secondary education in English was available in the Straits Settlements, and the Cambridge local examinations were first held in 1891. From 1886, the Queen's scholarship offered an opportunity for a select few to study at British universities. In 1905, the King Edward VII College of Medicine was founded in Singapore after the Straits Chinese raised the necessary funds. In 1928, the opening of Raffles College provided another local avenue for higher education.

Thus, from the beginning of the 20th century higher education was available locally for students of the English schools. With the expansion of Western commercial enterprises and the extension of British administration into all the Malay states, English had become the main language of government and

commerce. An English education thus offered the prospect of better jobs. Moreover, the English schools received the highest rates of government aid and had the best facilities. Not surprisingly, there were demands from the people for the establishment of more English schools.

Up to 1941, the British deliberately limited the expansion of English schools as they feared an English education would raise social and political expectations, thereby threatening the colonial order. The higher fees charged by the English schools further restricted enrolments.

Few Malays attended English schools as most were run by Christian missionaries and all were in urban centres. Also, colonial policy required Malay children to attend four years of Malay school before selection for English schools. Only the sons of the Malay rulers and aristocrats were exempted. For this privileged group, a boarding school, the Malay College, was set up in 1905 to groom them for the administrative service (see 'Education and the Malay Civil Service'. Thus, the Malays were largely cut off from the socioeconomic advantages that came with an English education.

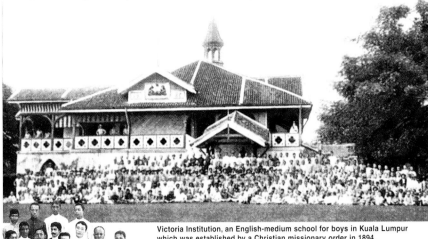

Victoria Institution, an English-medium school for boys in Kuala Lumpur which was established by a Christian missionary order in 1894.

LEFT: The first headmaster, Bennett Shaw (in gown), and the staff of Victoria Institution, Kuala Lumpur.

RIGHT: The children of Indian estate workers were educated in Tamil medium schools on the estates.

A Students Saving Scheme stamp valued at 10 cents.

A University of Cambridge certificate, 1932. The Cambridge local examinations were held for the first time in 1891.

PRIMARY SCHOOLS, PUPILS AND TEACHERS, 1938

MEDIUM	SCHOOLS	PUPILS	TEACHERS
Malay	788	56,904	2,810
English	271	41,917	2,350
Chinese	996	86,147	3,556
Tamil	607	26,271	864

A government Malay school in Merlimau, Melaka, which was established in 1931.

Glossary

A

Agency house: A type of mercantile firm first established in the 18th century by British merchants trading in Asia for the export of local goods. In the 19th century, they also imported British manufactured goods and raised capital for the tin and rubber industries in overseas markets such as the London Stock Exchange.

Agent: British official appointed to advise the Malay ruler of one of the Unfederated Malay States on all matters except Islam and Malay customs.

Anglo-Dutch Treaty: 1824 treaty which demarcated the British and Dutch spheres of influence by an imaginary line down the Strait of Melaka. The British sphere was the Malay Peninsula and Singapore; the Dutch, present-day Indonesia.

Anglo-Johor Treaty: 1885 treaty by which Britain recognized Abu Bakar as the sovereign ruler of the state, with the title of 'Sultan'.

Anglo-Siamese Treaty: 1909 treaty under which Siam relinquished suzerainty over the states of Kelantan, Terengganu, Kedah and Perlis, which were subsequently recognized as areas under British protection.

B

Borneo Company: Mercantile company granted monopolies in Sarawak by James Brooke.

British North Borneo Company: A chartered company set up in 1881 to administer the territory of North Borneo.

Burney Treaty: 1826 treaty which established Siam and Britain as joint guardians of law and order in the Malay states. Siam was predominant in Kelantan, Terengganu and Kedah (and Perlis from 1842); the British, the southern states.

C

Chief Secretary: New title for the Resident-General 1911–35.

Chinese Engagement: *see* Pangkor Treaty.

D

Decentralization policy: Policy introduced in the 1920s by the British to return to the Malay rulers of the Federated Malay States some of the powers they had lost to British officials.

Durbar: Meeting of Malay rulers of the Federated Malay States and their Residents with the Resident-General and the High Commissioner

E

East India Company (EIC): A private company formed in 1600 with a royal charter for a trade monopoly in the countries between the American and African continents. It established settlements in Penang (1786) and Singapore (1819), and acquired control of Melaka in 1824. The control of these Straits Settlements passed to the British government in 1858.

F

Federal Council: Legislative body of the Federated Malay States, established in 1909.

Federated Malay States (FMS): Federation formed in 1896 of Selangor, Pahang, Perak and Negeri Sembilan headed by a Resident-General (in the capital, Kuala Lumpur), whose superior was the High Commissioner (also Governor of the Straits Settlements) (in Singapore).

G

Governor: Head of the Straits Settlements. From 1896 he also held the position of High Commissioner of the Federated Malay States.

H

High Commissioner: Head of the Federated Malay States, who was also Governor of the Straits Settlements.

M

Malay nationalist movement: A 20th-century movement which sought to improve the economic position of the Malays through the faithful observance of Islam, and to create a sense of national consciousness which was lacking because of loyalty to individual Malay state rulers.

N

Naning War: 1831 uprising by the people of Naning (on the Melaka border) led by Dul Said after the Governor of the Straits Settlements tried to impose taxes on the semi-autonomous state. After winning, the British made Naning part of Melaka.

P

Pangkor Engagement: *see* Pangkor Treaty.

Pangkor Treaty: Treaty signed in 1874 consisting of two documents: the Chinese Engagement, which divided the mining areas of Perak between the two rival Chinese groups (Ghee Hin and Hai San); and the Pangkor Engagement, which compelled the sultan to accept the appointment of a British Resident to advise him and to collect and control revenue.

R

Resident: British official in each of the Federated Malay States whose role was to advise the Malay ruler on all matters except Islam and Malay customs.

Resident-General: British official in Kuala Lumpur overseeing the Federated Malay States. His superior was the High Commissioner (in Singapore). In 1911, the title was changed to Chief Secretary.

Residential System: The system of government introduced in the Malay states after the signing of the Pangkor Treaty in 1874. A British Resident advised the ruler of the state on all matters except Islam and Malay customs.

Revenue farm: Licence granting the monopoly on a particular service for a specified period, for example the collection of export duty or the sale of opium. These licences were often auctioned to the highest bidder, and rental had to be paid in advance.

S

Straits Settlements: The territories of Singapore, Penang and Melaka, which were administered by the East India Company in India until 1858, when control passed to the British government.

Sultan: Ruler of a Malay state.

T

Temenggong: Minister of defence, police chief. In Johor, the Temenggongs became rulers of the state, and in 1885 Temenggong Abu Bakar was recognized as sultan.

U

Unfederated Malay States (UMS): Kelantan, Terengganu, Kedah and Perlis (which until the signing of the Anglo-Siamese Treaty in 1909 were under the suzerainty of Siam) and Johor.

W

White rajah: Rulers of Sarawak from 1841 to 1941, the white rajahs were James Brooke, his nephew Charles Brooke and Charles's son, Vyner Brooke.

Bibliography

Abbreviations

JMBRAS   *Journal of the Malaysian Branch of the Royal Asiatic Society*

JSEAS   *Journal of Southeast Asian Studies*

MBRAS   Malaysian Branch of the Royal Asiatic Society

Abdullah bin Kadir, Munshi (1969), *The Hikayat Abdullah: The Autobiography of Abdullah bin Kadir (1797–1854)* (trans. A. H. Hill), Singapore: Oxford University Press.

Andaya, Barbara Watson **and** Andaya, Leonard Y. (2000), *A History of Malaysia*, 2nd edn, London: Palgrave.

Arasaratnam, S. (1970), *Indians in Malaysia and Singapore*, London: Institute of Race Relations.

Awang Had Salleh (1979), *Malay Secular Education and Teacher Training in British Malaya*, Kuala Lumpur: Dewan Bahasa dan Pustaka.

Barlow, H. S. (1995), *Swettenham*, Kuala Lumpur: Southdene.

Bird, Isabella (1883), *The Golden Chersonese and the Way Thither*, London: John Murray.

Black, Ian (1983), *A Gambling Style of Government: The Establishment of the Chartered Company's Rule in Sabah 1878–1915*, Kuala Lumpur: Oxford University Press.

Blythe, Wilfred (1969), *The Impact of Chinese Secret Societies in Malaya: A Historical Study*, London: Oxford University Press.

Bonney, R. (1971), *Kedah 1771–1821: The Search for Security and Independence*, Kuala Lumpur: Oxford University Press.

Buckley, C. B. (1902), *An Anecdotal History of Old Times in Singapore 1819–1867*, 2 vols, Singapore: Fraser and Neave.

Butcher, John **and** Dick, Howard (eds.) (1993), *The Rise and Fall of Revenue Farming: Business Elites and the Emergence of the Modern State in Southeast Asia*, London: Macmillan.

Butcher, John G. (1979), *The British in Malaya 1880–1941: The Social History of a European Community in Colonial South-East Asia*, Kuala Lumpur: Oxford University Press.

Cameron, John (1865), *Our Tropical Possessions in Malayan India*, London: Smith, Elder and Co.

Chai Hon-Chan (1964), *The Development of British Malaya 1896–1909*, Kuala Lumpur: Oxford University Press.

Cheah Boon Kheng (1994), 'Feudalism in Pre-colonial Malaya: The Past as a Colonial Discourse', *JSEAS*, 25(2): 243–69.

Chelliah, D. D. (1947), *A Short History of Education in the Straits Settlements*, Kuala Lumpur: Government Press.

Chew, Daniel (1990), *Chinese Pioneers on the Sarawak Frontier 1841–1941*, Singapore: Oxford University Press.

Chiang Hai Ding (1978), *A History of Straits Settlements Foreign Trade 1870–1915*, Singapore: National Museum.

Cowan, C. D. (1961), *Nineteenth Century Malaya: The Origins of British Political Control*, London: Oxford University Press.

Davenport, R. P. T. and Jones, G. (1989), *British Business in Asia since 1860*, Cambridge: Cambridge University Press.

Drabble, J. H. (1973), *Rubber in Malaya 1876–1922: The Genesis of the Industry*, Kuala Lumpur: Oxford University Press.

_____ (1991), *Malayan Rubber: The Interwar Years*, London: Macmillan.

Drabble, J. H. and Drake, P. J. (1981), 'The British Agency Houses in Malaysia: Survival in a Changing World', *JSEAS*, 12(2): 297–328.

Emerson, R. (1937), *Malaysia: A Study in Direct and Indirect Rule*, London: Macmillan.

Falconer, John (1987), *A Vision of the Past: A History of Early Photography in Singapore and Malaya: The Photographs of G. R. Lambert & Co. 1880–1910*, Singapore: Times Editions.

Furnivall, J. S. (1948), *Colonial Policy and Practice*, London: Cambridge University Press.

Gale, Bruce (1996), *1837: Tales of Pioneer Traders in the East*, 2nd edn, Kuala Lumpur: Malaysian International Chamber of Commerce and Industry.

Gallop, Annabel Teh (1994), *The Legacy of the Malay Letter; Warisan Warkah Melayu*, London: British Library for the National Archives of Malaysia.

Gopinath, Aruna, *Pahang 1880–1933: A Political History*, MBRAS Monograph No. 18, Kuala Lumpur: MBRAS.

Gullick, J. M. (1988), *Indigenous Political Systems of Western Malaya*, rev. edn, London: Athlone Press.

_____ (1989), *Malay Society in the Late Nineteenth Century: The Beginnings of Change*, Singapore: Oxford University Press.

_____ (1992), *Rulers and Residents: Influence and Power in the Malay States 1870–1920*, Singapore: Oxford University Press.

_____ (1993), *Glimpses of Selangor 1860–1898*, MBRAS Monograph No. 25, Kuala Lumpur: MBRAS.

_____ (1993), *They Came to Malaya: A Travellers' Anthology*, Singapore: Oxford University Press.

_____ (1994), *Old Kuala Lumpur*, Kuala Lumpur: Oxford University Press.

_____ (2000), *A History of Kuala Lumpur 1856–1939*, MBRAS Monograph No. 29, Kuala Lumpur: MBRAS.

Heussler, R. (1981), *British Rule in Malaya: The Malayan Civil Service and Its Predecessors 1867–1942*, Westport, Connecticut: Greenwood.

Hill, R. D. (1977), *Rice in Malaya: A Study in Historical Geography*, Kuala Lumpur: Oxford University Press.

Hose, Charles (1926), *Natural Man: A Record from Borneo*, London: Macmillan.

Hoyt, Sarnia Hayes (1996), *Old Malacca*, Kuala Lumpur: Oxford University Press.

_____ (1996), *Old Penang*, Kuala Lumpur: Oxford University Press.

Huff, W. G. (1994), *The Economic Growth of Singapore: Trade and Development in the Twentieth Century*, Cambridge: Cambridge University Press.

Jackson, J. C. (1968), *Planters and Speculators: Chinese and European Agricultural Enterprise in Malaya 1786–1921*, Kuala Lumpur: University of Malaya Press.

Jackson, R. N. (1961), *Immigrant Labour and the Development of Malaya 1786–1920*, Kuala Lumpur: Government Printer.

Kaur, Amarjit (1985), *Bridge and Barrier: Transport and Communications in Colonial Malaya 1870–1957*, Singapore: Oxford University Press.

_____ (1998), *Economic Change in Malaysia: Sabah and Sarawak since 1850*, London: Macmillan.

Kennedy, J. (1993), *A History of Malaya*, 3rd edn, Kuala Lumpur: A. Abdul Majeed & Co.

Keppel, Henry (1846), *The Expedition to Borneo of HMS Dido for the Suppression of Piracy*, 2 vols, London: Chapman and Hall.

Khasnor Johan (1984), *The Emergence of the Modern Malay Administrative Elite*, Singapore: Oxford University Press.

Khoo Kay Kim (1972), *The Western Malay States 1850–1873: The Effects of Commercial Development on Malay Politics*, Kuala Lumpur: Oxford University Press.

King, Victor T. (1993), *The Peoples of Borneo*, Oxford: Blackwell.

Kobkua Suwannathat-Pian (1988), *Thai–Malay Relations: Traditional Intra-regional Relations from the Seventeenth Century to the Early Twentieth Century*, Singapore: Oxford University Press.

Kratoska, P. H. (ed.) (1985), *Honourable Intentions: Talks on the British Empire in South-East Asia*

Delivered at the Royal Colonial Institute 1874–1928, Singapore: Oxford University Press.

Leong, Cecilia (1982), *Sabah: The First 100 Years*, Kuala Lumpur: Percetakan Nan Yang Muda.

Li Dun Jen (1982), *British Malaya: An Economic Analysis*, Kuala Lumpur: Insan.

Lim Chong Yah (1967), *Economic Development of Modern Malaya*, Kuala Lumpur: Oxford University Press.

Lim Teck Ghee (1977), *Peasants and Their Agricultural Economy in Colonial Malaya 1874–1941*, Kuala Lumpur: Oxford University Press.

Lockard, Craig A. **and** Kennedy, Graham E. (1992), *Old Sarawak: A Pictorial Study*, Kuala Lumpur: Dewan Bahasa dan Pustaka.

Loh Fook Seng, Philip (1975), *Seeds of Separatism: Educational Policy in Malaya 1874–1940*, Kuala Lumpur: Oxford University Press.

Loh Kok-Wah, Francis (1988), *Beyond the Tin Mines: Coolies, Squatters and New Villages in the Kinta Valley, Malaysia c. 1880–1980*, Singapore: Oxford University Press.

McNair, J. F. A. (1878), *Perak and the Malays: Sarong and Kris*, London: Tinsley Bros.

Makepeace, W., Brooke, G. E. **and** Braddell, R. St. J. (eds.) (1921), *One Hundred Years of Singapore being Some Account of the Capital of the Straits Settlements … to the 6th February 1919*, 2 vols, London: John Murray.

Marryat, Frank S. (1848), *Borneo and the Indian Archipelago, with Drawings of Costume and Scenery*, London: Longman, Brown, Green and Longman.

Milner, A. C. (1982), *Kerajaan: Malay Political Culture on the Eve of Colonial Rule*, Tucson: University of Arizona Press.

Moore, Donald **and** Moore, Joanna (1969), *The First 150 Years of Singapore*, Singapore: Donald Moore.

Mundy, Rodney (1848), *Narrative of Events in Borneo and Celebes Down to the Occupation of Labuan*, 2 vols, London: John Murray.

Ooi Keat Gin (1997), *Of Free Trade and Native Interests: The Brookes and the Economic Development of Sarawak 1841–1941*, Kuala Lumpur: Oxford University Press.

Parkinson, C. N. (1960), *British Intervention in Malaya 1867–1877*, Singapore: University of Malaya Press.

Puthucheary, J. J. (1960), *Ownership and Control in the Malayan Economy*, Singapore: Donald Moore.

Ramasamy, P. (1994), *Plantation Labour, Unions, Capital and the State in Peninsular Malaysia*, Kuala Lumpur: Oxford University Press.

Ranjit Singh, D. S. (2000), *The Making of Sabah 1865–1941: The Dynamics of Indigenous Society*, Kuala Lumpur: University of Malaya Press.

Rimmer, Peter J. and Allen, Lisa M. (1990), *Pullers, Planters, Plantation Workers: The Underside of Malaysian History*, Singapore: Singapore University Press.

Roff, William R. (1974), *Kelantan: Religion, Society and Politics in a Malay State*, Kuala Lumpur: Oxford University Press.

_____ (1994), *The Origins of Malay Nationalism*, 2nd edn, Kuala Lumpur: Oxford University Press.

Rutter, Owen (1930), *The Pirate Wind: Tales of the Sea Robbers of Malaya*, London: Hutchinson.

Sadka, E. (1968), *The Protected Malay States 1874–1895*, Kuala Lumpur: University of Malaya Press.

Sandhu, Kernial Singh (1969), *Indians in Malaya: Some Aspects of Their Immigration and Settlement 1786–1957*, Cambridge: Cambridge University Press.

Sandin, Benedict (1967), *The Sea Dyaks of Borneo before White Rajah Rule*, London: Macmillan.

Saunders, Graham (1977), *The Development of a Plural Society in Malaya*, Kuala Lumpur: Longman.

_____ (1994), *A History of Brunei*, Kuala Lumpur: Oxford University Press.

Sejarah Melayu or Malay Annals (1952), Raffles MS 18, translated by C. C. Brown, *JMBRAS*, 25(2–3).

Shaharil Talib (1984), *After Its Own Image: The Trengganu Experience 1881–1941*, Singapore: Oxford University Press.

Sharom Ahmat (1984), *Kedah: Tradition and Change in a Malay State, A Study of the Economic and*

Political Development of Kedah 1878–1923, MBRAS Monograph No. 12, Kuala Lumpur: MBRAS.

Sidhu, J. S. (1980), *Administration in the Federated Malay States 1896–1920*, Kuala Lumpur: Oxford University Press.

Smith, Simon C. (1995), *British Relations with the Malay Rulers from Decentralization to Malayan Independence 1930–1957*, Kuala Lumpur: Oxford University Press.

Song Ong Siang (1909), *One Hundred Years' History of the Chinese in Singapore*, London: John Murray.

Stenson, M. R. (1980), *Class, Race and Colonialism in West Malaysia*, Brisbane: University of Queensland Press.

Stevenson, Rex (1975), *Cultivators and Administrators: British Educational Policy towards the Malays 1875–1906*, Kuala Lumpur: Oxford University Press.

Tan Pek Leng (1983), 'Chinese Secret Societies and Labour Control in the Nineteenth Century Straits Settlements', *Kajian Malaysia*, 1(2): 14–48.

Tarling, Nicholas (1963), *Piracy and Politics in the Malay World: A Study of British Imperialism in Nineteenth Century Southeast Asia*, Singapore: Donald Moore.

_____ (1971), *Britain, the Brookes and Brunei*, Kuala Lumpur: Oxford University Press.

_____ (1978), *Sulu and Sabah: A Study of British Policy towards the Philippines and North Borneo from the Late Eighteenth Century*, Kuala Lumpur: Oxford University Press.

Tate, D. J. M. (comp.) (1988), *Rajah Brooke's Borneo: The Nineteenth Century World of Pirates and Head-hunters, Orang Utan and Hornbills, and Other Such Rarities…*, Hong Kong, John Nicholson Ltd.

_____ (comp.) (1989), *Straits Affairs: The Malay World and Singapore: Being Glimpses of the Straits Settlements and the Malay Peninsula in the Nineteenth Century…*, Hong Kong: John Nicholson Ltd.

Thio, Eunice (1969), *British Policy in the Malay Peninsula 1880–1910*, Kuala Lumpur: University of Malaya Press.

Tregonning, K. G. (1962), *Papers on Malayan History*, Singapore:

University of Malaya Press.

_____ (1965), *The British in Malaya*, Tucson: University of Arizona Press.

_____ (1965), *A History of Modern Sabah*, Kuala Lumpur: University of Malaya Press.

Trocki, Carl A. (1979), *Prince of Pirates: The Temenggongs and the Development of Johor and Singapore 1784–1885*, Singapore: Singapore University Press.

Turnbull, C. M. (1972), *The Straits Settlements 1826–67: Indian Presidency to Crown Colony*, London: Athlone.

_____ (1989), *A History of Singapore 1819–1988*, 2nd edn, Kuala Lumpur: Oxford University Press.

Wang Tai Peng (1994), *The Origins of Chinese Kongsi*, Petaling Jaya: Pelanduk.

Warren, James Francis (1981), *The Sulu Zone 1768–1898: The Dynamics of External Trade, Slavery and Ethnicity in the Transformation of a Southeast Asian Maritime State*, Singapore: Singapore University Press.

Winstedt, R. O. (ed.) (1923), *Malaya: The Straits Settlements and the Federated and Unfederated Malay States*, London: Constable.

_____ (ed.) (1934), 'Negri Sembilan: The History, Policy and Beliefs of the Nine States', *JMBRAS*, 12(3).

_____ (1992), *A History of Johore (1365–1941)*, MBRAS Reprint No. 6, Kuala Lumpur: MBRAS.

Winstedt, R. O. **and** Wilkinson, R. J. (1932), 'A History of Perak', *JMBRAS*, 12(1).

Wong Lin Ken (1965), *The Malayan Tin Industry to 1914*, Tucson: University of Arizona Press.

Wright, A. **and** Cartwright, H. A. (1908), *Twentieth Century Impressions of British Malaya*, London: Lloyds Greater Britain Publishing Co.

Wright, Arnold **and** Reid, Thomas H. (1912), *The Malay Peninsula: A Record of British Progress in the Middle East*, New York: Charles Scribner's Sons.

Wright, L. R. (1970), *The Origins of British Borneo*, Hong Kong: Hong Kong University Press.

Yeo Kim Wah (1982), *The Politics of Decentralization: Colonial Controversy in Malaya 1920–1929*, Kuala Lumpur: Oxford University Press.

Index

Picture Credits

Abdul Halim Mohd Noor, p. 9, *songket* sarong; p. 24, untailored woven ensemble. **A. Kasim Abas**, p. 112, Masjid Tinggi. **Ande, D.**, p. 24, procession of Queen of Patani.
Antiques of the Orient, p. 8, Fort Cornwallis, map of East Indies; p. 10, Malay stilt village; p. 15, Santiago Gate, Melaka Town Square, Portuguese coat of arms, Dutch East India Company flag, British East India Company coat of arms, spices; p. 31, sago factory; p. 34, George Town, pepper berries; pp. 36–7, Penang and Kedah; p. 38, Horsburgh's chart, plan of Singapore town; p. 39, early view of Singapore; p. 41, waterfront houses at Melaka; p. 50, Melaka in 1807; p. 56, Government House at Melaka; p. 58, home of Temenggong Abdul Rahman; p. 64, Governor Weld.
Anuar bin Abdul Rahim, p. 22, bullfighting; p. 28, collecting birds' nests; p. 41, picture frame; p. 48, Guan Di; p. 54, Raja Muda Hassim; p. 56, destruction of Portuguese fort at Melaka; p. 57, Naning War; p. 61, British attack; p. 90, photo frame; p. 100, Brooke at Brunei court; p. 132, Yap Ah Loy; p. 134, Malay school children. **Arkib Negara Malaysia**, p. 42 & 58, Temenggong Daeng Ibrahim. **Bank Negara Malaysia**, p. 12, quarter *penjuru*; p. 21, money tree, *tampang* and Islamic coin; p. 40, Straits Settlements coins; p. 67, Malaysian banknote; p. 88, rubber coupon; p. 92, *bunga mas*; p. 98, Sarawak coins. **Barlow, H. S.**, p. 86, Frank Swettenham. **The British Library**, p. 34, 'View of the North Point ...'; p. 39, letter from Temenggong Abdul Rahman, Singapore Institution; p. 56, letter from Dul Said; p. 96, page from *Sejarah Melayu*; p. 127, Munshi Ibrahim. **Brunton, John**, p. 31, soaking sago logs, shredding sago log, baking sago starch.
Centre for the Study of Built Environment in the Malay World (KALAM), Universiti Technologi Malaysia, p. 13, Istana Hinggap. **Chai Kah Yune**, p. 29, birds' nest soup.
Dew, Stephen, p. 40, town plan of George Town. **EDM Archives**, p. 3, elephant outing on Perak River in Kuala Kangsar; p. 4, noble Malay

ladies; p. 8, engraving of Sir Stamford Raffles, Murut warrior; p. 9, Perak chiefs and attendants, rubber tappers, tin mine; p. 10, houseboats on Pahang River; pp. 10–11, transport elephants, Kelabit metalsmiths; p. 11, Dusun women; p. 12, Selangor emblem; p. 13, Sultan Ahmad, Raja Yusuf and sons, bodyguards of Tuanku Muhammad; p. 14, early view of Melaka; p. 16, rice fields in Province Wellesley, durians; p. 17, coconut palm, gift for a princess; p. 18, Che Mida and Nakhoda Tiong, large house, boat; pp. 18–19, Sultan Abdul Samad and entourage; p. 19, Sakai; p. 20, sluice box, mine pit; p. 22, flowering rice plant; p. 23, water wheel; p. 25, mangosteen, tied warp threads, Iban woven skirt, Iban woman on backstrap loom; p. 26, Iban couple, Kenyah group; p. 27, communal area in Kayan longhouse, Charles Hose, Dusun man and jar; p. 28, birds' nest collectors, Segai-i warrior; p. 30 antimony processing plant, Borneo Company headquarters; p. 31, sago palms, washing shredded sago pith; p. 32, Iranun sea warrior, cover of *Pirate Wind*; p. 33, Iranun attack, skulls in longhouse, Iban women dancing with heads, Sultan of Gunung Tabor and entourage; p. 34, view of Singapore from Mount Wallich; p. 35, Singapore headquarters of Boustead & Co., Statue of Sir Stamford Raffles; p. 36, Kedah opium farm; p. 37, tin mine, elephants; p. 40, Chinese merchants, European overseer and Chinese workers, Glugor House and spice plantation; p. 41, Straits Trading Company office, Boat Quay, rubber factory, oil store; p. 42, Temenggong Abu Bakar, Temenggong's pleasure boat; p. 43, *surat sungai*; p. 45, Borneo Company boat, Borneo Company logo; p. 46, Chung family residence; p. 47, British officials, Pangkor Treaty proclamation; p. 50, Sultan Sulaiman and followers; pp. 50–1, view from Strawberry Hill, HMS *Rinaldo*; p. 51, Abu Bakar, James Brooke; p. 52, Siamese princes and Kedah nobles; p. 53, King Rama III; p. 55, HMS *Dido*, Sultan Omar Ali, Baroness Angela Burdett-Coutts; p. 56, map of Malay Peninsula; p. 57, Malay swords

and daggers; Temenggong Abu Bakar's palace; p. 59, Sir Frederick Weld; p. 60, Tunku Kudin's compound at Klang; p. 61, J. W. W. Birch; p. 62, sketch of Pekan; p. 63, Sultan Ahmad and retinue, labourers building embankment; p. 64, view of Klang; p. 65, Sultan Abdul Samad's *istana*, Istana Mahkota, Sultan Sulaiman, Kuala Lumpur in 1909; p. 67, Tuanku Muhammad with bodyguards; p. 68, opencast tin mine, smoking opium, Weld Quay; pp. 68–9, Hongkong and Shanghai Bank building; p. 70, group outside Government House in Singapore, Frank Swettenham's visit to Kamunting mine; p. 71, Sultan Idris and Frank Low, Istana Negara in Kuala Kangsar, members of the Perak State Council, Cecil Wray, Masjid Jamek; p. 72, Chinese labourers, Negeri Sembilan Miners' Association; pp. 72–3, opencast tin mine; p. 73, coolies removing ore, tin dredge; p. 74, fishing boats, ploughing fields, processing rattan; p. 75, water village, Malay village; p. 76, commercial crops (all pictures), tin mining, tin ingots, tapping rubber, rubber factory; p. 77, Loke Yew, Loke Chow Kit, spirit distillery, Selangor opium farm; p. 78, bullock carts, changes in transport, Netherlands Trading Society product advertisement, staff of Sandilands, Buttery & Co.; p. 79, Weld Quay, hydraulic machinery; p. 81, Sir Cecil Clementi Smith, Tuanku Muhammad, FMS guidebook, *Straits Produce* cartoon; p. 82, Penang port, Seremban railway station, Station Road in Ipoh, electric tram; pp. 82–3, Thai royalty; p. 83, Sir John Anderson; p. 87, *Straits Produce* cartoon; p. 88, *Straits Produce* cartoon, roll-call on estate; p. 89, Selangor Club, Old Market Square, Sultan Abdul Samad Building, railway yards, *Straits Produce* cartoon; p. 90, Sir Hugh Clifford; p. 91, postcards; p. 92, Syed Alwi, Sultan Abdul Hamid Halim, Sultan Abu Bakar, Sultan Muhammad IV, Sultan Zainal Abidin III; pp. 92–3, Kelantan state council; p. 93, Sultan Abu Bakar, Sultan Ibrahim; p. 94, Kuala Terengganu; p. 95, Sultan Abdul Halim Shah; p. 97, Sultan Iskandar; p. 98, 'Keeney-Ballo'; pp. 98–9, map of 'Part of the Malayan

Archipelago'; p. 99, Brooke stamps, oil rig; p. 101, HMS *Dido*, Captain Henry Keppel, attack on Padeh village, raid on Kanowit village, fort on Baram River; p. 102, Iban group, Francis and Harriette McDougall; p. 103, sketch by Thomas S. Chapman, peacemaking ceremony; p. 104, Alfred Dent, tobacco plant, Murut warrior; p. 105, view of Sandakan, Government House in Sandakan; p. 106, sketches of Victoria, capital of Labuan (all pictures); p. 107, Malay native; p. 110, Penang market, King Edward's School, lepers taking medicine, Petaling Street; p. 111, rice fields, opencast mine, clearing land for rubber; p. 112, European workers, wealthy Chinese family, Chinese Residency, Chinese cobblers, Malay man, Malay children; p. 113, Malay festival, Sultan Idris's daughter-in-law, Orang Asli, Indian music and dance troupe, bullock carts, Malay State Guides of Perak, moneylender, female rubber tapper, Hindu temple; p. 114, Malayan railways building in Penang, Malay village, plantation workers; p. 115, *Straits Produce* cartoon, *British Malaya* cartoon, packing processed rubber; p. 116, Penang fire brigade, Talbot motorcars; p. 117, Weld Quay, Perak Museum, bridge in Market Street, view of Ipoh town, Kuala Lumpur government offices, Kuala Lumpur's civic leaders; p. 118, coagulating latex, interior of rubber factory; p. 119, H. N. Ridley; p. 120, Padang Rengas Pass; p. 121, Kuala Lumpur Railway Station, early train on Sabah railway, Chinese vendors; p. 123, European Hospital, Tan Tock Seng Hospital, estate hospital, nursing staff, Maynard & Co. dispensary (interior and exterior); p. 125, Capt. Salleh bin Haji Sulaiman; p. 126, staff of Singapore Free Press, selection of Jawi newspapers; p. 128, *Al-Iman* journal, colours presentation; p. 129, *Utusan Melayu* article; p. 130, *kangany* licence, workers' quarters, rubber tappers; pp. 130–1, factory and staff at Gula Estate; p. 132, Japanese prostitutes; p. 133, Indian family; p. 135, Victoria Institution, staff of Victoria Institution; p. 139, Ipoh street scene; p. 143, rubber planter and staff.

143

Ferrero, John-Paul, p. 29, collecting birds' nests on ladders. **Fong, P. K.**, p. 30, antimony mine; p. 54, document from Raja Muda Hassim; p. 55, view of Kuching; p. 98, 'Mr Brooke's First Residence'; p. 102, James Brooke; p. 107, signing of Labuan treaty; p. 109, Chinese gold miners. **Foreign and Commonwealth Office Collection, London**, p. 34, view of Taiping; p. 65, Sultan Abdul Samad and retainers; p. 66, Negeri Sembilan nobility; p. 68, participants of second Malay Durbar; p. 70, visit to Batak Rabit; p. 71, Sir Hugh Low's Residency; p. 80, 'Carcosa'; p. 81, view of Kuala Lumpur in 1897; pp. 84–5, group at second Malay Durbar; p. 85, Prince of Wales theatre group, football match, garden party; p. 86, British officials; p. 89, view of Kuala Lumpur in 1884; p. 97, Sultan Idris with staff. **Hon Photo**, p. 118, rubber estate. **Hongkong Bank Malaysia Berhad**, p. 69, banknotes; p. 78, 19th-century currency notes; p. 79, Mercantile Bank in Penang, HSBC in Penang; p. 99, Brooke banknotes. **Institute for Medical Research**, p. 122, Institute for Medical Research building. **Khoo Salma Nasution**, p. 77, Loke Mansion. **Kobkua Suwannathat-Pian**, p. 94, Sultan Zainal Abidin III; p. 95, King Chulalongkorn. **Kratoska, Paul**, p. 16, boats at Manai fruit market, Malay women selling vegetables; p. 21, water buffalo; p. 23, ploughing rice fields, flooded rice fields, winnowing padi; p. 41, product advertisements; p. 44, Alexander Guthrie, William Adamson, Samuel Gilfillan and H.W. Wood; p. 45, Behn, Meyer & Co. office; p. 73, hydraulic eleva-tors; p. 74, selling fish; p. 81, *Raffles Hotel Tourist's Guide*; p. 86, Sir John Anderson in Kota Bharu; p. 88, min-eral train; p. 89, third Kuala Lumpur railway station; p. 90, Sir Laurence Guillemard, Sir Shenton Thomas, cartoon; p. 115, W. W. Bailey; p. 117, Port Swettenham; p. 121, Keppel Road Railway Station, buffet car, railway and hotel posters; p. 129, exercise class. **Leong Yee Fong**, p. 131, N. Raghavani. **Library of Congress**, p. 57, letter from Farquhar. **Lim Chong Keat** (illustration now with Balai Seni Lukis), p. 76, ferry boat-men. **Lim, Lawrence**, p. 39, opium pipe; 72, opium pipe. **Lim, Suan I.**, pp. 6 & 47, Muzium Negara wall mural. **Lydbury, Jane**, pp. 1 & 133, Chinese women workers; p. 27, Ong Ewe Hai, Wong Nai Song; p. 46, Chung Keng Kwee; p. 120, railway

railway tunnel construction; p. 133, Cantonese women, domestic helpers. **Malay College Old Boys Association**, p. 124, examination ticket, Tuanku Tan Sri Mohamad bin Tunku Besar Burhanuddin, Tan Sri Nik Ahmed Kamil, Tuanku Jaafar Ibni Al-Marhum Tuanku Abdul Rahman; p. 125, cadet corps, theatre production, cricket team. **Malaysian Rubber Board**, p. 115, sorting rubber seeds; p. 130, *kangany*, pay day; p. 135, Tamil school classroom. **Miksic, John N.**, p. 39, opium pots; p. 72, opium pots. **Mohd Kassim Haji Ali**, p. 68, immigrant workers disembarking; p. 119, landing pier in Penang. **Mohd Nor bin Khalid**, p. 109, oil search cartoons. **Mohd Yunus Noor**, p. 61, Pasir Salak Historical Complex, memorial plaque. **Muzium DiRaja Abu Bakar, Istana Besar, Johor**, p. 59, Sultan Abu Bakar. **Muzium Negara**, p. 12, seal of Sultan Muhammad IV of Kelantan, seal of Sultan Mahmud Shah of Perak; p. 13, Dato Jaafar bin Muhammad; p. 19, Hugh Low; p. 87, Malay rulers and British officials; p. 134, Malay school; p. 135, government Malay school; p. 44, John Buttery, A. A. Anthony; p. 46, brick shophouses in Kuala Lumpur; p. 47, Pankgor Treaty signing table; p. 52, East India Company headquarters; pp. 52–3, *bunga mas*; p. 60, Pangkor Treaty; p. 61, Sultan Abdullah; p. 62, Hugh Clifford; p. 67, Tuanku Abdul Rahman; p. 81, Sultan Abdul Samad; p. 80, Gopeng contingent; p. 81, Sultan Idris, Sultan Ahmad; pp. 82–3, group at first Malay Durbar; p. 86, Sir John Anderson; p. 90, Sultan Sulaiman and Sir George Maxwell, Sir George Maxwell, Sir Cecil Clementi; p. 96, Legislative Council group photo; p. 97, Perak State Council; p. 112, Chinese miners, Yap Ah Loy; p. 125, Malay College football team, Malay College prefects; p. 131, Nehru addressing gathering. **National Archives of Singapore**, p. 18, bodyguards; p. 38, Sir Stamford Raffles, William Farquhar, John Crawford. **National Heritage Board of Singapore**, p. 38, diorama of meeting; p. 39, diorama of clan mediation, opium smoking; p. 52, letter seal; p. 72, opium smoking; p. 75, land title; p. 78, Commercial Union policy; p. 79, Lloyds insurance certificate; p. 80, gold mine in Raub; p. 115, bullock cart; p. 116, rickshaw pullers, motorcyclist; p. 117, Melaka town centre; p. 118, carrying buckets of latex; p. 122, diorama of coolie

quarters; p. 123, medicine sellers, medicine bill, prescription, vaccin-ation notice; p. 129, basket making; p. 133, diorama of female workers, Chinese amah, Indian women; p. 135, Students Saving Scheme stamp, University of Cambridge certificate. **National Library of Singapore**, p. 126, *Straits Produce* cartoon; p. 127, pages from *Hikayat Abdullah*, cover of *Chermin Mata*, illustration from *Cherita Orang Yang Chari Selamat*; p. 137, cover of *Straits Times Annual*. **National Maritime Museum, Greenwich**, p. 98, watercolour of British ships. **National Museum of Singapore**, p. 42, 'The view from Government Hill'. **National Portrait Gallery**, p. 54, James Brooke; p. 69, Sir Frank Swettenham. **National University of Singapore Library**, p. 113, Malay ladies with textiles. **New Straits Times Press (Malaysia) Berhad**, p. 37, Wan Saman Canal; p. 58, Istana Kampong Glam; p. 126, Abdul Rahim Kajai; p. 134, *pondok* school. **Osman Asari**, p. 16, durian sellers; p. 30, tramway; p. 38, picture frame; p. 43, Tan Yeok Nee. **Pejabat Sultan Kelantan, Kota Bharu**, p. 12, kris, betel nut container. **PETRONAS**, p. 24, *songket* motifs, *songket* waist cloth. **Picture Library**, pp. 6–7, rubber estate (background); p. 37, pepper culti-vation; p. 118, rubber seeds. **Pos Malaysia Berhad**, p. 84, Conference of Rulers stamps; p. 122, Institute for Medical Research stamps. **Public Record Office, London**, p. 108, letter from Sultan Omar Ali Saifuddin. **Radin Mohd Noh Saleh**, p. 13, Balai Besar; p. 24, *kain limar* sarong; p. 67, Istana Sri Menanti; p. 95, Wat Uttamaran; p. 96, Johor coat of arms; p. 130, Loo Pan Hong. **Raffles Hotel Collection**, p. 43, pepper crop, gambier estate; p. 86, Raffles Hotel advertisement; p. 111, FMS Railway posters; p. 118, plainter's journal, Raffles Hotel; p. 119, rubber tree; p. 120, FMS Railway poster; p. 121, baggage tag, FMS Railway poster. **Roff, William R.**, p. 126, Sayyid Shaikh Al-Hadi; p. 128, Shakih Mohd Tahir bin Jalaluddin al-Azhari; p. 129, Mohd Eunos bin Abdullah. **S. C. Shekar**, p. 48, kongsi houses, ancestral tablets; p. 78, Commercial Union firemark; p. 94, Istana Tengku Nik. **Sarawak Museum**, p. 29, rattan collectors, cleaning birds' nests, packing and weighing birds' nests; p. 75, group of Sarawak Malays; p. 99, Chinese gold miners; p. 102, Charles Brooke, Vyner Brooke, Chinese

camphor traders; p. 107, hoisting of British flag. **Selvanayagam, Grace**, p. 25, *songket* motifs (all pictures). **Shell Companies in Malaysia**, pp. 7 & 108, Miri Well No. 1; p. 115, pineapple canning factory; pp. 124–5, Malay College. **Shell Companies in Singapore**, p. 109, advertisement, lorry tankers, p. 117, warehouses along Collyer Quay. **Shell Sarawak**, p. 109, labourers collecting wages. **Sime Darby Berhad**, p. 44, John Middleton Sime, immigrant coolies, Sime Darby's first office, first logo; p. 91, Sime Darby group photo. **Soong Ching-yee**, p. 29, swift and nest. **Straits Trading Company Limited**, p. 41, James Sword, Herman Muhlinghaus. **Sultan Idris Training College**, p. 129, college campus, O. T. Dussek. **Tan Hong Yew**, pp. 5 & 17, fishermen with baskets; pp. 10–11, boat building; p. 17, collecting sea cucumbers, drying fish; p. 20, panning for tin, cross-section of mining pit; p. 21, smelting tin ore; p. 25, weaver and loom; p. 27, Iban sword; p. 32, *lanong, garay*; p. 33, Iban war cap; p. 46, villagers and runaway elephant; p. 60, British flotilla on Perak River, British army camp, encampment at Bandar Bahru; p. 63, William Fraser; p. 66, interior and exterior of stockade; p. 67, Martin Lister; p. 73, chain pump and water wheel; p. 74, boat building; p. 100, Sultan Omar Ali, Sultan Abdul Mumin, Sultan Hashim; p. 103, Sebuyan Dayak; p. 105, Mat Salleh, police barracks, police on water buffaloes; p. 120, elephant on railway track. **Tan Kim Hong**, p. 48, Chinese Protectorate office. **Tan Liok Ee**, p. 123, children waiting for vaccination; p. 134, Chinese school, Fukien Girls' School students. **Tan Pek Leng**, p. 49, Ghee Hin head-quarters, Hai San headquarters. **Teo Eng Hean**, p. 44, picture frame; p. 69, map of Federated Malay States. **Tommy Chang Image Produc-tions**, p. 105, Mat Salleh memorial. **Universiti Kebangsaan Malaysia**, p. 127, cover of *Putera Gunung Tahan*. **Warren, James Francis**, p. 28, Sulu overlord. **World Wide Fund for Nature Malaysia**, M. N. Azwad, p. 118, tapping latex; S. Sreedharan, p. 19, harvesting rice. **Yamashita, Mike**, p. 23, transplanting seedlings. **Yeap Kok Chien**, p. 29, Manchu man; p. 35, bust of Captain Francis Light; p. 49, Khaw Boo Aun, Ghee Hin society certificate, Chung Keng Kwee, Ch'lu Chao-pang, Khoo Thean Telk, Toa Peh Kong society certificate; p. 69, vegetable and fruit sellers.